Clarence Thomas and the Tough Love Crowd

# Clarence Thomas and the Tough Love Crowd

## Counterfeit Heroes and Unhappy Truths

Ronald Suresh Roberts

*New York University Press*
NEW YORK AND LONDON

NEW YORK UNIVERSITY PRESS
New York and London

Library of Congress Cataloging-in-Publication Data
Roberts, Ronald Suresh.
Clarence Thomas and the tough love crowd : counterfeit heroes and
unhappy truths / Ronald Suresh Roberts.
p.  cm.
Includes bibliographical references and index.
ISBN 0-8147-7454-7
1. Conservatism—United States.   2. Afro-American intellectuals—
Attitudes.  I. Title.
JC573.2.U6R63  1995
320.5'2'08996073—dc20          94-29895
                                      CIP

New York University Press books are printed on acid-free paper,
and their binding materials are chosen for strength and durability.

Manufactured in the United States of America

10   9   8   7   6   5   4   3   2   1

*For brothers Anil and Shastri, who are not ordinary.*
*And for my parents, who account for that fact.*

# Contents

## V. Tough Love International

# Acknowledgments

Without Patricia Williams' encouragement, and Rob Nixon's advice and support, this book would still be an idea. I am also grateful to Richard Delgado, Andrew Ross, Drucilla Cornell, Antony Anghie, and Stephen Vascianne. Girardeau Spann's suggestions on an earlier draft account for a range of important improvements. Duncan Kennedy was provocative, and I am grateful to Steven Winter and Joan Williams for discussing with me my discussion of their work.

The book began, at Harvard Law School, with Randall Kennedy's suggestion that I address, generally, the political responsibilities of intellectuals, and examine the (he felt) competing duties of political loyalty and truth-telling. But Kennedy was soon in an unusual position: both supervisor and subject. While his enthusiasm may have waned, his cordiality has not. Just after that early draft was finished, in mid-1991, Clarence Thomas was nominated to the Supreme Court.

I am hugely grateful to Niko Pfund, editor-in-chief of New York University Press, who took an early and instructive interest in the book, and to Roger Normand and Chris Jochnick who first told him about it. Danzy Senna and Omar Wasow taught me lots about America. Stephanie Flanders bravely read and commented incisively on earlier drafts. I am also grateful to Sarah Leah Whitson, Balram Kakkar, April Tash, Jen Stein, Guy Evans, Margaret Minister, Isabel Karpin, David Ellison, Armen Merjian, Stephen Blacklocks, and Dan Harris. Susan Kohlmann and John Pritchard provided indispensable support. Daphne Heywood taught me literature; Jane Stapleton, Paul Davies, and Andrew Ashworth taught me law; Nicola Lacey, legal theory; John Gardner and Stephen Mulhall, moral and political philosophy.

# Preface: The Tough Love Crowd: Disciplined Heroes

Luckily, we have a fighting tradition.... The chain will never be accepted as a natural garment.

—Alice Walker

"The multiple cleavages within racial minority groups undermine the notion of a singular, subordinated racial minority interest." This comment appeared in 1993 in the *Harvard Law Review,* and black neoconservatism is widely taken as evidence of its truth. A number of African American professionals have made black neoconservatism seem more a movement than an eccentricity. Yet while there have been suggestions that upwardly mobile blacks will comfortably adopt the politics and outlook of middle America, others have emphasized the enduring rage of African America's privileged class. Is this rage a problem that ought to be contained or a valuable political resource? Is it dysfunctional or rational? Does it reflect truth or delusion?

The performance of Justice Clarence Thomas on the Supreme Court has given such questions a renewed urgency. The Thomas appointment has given black neoconservatives their first conspicuous political power. The group's defining trait is Tough Love. They dish out harsh truths for other people's good. They would elevate the familiar wisdom, "spare the rod and spoil the child," to the policymaking arena. But does this homespun wisdom serve well in the charged setting of contemporary politics? Answering this question requires a close look at the work of several prominent Toughs.

Thomas Sowell (see chapter 4, "Tough Love Economist") is a central figure in any discussion of black neoconservatism. He is a senior fellow at the Hoover Institution on War, Revolution, and Peace. A frequent columnist, he has taught at universities around the world. In 1983, the *New Republic* commented that Sowell was "having a greater influence on the discussion of matters of race and ethnicity than any other writer of the past ten years." Shelby Steele (with Stanley Crouch, one of the "Tough Love Literati" discussed in chapter 3) is an essayist and a professor of English at San Jose State University. He is best known for *The Content of Our Character,* published in 1990. Stanley Crouch is a freelance writer and former jazz critic for the *Village Voice.* A collection of Crouch's work was published in 1990 as *Notes of a Hanging Judge.* Stephen Carter (with Randall Kennedy, one of the "Tough Love Lawyers" described in chapter 5) is a professor at Yale Law School. He has written extensively on constitutional law, intellectual property, and other legal issues, and he first attracted widespread attention with the 1991 publication of *Reflections of an Affirmative Action Baby.* On the appearance of Carter's second book, *The Culture of Disbelief,* President Clinton publicly suggested that everyone concerned with the place of religion in American politics ought to read it. (Carter's subsequent *Confirmation Mess,* examining the Senate's role in confirming presidential nominees, was also widely noticed.) Randall Kennedy is a professor at Harvard Law School and editor of *Reconstruction,* a journal on African American politics, society, and culture. He has written widely on American race relations law and issues of American legal history. His 1989 article, "Racial Critiques of Legal Academia," attracted much attention for its criticisms of "critical race theory," a school of thought with which Lani Guinier and Derrick Bell are associated. Vidia Naipaul (see part 5, "Tough Love International") was born in the Caribbean and has written both fiction and nonfiction concerning India, the West Indies, the Middle East, Africa, Britain, and the United States, among other places. Naipaul has won numerous British literary awards, and the British press routinely calls him the country's greatest living writer. In 1990, Naipaul was knighted by the queen of England. With the publication of his latest book, *A Way in the World,* Sir Vidia continues to be revered by many of his British readers, and reviled by many of the postcolonial people he calls barbarians.

Without exception, these individuals present themselves as harsh truth tellers, motivated by *concern* for those they criticize. They urge that various orthodoxies are blind to harsh facts and therefore unable to offer meaningful solutions. A blurb on the back of Thomas Sowell's book, *The Economics and Politics of Race* (1983), assures the hesitating book purchaser that "Sowell has become one of the most ruthlessly honest social critics of our time. He may eventually be recognized as a *partisan of the poor* because his willingness to face bitter facts can contribute to our ability to help the poor in fundamental and lasting ways" (emphasis added).

All the Toughs make claims like this. Even Naipaul, the Tough Love Crowd's fiction writer, is often called a remarkable teller of *social truth*, and he has written more nonfiction than novels. Naipaul declared in a 1993 interview in the London *Independent* that "several generations of free milk and orange juice have led to an army of thugs.... They seem to think we should do something for them.... I think people should earn their own regard."

Yet the Toughs attempt such diagnoses in a precarious setting. Parodying a Clarence Thomas favorite, Winston Churchill, one might put the point like this: never in the history of human communication have so many depended so much on so few. In this setting, where news organizations and political handlers manufacture truth, the Toughs get a free ride. Critics say they deliberately betray the groups they claim to champion. They reply, offended, that their good faith is unquestionable. Justice Thomas, since joining the Court, has continued to complain about the pressures imposed by a hyper-critical "new orthodoxy." He has complained that "where blacks were once intimidated from crossing racial boundaries, we now fear crossing *ideological* boundaries" (Thomas's emphasis). The usually incisive Henry Louis Gates, Jr., has occasionally been overtaken by such rhetoric, as when he wrote—on the *New York Times* op-ed page—of the hazards posed by African American "thought police." Others, too, sometimes find the betrayal claim unfair to the Tough Love Crowd. Even when such persons disagree with the Tough Love Crowd's agenda, they praise the Crowd's courage in standing up to the unjustified abuse and vilification of civil rights traditionalists. Such praise is encouraged by the Tough Love Crowd's own rhetoric. "Dissent bore a price—one I gladly paid," announced Clarence Thomas while head of the EEOC. With such rhetoric, the Toughs pass as martyrs even as they burnish sacred cows.

# The Truth Trap

# Reality: The Opium of Progressives

I represented an important and mainstream tradition [of] vigorous enforcement of the civil rights laws as passed by Congress.

—Lani Guinier

There is a battle for truth.... The political question ... is truth itself.

—Michel Foucault

The Tough Love Crowd's solutions to many problems resemble—though they would be alarmed by the comparison—the Maoist creed of self-criticism. The Toughs object to calls for societal reform when in fact what may be necessary is self-reform. And the Toughs are a paradoxical crowd. They present themselves as critics, yet their work is anything but critical. They present themselves as heroes, yet their performance is anything but self-sacrificial. They claim to be outsiders even while they are sustained by the culture's most powerful institutions. And, crucially, they insist on being counted among the racially progressive. *That* claim can usefully be challenged. The Toughs disparage passion in the name of various ideals of disinterest, and this locks them, whatever their intentions, into conservative politics. The Toughs' dispassionate reckonings always omit important moral questions. They are undone by an unexamined belief that partisanship has no place in honest thinking. They believe (or, worse, pretend) that partisanship is an avoidable taint, whereas partisanship is neither avoidable nor a taint.

The Tough Love Crowd's belief that partisanship is bad is a particular failing *for them,* since each Tough is partisan in an important sense. Each has a declared concern for the well-being of the dispossessed. Clarence Thomas, Shelby Steele, Thomas Sowell, Stephen Carter, and Randall Kennedy all declare a concern for African Americans; V. S. Naipaul declares a concern for postcolonial peoples. Another thing the Toughs have in common, however, is that they might loosely be described as conservatives. Clarence Thomas, Shelby Steele, and Thomas Sowell endorse variants of a self-help ideology that sometimes resembles the politics of the U.S. right wing. Stephen Carter and Randall Kennedy pursue ideals of impersonal intellectual excellence that often resemble the politics of America's cultural conservatives. Likewise, when V. S. Naipaul tells the harsh truths that he thinks his audience needs to hear for their own good, his truths reflect values that underwrote centuries of European empire building. Consequently, many have argued that the Tough Love Crowd betrays the people it supposedly wants to help.

But what *accounts for* the Toughs' harsh stuff? Is it some kind of deep psychic bitterness? Armchair psychoanalysts have suggested, for instance, that Thomas's Supreme Court performance constitutes a deliberate vendetta against those who opposed him at the confirmation hearings. The *New Yorker* has speculated that Thomas's "jurisprudence seems guided to an unusual degree by raw anger" against his confirmation-hearing opponents, and by his refusal to "let bygones be bygones." It is hard, however, to imagine this sort of analysis being rendered of Scalia or of Rehnquist (and, as the *New Yorker* itself notes, Scalia and Thomas have voted together more than 85 percent of the time).

Another form of mind gazing claims that Justice Thomas is a "Tom," craving white approbation. While plausible, this is an unhelpful way to explain how Thomas decides cases. There are lots of ways to be sycophantic to whites, several of which might not so surely incur the scorn of blacks. "Tom" could probably satisfy any desire for white approval at less cost. Indeed, this view of Thomas is a precise mirror image of the Tough Love Crowd's projection of personal distress across entire peoples. Witness Shelby Steele: "Somewhere inside every black is a certain awe at the power and achievement of the white race."[1]

A further psychological claim—that Thomas places self-advancement above group allegiances—may be harder to dismiss. Opportunism might even genuinely illuminate the earlier stages of Thomas's career, and his rise to the Court. But opportunism fails to account for his continuing performance as a life-tenured public official. Thomas is now beholden to nobody, yet his course remains the same. Likewise, Carter and Kennedy are now life-tenured law professors, and Naipaul is arguably the single most decorated author in the United Kingdom. Thomas Sowell has been issuing Tough Love publications since at least 1972, long before black neoconservatism was the lucrative affair it has since become. Opportunism is a significant *but incomplete* explanation of the Tough Love Crowd's continuing conduct. Moreover, the claim that the Tough Love Crowd is simply self-interested raises unsolvable questions of motive. Since no one can know what *really* makes them tick, their good faith may, for the purposes of the present argument, be assumed. Far from being naive, this assumption simply acknowledges the complexity of human psychology. The opposite assumption—that the Toughs are deliberately evil—unrealistically credits them with superhuman stamina. As Jean-Paul Sartre has remarked, "Evil is fatiguing, it requires an unmaintainable vigilance."

In the present account, the Tough Love Crowd's allegiance to a variety of inherited methods (of judging, writing, investigating) looms large in explaining both how and why their dissent goes wrong. Clarence Thomas's search for African American well-being is guided by a belief that the requirements of reason are uncontroversial and are superior to passionate political activism. Thomas says that passion blights the civil rights movement and its leaders, who, ignoring rationality and truth, merely "bitch, bitch, bitch, moan and moan and whine." While Thomas has criticized an allegedly all-powerful "civil rights aristocracy," he insists that he has done so not primarily because of the civil rights movement's alleged elitism but rather because the movement is "really out of touch with reality."[2]

Stephen Carter, too, consistently conflates politicization with distortion (partisanship with taint), and calls for depoliticized ideals in everything that catches his eye (the Senate confirmation process, judicial decisionmaking, legal practice, law teaching, intellectual life generally, religious practice). Carter's most recent writing on the judicial confirmation process continues to champion his long-standing view that Supreme Court justices ought to work "without a scintilla of loyalty to movement or cause." Carter has, moreover, confessed to having produced bad analysis because of having "fallen into [a] trap" of hoping "to describe history with a sort of certainty that natural scientists bring to the task of describing the physical world." Carter tells us the "essential" truth (his frequent term) about any number of things. And this truth seldom unsettles anything. Carter's dispassionate inquiry into what really happened in the Watergate litigation begins as a "quasi-scientific" search, yet ends in a view that "conforms to tradition and intuition." Encouraged by this supposed coincidence of science and intuition, Carter consistently urges factual investigation and dispassionate search, whether in scholarship, judging, *or politics.*[3]

Likewise, Shelby Steele, in an insufficiently noticed feature of his work, adopts the language of clinical psychology to separate mere ideas (which are, in his phrase, "a dime a dozen") from his own views, which represent reality. And the back cover of *The Content of Our Character* claims that Steele's is "the perfect voice of reason in a sea of hate."

Thomas Sowell, meanwhile, has for decades been preaching the disciplinary realities of the marketplace, and the futility of civil rights. Sowell's book *Is Reality Optional?* answers—emphatically—that it is not. And Randall Kennedy advocates impersonal intellectual ideals of disinterest coupled with the impersonal testing of competing hypotheses—even concerning the most politically controversial issues. V. S. Naipaul, too, is forever claiming access to a bitter truth that eludes his critics. His earliest recorded piece of journalism is a 1956 article, published in the *Trinidad Guardian* and entitled "Honesty Needed in West Indian Writing." Naipaul has since consistently accused postcolonial opponents of turning away from a too overwhelming reality.

Yet the distinctions on which all this truth finding relies are complacent. These distinctions—between reason and passion, appearance and reality, political and apolitical, personal and impersonal, partisanship and disinterest—are entirely unreliable. The NAACP Legal Defense Fund (LDF), having reviewed the writings and speeches Thomas made while he chaired the EEOC, commented on the "extraordinary series of shifts" in Thomas's views on numerous issues. Thomas shifted a dozen times on affirmative action, in half as many years (1982–1988). Despite the instability of his views, the LDF noted, "whatever Thomas believes at a given point is to him an obvious, eternal truth. . . . He insists that whatever he says, even if different than what he said before, is the only possible conclusion any responsible person could come to."[4] The other Toughs also espouse unstable dogmas. Carter advocates more religious passion, but less egalitarian passion, in public debate. Thomas Sowell disparages the statistical and economic analysis performed by his opponents but reveres it when performed by himself and his allies. Randall Kennedy debunked impersonal scholarship in 1986, advocated it in 1989. Naipaul trashed Indian village life in 1964 and 1977, celebrated it in 1990. The Toughs' opinions shift over time and under the pressures of political controversy, but always they claim they speak the simple *truth*. And Tough truth finding, they assert, is vital in order to navigate the contemporary social landscape.

This search for a social landscape frequently leads the Tough Love Crowd to dignify antiprogressive politics as fact. Stephen Carter's widely discussed

*Wall Street Journal* op-ed article on affirmative action is a good example. Carter's piece entirely ignored his own concession, made elsewhere, that meritocracy is a myth. Carter argued instead that "racial preferences" simply *have* beneficiaries and that this conclusion is "not normative in any sense. It is simply a fact." But affirmative action (*quare*, "preferences") only creates issues of beneficiaries and of innocent victims if it involves lowering the very standards that Carter elsewhere admits are already displaced by various shams like a "star system." Carter's preferences, then, are not factual but controversial. Carter subsequently stated that he "never imagined" that simply publishing the article (in the *Wall Street Journal*) "would itself be a political act." Even if one here sets aside accusations of bad faith, what remains is such astonishing naivete in a prominent scholar that one wonders which is the harsher criticism—bad faith or stupidity. When the avalanche of correspondence responding to his op-ed piece arrived, it was predictably (to everyone but Carter) split on racial lines. White readers, Carter discloses, were generally appreciative; black readers were generally hostile. The disparate impact of Carter's column on his audience moved him to confess to "a degree of guilt" since he had not intended to give racist readers comfort.[5] Nevertheless Carter insists that it is unfair to call his Tough stuff anything but loyal dissent. And the usually incisive Henry Louis Gates, Jr., seemed to have this Crowd in mind when he said, on the *New York Times* op-ed page, "Critique, too, can be a form of caring."[6] The immediate context of the Gates article was a criticism of black antisemitism. It is unquestionably vital to condemn those who embrace anti-Jewish bigots—Pat Buchanan, Louis Farrakhan, *and Clarence Thomas.* Thomas has said that Farrakhan is "a man I have admired for more than a decade."[7]

Yet this does not mean that *every* self-styled critique of African America is always and inherently caring. The Toughs offer politically charged pronouncements on a range of issues that are far more debatable than antisemitism. It may indeed be that Judas is defunct in African America, and in the former colonies, but that conclusion requires argument, not assertion.

## The Atrocity of Tough Love

In bygone days, it might have been sufficient for the Tough Love Crowd's critics to rest with the complaint that the Toughs are moral but misguided, or naive but caring. This is no longer enough. The supposedly apolitical ideals that the Toughs follow stand too long exposed. Long ago the "strident" work of Franz Fanon or the "angry" autobiography of Malcolm X had to be championed and rescued as respectable work. Decades ago, Audre Lorde, Derek Walcott, Franz Fanon, Eric Williams, and C. L. R. James, resisting confining protocols in an array of academic "disciplines," had to explain and justify the intrusion of politics in scholarship and in art, much as one might excuse one's muddy feet on someone else's rug. Today, however, it is the defenders of quaint ideals who carry the burden of scholarly embarrassment.

The Tough Love Crowd's insistent claims of loyalty depend on the soundness of the very same ideas that the Toughs' new critics have successfully thrown into question. These new critics, Negro Crits, build on "The New Black Aesthetic"[8] and are further inspired by Gayatri Spivak, bell hooks, and Cornel West. Not only have Negro Crits applied old methods to previously neglected materials on the model of Henry Louis Gates Jr.'s masterful work *The Signifying Monkey* and Derrick Bell's treatise *Race, Racism, and American Law*; they have also gone further. Negro Crits have begun the hard work of creating new methods to resist the particular blind spots of the inherited ways. Where Gates "reverse[d]" Audre Lorde and asserted emphatically that "*only* the master's tools will ever dismantle the master's house,"[9] Negro Crits have successfully pressed further. In path-breaking work like Patricia Williams's *Alchemy of Race and Rights* and Derrick Bell's *And We Are Not Saved,* Negro Crits have begun to reshape the tools themselves by resisting impersonal ideals and emphasizing the inevitable links between autobiography and scholarship. Older approaches aimed to produce timeless monuments of pure intellect undefiled by the author's personal story; there the author stood outside the work and pared her fingernails, like Stephen Dedalus. Negro Crits, in contrast, insist that identity and creativity *have always been* inseparable. When Samuel Beckett was asked why his country produced a wealth of literature, he commented that the British had left the Irish in a ditch, with no other option but to sing. African Americans, too, know why the caged bird sings. And in Trinidad Spree Simon, descendant of a slave, rummaged in a garbage dump, salvaged an oil drum, and created the twentieth century's only new musical instrument: the steel pan. Negro Crits, pressing this insight in areas previously closed to them, are inventing new tools, like law-and-autobiography. There has been progress, but also resistance. Conservative Allan Bloom (author of *The Closing of the American Mind*) has described Negro Criticism as "unprofitable hokum." And this resistance extends beyond such zealots. Negro Crit progress and the continuing resistance to it are both captured in a recent *Stanford Law Review*'s comment, authored by two reputedly progressive lawyers: "What is new and noteworthy is that *[Alchemy]*, a book consisting of a series of such autobiographical narratives would be hailed as a major work of legal scholarship. ... *Scholars should not be readily allowed to offer their own experiences as evidence*" (emphasis added).[10]

The Tough Love Crowd is an important additional part of this resistance. Clarence Thomas: "I heartily approve of [Bloom's] critique of black studies."[11] The Toughs thus enter a *political* struggle over what counts as culturally valuable. V. S. Naipaul has urged—in *What's Wrong with Being a Snob?*— that to civilize a place "you recognize the primitive and try to eradicate it." The erection and sustenance of the Toughs' intellectual tastes absolutely require such combative political effort. The Toughs can press their ideas upon us only at the expense of a ravished "culturally disenfranchised" (Edward Said's phrase). In this setting, the choice of an intellectual approach *is itself* a moral and political choice with moral and political consequences.

Talk of intellectual morality is sometimes felt to be hopeless given that so many people today believe that everything depends on subjective opinion. Yet contemporary skepticism has exactly the opposite significance: skepticism does not mean that talk of morality in scholarship is gibberish. Rather, *skepticism makes moral choice unavoidable.* We can no longer run from ethics by claiming to offer simple truth. Drucilla Cornell has, for instance, emphasized the neglected moral imperative generated by what is flaccidly called "postmodernism." In *The Philosophy of the Limit,* Cornell emphasizes that "the identification of deconstruction with ethical skepticism is a serious misinterpretation." Cornell persuasively suggests that attention to the culturally dispossessed is the "ethical aspiration" behind Jacques Derrida's work. And Edward Said has long emphasized that the chosen manner of beginning scholarship, of choosing what to let in and what to exclude, is "*ethical* in the widest sense of that term" (Said's emphasis).[12]

In this setting, the Tough Love Crowd's old thinking is a *moral* failing, and it directly raises questions of political loyalty and, alas, of political betrayal. The Toughs are aware of the serious challenges to their old ways. They simply choose to ignore these challenges rather than to engage them. Stephen Carter, who among the Toughs has come closest to facing these issues, only glimpses the problems and retreats. Carter frequently refers to his preferred disinterested intellectual ideal as a dinosaur technique. Carter concedes that his constitutional theory of original intent is "practically anathema" among serious legal theorists. And Carter concedes that his own arguments in favor of a moral obligation to obey the law (of obvious relevance to the de jure oppressed) revivify "a quaint relic of a more primitive era in the development of political philosophy."[13] Yet, as though such confessions confer immunity, Carter persists in his self-disparaged ways. Carter has yet to grasp the ethical self-immolation of his ritual admissions.

More generally, the Tough Love Crowd adopts an old ideal best expressed by Julien Benda's classic work, *The Betrayal of the Clerks* (1927). The Toughs all assume that intellectual loyalty is always and inherently fulfilled by Julien Benda's creed of independence. They do not pause to consider the questions, Independence from *what?* In the service of *what?* The Tough Love Crowd assumes that an intellectual has fulfilled her moral and political loyalty if she participates "independently" within the prevailing academic culture. Yet mightn't one suspect that a vague independence is an ideal egoist's garb? And perhaps egos are in ample supply among intellectuals? Are egotism and political loyalty, then, always compatible? Stephen Carter openly "plead[s] guilty" to being influenced by the "professional reception" of his work.[14] Is this concern really always and automatically compatible with moral and political loyalty to the dispossessed? Carter believes that "to succeed in a profession, one adopts the profession's ethos, its aesthetic, its culture. One remakes significant aspects of oneself." He concedes that this will often "feel like a surrender to white power." Even while declining to join those who are challenging that power's hold on the criteria of professional conduct, Carter asserts without argument that his position is not *really* surrender and is consistent with solidarity. The tension between racial-justice concerns and the perceived demands of professional success is entirely explicit in a 1980 Thomas interview. There Thomas said that if

I ever went to work for the EEOC or did anything directly connected with blacks, my career would be irreparably ruined.... The monkey would be on my back to prove that I didn't have the job because I'm black. People meeting me for the first time would automatically dismiss my thinking as second rate.[15]

Again, what about the paradoxical animal, ivory-tower careerism, that Randall Kennedy has recently brought into the open? Among the multiple lessons that Kennedy announces he has learned from the Guinier affair is that "intellectuals who anticipate appointment to high office" should beware that their writings will be taken literally. Guinier herself took a rather different lesson from the experience. Her first law review article to appear since the debacle thanks those who "encouraged me to pursue my ideas, despite the apparent political cost." Guinier's resistance to the demands of the jobkeepers is perhaps what led the *Wall Street Journal* to describe her as a "young, black tart-tongued law professor."[16] The Toughs are evidently more mannerly.

There is much to suggest that the incentives prevailing in the civic guilds (of law, literature, economics, the judiciary) are frequently opposed to progressive politics. Yet the Toughs rest content with a lethargic faith in the inherited ways. In this, many of the Toughs are political casualties of the quietly oppressive ideals of amateur humanism:

Humanism's inability to attend to its own involvement, contrary to its expressed desires, in the concrete operations of power—in other words, its naive faith in aesthetic and moral "disinterest" as well as its refusal to recognize the "origins" of reason in power—frustrate its confessed desires for moral or ideological reform.[17]

This formulation entirely—albeit abstractly—captures a claim that the following pages will flesh out in detail: the political allegiances of the Tough Love Crowd are frustrated by a relatively unquestioning entry into prevailing ways of doing things (whether in law, literature, or economics). V. S. Naipaul has, for instance, conceded that his harshest opinions about postcolonial places were caused by an unfortunate "romantic 19th Century notion of the Writer . . . as the reader of externals."

The conservative political significance of pursuing old ways is obvious in the Tough Love Crowd's work. Clarence Thomas adopts the generally conservative legal theory of original intent. Stephen Carter (avowed originalist) and Randall Kennedy (arguably originalist)[18] adopt not only originalism itself but also a manner of legal scholarship that lies well within the old ways. Carter and Kennedy reject not only Negro Criticism but also any other kind of lawyering that challenges inherited custom. They choose to be among law's tweediest professors and yet assert, without argument, that this choice is morally and politically responsible.

Thomas Sowell, meanwhile, stands by the imagined ability of social scientists (especially economists) to detect underlying realities about the world. Sowell refuses to contend with powerful contemporary arguments that scientific method, too, is drenched in value judgments—that scientists are able to solve problems only because their guilds set solvable problems and suppress askable questions.[19] Meanwhile V. S. Naipaul, in both his fiction and his nonfiction, asserts a degree of freedom from ideology that for a long time—and certainly before "postmodernism"—has been questionable within literary practice. Throughout Naipaul's career, the deludedness of postcolonial peoples has been a constant theme. And he has rejected a vibrant tradition of oppositional writing that has thrived alongside his own offerings. Finally, as we approach the twenty-first century, Shelby Steele would extend nineteenth-century laissez-faire economics to new terrain. He advocates an "Adam Smith vision of culture."[20] These guys would ensnare us forever in the way things were.

## The Tough Love Fact Trap

Are we free to believe whatever we choose or whatever is consistent with our prejudices, whether about Western civilization, the economy, or the credibility of Anita Hill? Is there no independent reality that we need to check these beliefs against?
—Thomas Sowell, *Is Reality Optional?*

Tough Love has political costs. These costs happen every time the Toughs present as a closed issue of fact what is and ought to be an issue open for debate. Take, for example, racist backlash. The Toughs uniformly claim that such sentiment is caused by the various excesses of the civil rights movement. If, for instance, you thought the Guinier debacle reflected presidential abdication and ill-informed journalists who became, in Guinier's phrase, "stenographers to the powerful," think again. Where Guinier protested that "my opponents were successful in defining me in a way that even my own mother does not recognize," Randall Kennedy assures us, in an article entitled "Lani Guinier's Constitution," that Guinier's opponents "accurately perceived her racial politics." In Kennedy's neutral description, Guinier's thought just *really* was ahead of the curve. Clint Bolick, who supported the Clarence Thomas nomination, opposed the 1991 Civil Rights Act, wrote an article under the headline "Clinton's Quota Queens" criticizing Lani Guinier, and characterized subsequent Clinton nominee Deval Patrick as a "Stealth Guinier," clearly agrees with Kennedy. Bolick said, in a MacNeil/Lehrer panel discussion the day the Patrick nomination was announced, that Kennedy and Carter would make acceptable civil rights nominees because they were both "very thoughtful," whereas Guinier and Patrick were not "mainstream." And while Kennedy criticized the low intellectual standards of the press coverage of the Guinier affair, his own treatment of Guinier's work— asking whether she was mainstream and answering that she was not— *exactly* duplicates the flaws that, according to Laurel Leff in the *Columbia Journalism Review,* were the central defect of press coverage of the affair.

Media fixation with Kennedy's question (is she "mainstream"?) was *itself* the problem, according to Leff, since the idea of "a" noncontroversial mainstream in the abstruse and politically charged area of voting rights law is itself entirely illusory. Kennedy offered entirely unspecified "intellectual" criticism of the Guinier press coverage, even while his own writing duplicated the skewed agenda (is she mainstream?) and the questionable conclusions of the press stenographers themselves. Kennedy, like the press corps, claims the ability to provide a factual description of Guinier, and of the mainstream that she is outside. What gets entirely lost, in Kennedy's deceptively temperate critique of Guinier's scholarship, is Guinier's own claim that she is and was mainstream (if that term has any meaning) and that the proper moral and *prescriptive* goal is to make *that* fact clear. This claim was erased in both the *Wall Street Journal*'s criticism of the "pervasiveness of the racial prism through which [Guinier] views every issue" and Kennedy's own remark that Guinier's writings "recklessly . . . overplay[ed] the racism card." Again, we may have thought Clint Bolick's view that Guinier belonged to "a profoundly left-wing school of thought that has redefined the outer boundaries of radicalism in legal academia" was his zealotry speaking. Think again. Kennedy now tells us that "intellectuals on the left supplied a real basis to fuel the anxieties wrongly loosed upon Guinier."[21] Suddenly the *Journal* itself seems sane. Kennedy's truth works wonders. Kennedy has not yet openly endorsed the Democratic Leadership Conference (DLC) agenda: the removal of race from U.S. politics for the benefit of the Democratic party organization. Yet it is hard not to read his discussion of the Guinier affair as implicit cheerleading on the DLC's behalf.[22] Indeed, for Kennedy, no less than for the *Washington Times* (Clint Bolick, David Brock, William F. Buckley, Jr., the pre-judicial Clarence Thomas, et al.), Guinier inhabited an "idiosyncratic ideological universe."[23]

Both Kennedy's taste for investigation into whether Guinier was mainstream and his conclusion that she was not reflect his more general preference for a process of empirical testing in legal and other scholarship, and elsewhere. Kennedy's implicit vindication of Guiner's opponents, when he pronounced that *she* was indeed not mainstream, reflected this more general Tough trait: the Toughs are confident that they have a finely tuned grip on political reality. Kennedy, for instance, appears to think he possesses the becalmed political "skill of a tightrope walker."[24] While this circus metaphor is unintentionally astute, Kennedy's political savvy may nevertheless be doubted.

Stephen Carter, too, claims to have a firm grip. Carter frequently announces that a particular argument "carries a good thing too far"—or that beyond a line discerned by himself, the interplay of politics and religion becomes "not cross-pollination but pollution." In a phrase that wonderfully captures the sleight of hand generally involved in Tough Love truth claims, Carter unveils an "empirical hunch" (!) crucial to his constitutional law analysis, that most Americans believe their society is "essentially just." Such impressionistic certainty is the central problem with Carter's crowd. Carter instinctively claims that his well-tutored sensibility reflexively grasps the true line between numerous sanities and various excesses. He endorses ideals of professionalism and expertise to the precise extent that they enlarge his personal authority. Carter resists "concepts of government-by-the-most-qualified" as "anathema" to America whenever his own legal or religious ox stands to be gored by other experts, such as those in the physical sciences. On the question of a domain of *legal*-professional expertise, however, Carter's views are diametrically the opposite. He has faith in legal expertise. He insists that members of the Senate and the general public lack the competence to assess a Supreme Court nominee's judicial philosophy. He says that that job of assessment should be left to lawyers. Yet Carter's faith in lawyers is itself interestingly flexible. Elsewhere, when bar associations and law professors inconveniently endorse *Roe v. Wade* as a correct reading of the Constitution, Carter suddenly warns that the mere politically motivated prochoice views of lawyers should not be given too much credence, or else "there is scarcely any need for *judges*" [25] (emphasis added). Tough truth is a wonderful trick.

## Tough Professional Trafficking

Professionalism works, in the Tough Love fact trick, like one view of the societal function of religion. A familiar line of thought argues that religion is the opium of the masses—that despite its supposed concern for the well-being of people, religion distracts the faithful, making them pay too much attention to abstractions and afterlife, too little attention to worldly injustice. People are taught to turn the other cheek. Political energies are consumed in private rapture rather than public protest. And the status quo stays unscathed. Whether this picture of religion is accurate or not, there is now a more powerful opiate: reality, today disclosed by professionals, not priests. The Toughs are prominent peddlers of this new thing.

And their new opium gets a great press. Every day newspaper commentary on political events contrasts blundering idealism with savvy realism. Competent academics, politicians, writers, and judges face facts. Idle dreamers ignore reality. One Tough reality we all ought apparently to face is the ameritocracy of American meritocracy. The Toughs themselves emphasize that American meritocracy is, and probably always will be, "a sham arrangement" or a "star system," removed from measurable performance indicators.[26] Yet, despite their own concession that ameritocracy is certainly prevailing and probably permanent, the Tough Love Crowd urges us to drop such issues and, like the Nike sportswear slogan, Just Do It. This might be brilliant parental advice, but Clarence Thomas is not my mother. Supreme Court justices, lawyers, writers, and intellectuals exercise public *power* in various ways that people's parents generally cannot. Moreover, Tough Love reality is itself only a list of incorrect or fallible hunches. Tough truth frequently turns out to be *bad* parental advice. For instance, on the meritocracy question, Carter says that to debate performance criteria is futile because "committed professionals" are too busy meeting self-evident demands to "spend time quibbling" over things like "the standards ... for law firm partnership."[27] Yet Carter, from his academic vantage point, understates the degree to which there currently *is* quibbling over precisely the things that he would set beyond debate. Law firms are, today, very much occupied by questions like: Should a part-time arrangement for parent-professionals— the so-called mommy track—necessarily be a downward climb? What exactly are technical legal skills? Is the distracted Ivy League genius really more skillful than the reliable second-tier drone? Are drafting skills more important than client rapport? Are any of these as important as political connections? Moreover, several Wall Street law firms continue to make deliberate tradeoffs *against* increased profits and in favor of what Carter would, apparently, call an unprofessional collegiality. In this setting, it is the *failure* to stop and think about a firm's manner of measuring performance that is, today, a hallmark of professional incompetence. *In the laudable drive to be good lawyers, writers, economists, or judges, the Toughs neglect the fact that the best professionals are those who effectively question and reshape the very idea of what it means to be a good professional. The best are those who, in the journalese of the business press, "change the rules of the game," whatever their field of expertise.*

Rather than pursue this kind of vibrant and transformative excellence, Carter is contentedly "seduced by the standards under which my white professional world judges achievement." Despite the numerous and controversial questions around what "professionalism" means, Carter urges that *"the disciplining rules that define the profession itself [are not] in any comprehensible sense, ideological"* (emphasis added). Carter's static and romanticized picture of legal and other professionals is hardly undebatable truth. And Carter's unawareness that politics defines professionalism is, on its own merits, entirely unattractive.[28]

Always, despite the Tough Love Crowd's faith in apolitical ideals, the political and professional reality that they would map for us is inherently far from objective. Was Lani Guinier really scary? Was Ronald Reagan really not? Old certainties about justice, rationality, and family values have given way to energetic debate over questions like, Whose Justice? Which Rationality? Whose Family? Which Values?[29]

In such a context, people who care about professional standards, justice, rationality, and family values ought not to let hostile interpretation sit like unchallengeable fact. We ought to be relentlessly skeptical. *This call for skepticism is not just a piece of useful advice, but rather an ethical obligation.* If we countenance "painful" facts, we may have committed secular sin. The media, the courts, the academic institutions, and the literary establishment actively construct society's "regime of truth."[30] And the Tough Love Crowd neglects the fact that this regime of truth is the site of political struggle, not a preexisting order to be unveiled.

The question of whether, for instance, Anita Hill's disclosures in the Clarence Thomas confirmation hearings were credible or not is not likely to be settled by a thing called fact. "Credibility" hinges on numerous irrational factors, including cultural assumptions about the reliability (or lack thereof) of black women. It is thus interesting to watch the various attempts to treat the confirmation hearings as a subject of factual investigation, an approach to the Hill-Thomas affair specifically advocated by Stephen Carter. Thomas Sowell affirms that David Brock's book, *The Real Anita Hill,* offered only "facts and careful analysis."[31] Brock's assessment of Hill's testimony hinged on attacking the credibility of her story in various of its details. Ironically, Brock's own factual inaccuracies were promptly exposed by his ideological opponents.[32] The credibility of Brock's text quickly became the issue. Brock's believers probably dismiss his occasional inaccuracies as mere blemishes that do not cast doubt on the believability of his narrative as a whole. Yet this is precisely the defense that Anita Hill's supporters offer when confronted with the sort of minor inaccuracies that Brock makes it his business to assemble. Professional investigation has thus settled very little. Yet Brock's truth

continues to play a remarkably direct role in the political process, for instance, assisting a delay in the Senate's confirmation of a Clinton nominee.[33]

Take, next, a far more objective issue: Did Clinton live up to his campaign
pledge to cut the White House Staff by 25 percent? It's almost impossible to
frame an easier or more verifiable political question. The answer to this
clear-cut empirical question appeared in the *New York Times,* and the headline
speaks for itself: "Clinton Says He's Met Pledge to Cut Staff by 25%:
Republicans Accuse the President of Gimmickry."[34]

Clearly, then, the investigative approach to politics will be inconclusive
because the investigator's own values will inevitably shape her curiosities
and influence her conclusions, while her audience may have different values.
For identical reasons, the facts supplied by an investigator will not command
the kind of universal agreement possible with uncontroversial facts like the
opening hours of a supermarket or the operating hours of an abortion clinic.
The attraction of facts is that, where available, they are universally binding.
They are thought to provide *everyone* with reasons for belief and for action,
regardless of strong differences on questions of value. Whether one's intention is to use the facilities of a Florida abortion clinic or to kill the person in
charge, the *fact* that the clinic's operating hours are nine to five is useful
information. But such facts are rarely if ever the subject of political or
intellectual controversy. Even the most fact-resembling political controversies are inseparable from questions of value and from the vagaries of impres-
sions and appearances. Think of John Sununu, John Tower. Think especially
of Ronald Reagan's eight teflon years, and of the disgraced Oliver North's
bid to become a Virginia senator. Somehow William Kennedy Smith was not
guilty of rape, and David Gergen was never really a Republican.

As people concerned with helping the less well off, we ought to recognize
the limitedness of political fact and face the choices this predicament presents, choices about which values we wish to pursue. When the Toughs
declare their own dissenting "truths," they are dealing in the currency of
values. And doling out counterfeit fact.

### Why the Toughs Need Truth

Almost everything written about "black conservatism" concedes that it lacks
a constituency. The real-fact trick is thus indispensable for the Toughs in a
way that it is not for those with popular support. Lacking a constituency, the
Tough Love Crowd needs the claim of *truth* in order to stay aboard the

progressive project. The Toughs think oppression is immoral. Yet to many people their own agenda looks oppressive. They concede that their agenda involves bitter medicine, but they deny that it departs from their commitment to the dispossessed, claiming that it simply faces truth. They need this claim of truth to discipline a recalcitrant constituency and make it see its real best interests. But suppose their truth is a Trojan horse? The fact that many people doubt claims of objective truth creates an uneven playing field, *to the disadvantage of the Tough Love Crowd.* They speak on our behalf except they sound like our opponents. If their truths are ideological fetish, their love is rough self-pleasuring. And we be* more protected with their Trojan swords sheathed.[35]

---

*The conjugation "we be" is a grammatically correct African American usage. See Clarence Major, *Juba to Jive: A Dictionary of African American Slang* (New York: Penguin, 1994), 25.

# Julien Benda's Constitution

Never were there so many political works among those which ought to be the mirror of disinterested intelligence.

—Julien Benda, *The Betrayal of the Clerks*

I am an intellectual not a leader. I observe what others are doing and try to stand apart from it as I analyze it.

—Stephen Carter, *Reflections of an Affirmative Action Baby*

Julien Benda (1867–1956) was a French writer and philosopher who powerfully defended the purity of reason against what he saw as decadent contemporary intellectual movements. He belittled emotion, intuition, and sensation. Benda's *La Trahison des Clercs* is easily the most influential rendition of the tradition of disinterested truth seeking. Roland Barthes has commented that "a small study could be done on the contemporary descendants of Julien Benda" and that Benda's intellectual ideal seems "an attitude of mind destined to travel imperturbably across the ages."[1] Yet this ostensibly disinterested tradition was, *for Benda himself,* frankly intended to promote a conservative political agenda and to suppress what he viewed as misguided utopian activism. Benda scathingly dismissed those who sought to change the political world. He instead addressed those "whose activity essentially is not the pursuit of practical aims, all these who seek their joy in the practice of an art or a science or metaphysical speculation, in short in the possession of non-material advantages, and hence in a manner say 'My Kingdom is not of this world.' "

Stephen Carter, too, is concerned to shore up "the wall that traditionally kept those who lived the life of the mind separate from the world in which they lived it."[2] Having ostensibly renounced the affairs of the world, having ostensibly opted for nonmaterial advantage even while living in manifest material comfort, Julien Benda advocated impersonal ideals: "Man belongs neither to his language nor to his race; he belongs only to himself, for he is a free being, that is, a moral being."

Randall Kennedy, too, has argued that in meritorious scholarship "race, nationality, religion, class and personal qualities as such are irrelevant." Justice Thomas described his debates at the EEOC as "unfettered" and "liberating."[3] For Thomas, as for Benda, lay passions fetter truth. V. S. Naipaul, for his part, dismisses entire genres of writing because they are "missionary stuff being passed off as scholarship." And at the height of the Guinier controversy, Harvard Law School professor Mary Ann Glendon took to the pages of the *Wall Street Journal* to accuse Guinier of a sacrilegious confusion of advocacy with scholarship. Meanwhile, the *New York Times* opened up its coverage of the Guinier affair with the headline, "Guerrilla Fighter for Civil Rights." Guinier, it was widely argued, transgressed ideals of impartiality and of disinterested professionalism.

Yet there is much evidence, in the Guinier affair, in political clashes generally, and in Benda's essay itself, that this rhetoric of impartiality is itself avowedly a political tactic. Benda was, despite contrary appearances, entirely concerned with the real world: "My subject is the influence that the clerks have had in the world, and not what they were in themselves." And he believed that intellectuals could exert actual influence in society since the "adhesion of the 'clerks' to the passions of the layman fortifies these passions in the hearts of the latter." Benda urged that, rather than fortify lay passions, the intellectual's true function is to deflate social unrest: "In bringing this partiality to historical narrative the modern 'clerk' most seriously derogates from his true function, if I am right in saying that *his function is to restrain the passions of the layman.*"

The Toughs work within this ideal. For Benda, the civic sphere was inveterately consumed by passions (Step One); but the clerks could (and ought) to resist this taint as the best way to restrain those unfortunate, inevitable passions (Step Two); and the question of remedying the underlying grievances never arose, because those grievances were not rational, merely passionate (Step Three). For Thomas, society is inveterately race conscious (Step One); but the policymaker can (and ought) to resist this taint as the best way to restrain those unfortunate, inevitable racial passions (Step Two); and the question of remedying the grievances underlying racial passions is suppressed because impassioned grievances are not "rational," merely passionate (Step Three). These three steps are entirely explicit in Thomas's response to Derrick Bell's work, printed in the *Wall Street Journal* and suggestively headlined "The Black Experience: Rage and Reality."[4] The remaining question is whether the Tough Love Crowd's Bendaresque pedigree and the antipassion campaign that goes along with it perhaps undo their racial-justice allegiances.

## *Julien Benda's Politics*

When Julien Benda flaunts his credentials he does so as the savvy Machiavellian, not the donnish recluse. Benda berates his opponents for *political* clumsiness, not hapless truth finding: "Modern equalitarians, by failing to understand that there can be no equality except in the abstract and that inequality is the essence of the concrete, have merely displayed the extraordinary vulgarity of their minds as well as their amazing political clumsiness."

Likewise Stephen Carter criticizes the reasoning in *Roe v. Wade,* not primarily for its analytical defects but because it "stands out as a *political* failure." *Roe* is, for Carter, a political failure because of the persistence of open opposition to the decision. Carter's message is that if your political goals will occasion open and resilient opposition, you should adjust your ideals: "One receives only imperfect justice in the world; only fools, children, left-wing Democrats, social scientists, and a few demented judges expect anything better."

This language is the epigraph of an article that is the cornerstone of Carter's constitutional theory. The passage is, ironically, the invented speech of a fictional judge in Walter Murphy's novel *The Vicar of Christ.* Carter concedes that the judicial restraint—apolitical, somehow nonactivist decisionmaking—counseled in his epigraph is a "sad and somewhat unfashionable philosophy" among lawyers.[5] So, in order to manufacture the harsh truth about judges that we all *ought* afterward to face, Stephen Carter turns to fiction. Carter's counsel of judicial restraint is harsh prescription rather than dispassionate description. For Benda and the Tough Love Crowd, the thinker *ought* to peddle opium to the masses. Benda applauds the Church for grasping "that love between men can only be created by developing in them the sensibility for the abstract man, and by combating in them the interest for the concrete man; by turning them towards metaphysical meditation and away from the study of the concrete."

This robust agenda is rather a long way from the disinterested, insular musings with which we began. A legal-constitutional version of Benda's view can, moreover, be found in the Tough constitutional doctrine of original intent. Clarence Thomas has referred favorably to an original-intent picture of the Constitution in which "equal opportunity—*with all the inequalities of result this necessarily produces*—was the goal, and the Declaration of Independence was the guide." Thomas elsewhere wrote that this *true* equal opportunity America, the one with necessary inequalities, has been hijacked: "The tragedy of the civil rights movement is that as blacks achieved full exercise of their rights as citizens, government expanded, and blacks became an interest group in a coalition supporting expanded government." [6]

The idea that Blacks are now simply a special interest group where before they had legitimate claims is obviously not a value-neutral observation but a slice of Reagan-era ideology. The Toughs have an urgent, explicit agenda. Constitutional law professor Kathleen Sullivan has written that David Brock's book, *The Real Anita Hill*, is less a work of investigative journalism than "a tract in a cultural war" against progressive policies. [7] In such a context the Tough Love Crowd's mantra, "unhappy truth," is a hapless oxymoron.

## The Consequences of Benda's Ideal

Despite Benda's conservative social vision, sustained progressive resistance to his ideal is difficult to find. While Noam Chomsky laudably resists fake claims of objectivity in scholarship, his response is not to abandon the intellectual ideal of somehow-pure truth, but rather to seek it in "far-reaching, deep-seated universal principles of language structure." This pursuit accounts for an entire school of linguistics to which Chomsky has given his name. And, beyond linguistics, Chomsky's investigations occasionally unearth questionable political generalizations like the following: "Class transcends race." [8] Ellis Cose's *Rage of a Privileged Class*, documenting the persistence of race-related grievance among African America's successful, suggests the contrary.

Edward Said, too, discussing Julien Benda, understates Benda's ideological agenda. Said suggests that according to Benda the intellectual's vocation was "to tell the truth regardless of material consequences." [9] Yet this is a sanguine interpretation. Benda very deliberately pursued the ideal that intellectuals ought to peddle opium to the masses. Moreover, it is entirely possible to oppose lies, as Said wishes to do, without dignifying the notion of an absolute intellectual vocation, ostensibly above civic controversy.

Again, a prominent strand of the critical legal studies movement (henceforth, "Café Crits")[10] also adheres to Benda's transcendental standard of rationality, despite all the energy the Café Crits spend exposing the questionableness of institutions and of laws that pose as natural. This loyalty to the tradition of authoritative investigation, which is at the heart of important Café Crit disagreements with Negro Crits,[11] is most visible in the "structuralist" strand of Café Crit thought. Café Crits of this variety were convinced, in the midseventies, that they could discern what *really* makes law tick. They thought they had discovered a universal "fundamental contradiction" in all legal issues. Even after this audacious claim was renounced, the Café Crit search for truth did not disappear but was merely reblended into a supposedly more concrete "phenomenology of being."

The habit of faith in investigation and truth is a feature of Café Crit thought, well beyond Café Crit's structuralists and phenomenologists. Roberto Unger believes that fruitful activism requires an overarching "credible theory of social transformation" that the discerning critical scholar produces through brilliant scrivening. Much of Café Crit thought purports to deliver sweaty activists from untutored folly. Peter Gabel, for instance, unabashedly suggests that legal scholarship and political activism must wait upon "a general theory of life."[12] While such Café Crit writing makes wonderful reading, it too often ignores the possibility that political transformation must draw its energy from someplace mundane rather than transcendental.[13] Andrew Ross has commented that such ethereal theorizing is about as likely to mobilize change as "the spells of medieval witches or consultations of the I Ching."[14]

Yet, harrowingly, the suppressed fault line posed by the solitary investigative tradition of Julien Benda remains dimly perceived. Professor Derrick Bell has, for instance, added a preface to the paperback version of his inspirational and far from pessimistic book, *Faces at the Bottom of the Well.* In this new preface, Bell likens himself to a solitary prophet wandering unheeded in a wilderness. It is clear, both in the context of the book and in light of Bell's long-standing resistance to rhetorics of impartiality, that he is not advocating anything resembling the ideal of untethered scholarship to which the image of solitary truth bearer that he invokes is usually hitched. Yet Benda's metaphors are so well entrenched that the model of lonely truth spills as easily from Bell's pen as it did from Said's, from Chomsky's.

This invisible and widespread influence of ideals of disinterest and of solitary truth finding gives unnecessary credence to the Tough Love Crowd's idea that one can both work within the received ways of the academy and *thereby* render best political service to one's community. This paradox—the pursuit of racial justice through relatively raceless models—gives rise to some interesting wrinkles *within* the Tough Love creed. The Toughs all attempt to contain the varying degrees of race consciousness to which they admit. They assert that racial allegiances, whether inherently unhealthy (Steele) or potentially nurturing (Carter), ought not to enter the practice of the individual's craft. They assume that race-conscious craft is tainted craft, because the rules of good craft are race neutral. Good craft, they assert, restrains racial and other passions. They are Julien Benda's progeny.

## The Tough Love Crowd's Troubled Loyalty to Julien Benda

When the soul of a man is born in this country there are nets flung at it to hold it back from flight. You talk to me of nationality, language, religion. I shall try to fly by those nets. . . . Ireland is the old sow that eats her farrow.
—Stephen Dedalus, in *Portrait of the Artist as a Young Man*

Varying degrees of allegiance to untainted truth define the Tough Love Crowd. Clarence Thomas advocates a public sphere governed by reason and untainted by mere passions. Likewise, Thomas Sowell venerates those who "put truth above popularity." For Stephen Carter, the exemplary intellectual resists "the seductive call of group identity." Carter allows that racial solidarity is generally permissible, even beneficial, but he objects that race consciousness is treacherous in a person's role as intellectual. Carter says, "The entire point is that the majority view is irrelevant to the intellectual, whose authority must be the authority of reason. . . . We must worship no authority as absolute, except for the authority of truth itself."

Carter endorses Benda's notion that intellectualism is legitimately "an end in itself." Yet Carter does not renounce group allegiances. Rather, he slides from assertions that constituencies are irrelevant to intellectuals (as quoted above) to assertions that untethered truth seekers are, after all, serving their constituencies' best interests: "Free thinking is . . . the greatest service individuals can perform for their communities."

Randall Kennedy, with a similar ostensible heroism, resists the "powerful demand for loyal conformity." Kennedy instead endorses the "independent claims of intellectual craft" above the methods of those "self-conscious progressives" who fashion their scholarship "into ideological weaponry serving immediate political ends." Kennedy endorses a Bendaresque "commitment to truth above partisan social allegiances." Yet, like Carter, Kennedy's renunciation of "partisan social allegiances" is unstable. Kennedy has conceded that "*all* writers seek to make an impact on the world and [that] *all* writings that reach an audience create some impact—even if nothing but boredom" (Kennedy's emphasis). Kennedy added that "one surely ought to be concerned with the political implications of one's work." Kennedy ceded nearly ten pages of his "Racial Critiques" article to a discussion of whether, politically, he ought to have published the article, given that it was widely criticized within the community of minority scholars and was potentially useful to opponents of racial justice. But whether to publish or not is, in this context, an easy and uninteresting question (just do it). The interesting question is not whether one publishes what one arrives at, but how and why one arrives there in the first place. The interesting aspect of Kennedy's nine-page discussion is not the question he thinks he is addressing, but the very fact that he is addressing it: the fact that he is ostensibly concerned with group welfare. His kingdom *is* of this world. Kennedy's ultimate claim is not that group well-being is irrelevant to his intellectual pursuits, but that the group is *better served* by his chosen methods.

V. S. Naipaul, likewise, consistently adopts the view that "people with a cause inevitably turn themselves off intellectually." He proclaims that "I have no enemies, no rivals, no masters; I fear no one." Yet he, too, is very much of this world. He insists that novel writing necessarily "has to do with a concern for human existence." Naipaul asserts that his harsh diagnoses are in the true best interests of the peoples he surveys.[15] While Shelby Steele asserts that "politics bore me to tears," he also asserts that he is thankfully "in the same camp as Martin Luther King," and he insists that he writes out of love for African America.

Thomas, Kennedy, Carter, Naipaul, Steele, and Sowell can illuminatingly be contrasted with a certain picture of Stanley Crouch. Stephen Carter tendentiously describes Crouch as a reveling iconoclast, exultant in his outcast status and "proud to be a traitor to the black nationalist movement of the late 1960s." Yet there is another Stanley Crouch. This other Crouch (the one Carter ignores) is in no doubt that "the Negro is still at the moral center of American writing." This other Crouch has unusually thoughtful praise for, as well as unusually insightful criticism of, Jesse Jackson. This other Crouch claims, however (exactly like Carter and the other Toughs), that there have been such marked changes in America that traditional civil rights groups have been overtaken and are still fighting yesterday's war. This

Crouch, like the other Toughs, considers that his duty as an intellectual is to resist "the martial cattle car of presuppositions and clichés" and the blinkering "mud of racial limitation."[16]

Carter thus exaggerates the difference between Crouch and himself. Carter creates a Stanley Crouch in the image of the treacherous Other—and Carter recoils in horror from this vision of treachery. Carter's Crouch is invented so that Carter's reader can see someone crossing a line that Carter ostensibly refuses to cross. Thomas, Kennedy, Carter, Naipaul, Steele, and Sowell each reject the specter of betrayal and instead embrace a rhetoric of concern for the dispossessed.

Carter's invented Crouch is very like James Joyce's invented hero, Stephen Dedalus. The young Dedalus is determined to discover "the mode of life or art whereby [his] spirit could express itself in unfettered freedom." Carter's Crouch might easily join Joyce's Dedalus in declaring that "I will not serve that in which I no longer believe, whether it call itself my home, my fatherland, or my church. . . . I do not fear to be alone or to be spurned for another or to leave whatever I have to leave."[17]

The Tough Love Crowd ultimately recoils from such abandon. Although for strategic reasons they employ the language of neobohemian individualism, the Tough Love Crowd embraces, rather than disowns, the political burdens of racial allegiance. It is *important* to the Tough Lovers that they serve racial justice. They are partisans of racial justice. Carter's invented Crouch is illuminatingly different. Like Joyce's Dedalus, this Crouch tweaks the nose of damnation. Dedalus declares, "I am not afraid to make a mistake, even a great mistake, a lifelong mistake, and perhaps as long as eternity too." Joyce's Dedalus and Carter's Crouch espouse a partisanship to themselves, their art, and only very obliquely, if at all, to any collective (whether family, nation, or church). Their renunciation of American civil rights (Carter's Crouch) and Irish nationalism (Joyce's Dedalus) is explicit. Carter's horror at this idea of renunciation makes him a partisan. Renunciation is, for him and for the rest of the Tough Love Crowd, immoral. When, however, one looks more closely at the work of Stanley Crouch, rather than at Carter's anxious reconfiguration of Crouch, the sharp distinction on which Carter relies dissolves. Stanley Crouch thus affords Carter no comforting line in the sand. Carter and Crouch share a considerable kinship, despite Carter's protestations to the contrary.

# Tough Love U.S.A.

# 3

# Tough Love Literati

Shelby Steele, English professor, has written little significant literary scholarship. He is nevertheless known for his book *The Content of Our Character,* in which he castigates blacks for underperforming, harboring low self-esteem, and guilt-tripping whites. According to the book's front cover, Steele presents "A New Vision of Race in America."

Although Carter and Kennedy have each defended Steele and relied upon his work, Steele's rhetoric of individualism goes significantly beyond their own. Steele proclaims, for instance, that "the individual is the seat of all energy, creativity, motivation, and power." African American cultural affinity is, for Steele, a "bondage to collectivism at the expense of individual autonomy." Steele's alternative to this bondage, offered with no mitigating irony, is "an Adam Smith vision of culture" in which individuals are freed from the fetters of group identity. Yet the affinities Steele calls limiting are perceived differently by others. Nobel Laureate Toni Morrison has remarked, for instance, that "my world did not shrink because I was a black female writer. It just got bigger."[1]

Steele, far from Morrison, is nearer James Joyce's character Stephen Dedalus in *A Portrait of the Artist as a Young Man.* Under Joyce's gently ironic gaze Dedalus, like Steele, champions the idea that culture might emerge from the individual soul's presumably spacious crucible. Stephen's audacious goal is "to forge in the smithy of [his] soul the uncreated conscience of [his] race." However, even as Dedalus here proclaims his uncompromising independence and untetheredness, he lets slip that "Mother is putting my new second-hand clothes in order."[2]

James Joyce's ironic awareness of the (perhaps regrettable) limits of heroic individualism is entirely absent in Shelby Steele's earnest pursuit of an "Adam Smith" model of culture and an America that is "passionately raceless."[3] Steele's ideal people might well resemble what Henry Louis Gates, Jr., has called "bodiless vapor trails of sentience" such as might appear on a *Star Trek* episode. Steele's vision of a bloodless ethnic cleansing proved, in the end, too much even for Tough Stephen Carter. Carter's *Reflections of an Affirmative Action Baby* included "a dissenting view about dissenting views" specifically to distance himself from Steele. Carter embraced "racial solidarity" as an opportunity rather than a curse: "It does not strike me as either plausible or desirable for intellectuals to say, in effect, 'We put behind us all that we are. We have no interest in our backgrounds, in our communities and cultures that gave us birth.' Besides, to put the matter bluntly, our people need us."[4]

Again, Steele wishes to free African American individuals from what he tendentiously calls "the tyranny of wartime collectivism in which they must think of themselves as victims in order to identify with their race." Yet Tough Love lawyer Randall Kennedy apparently rejects Steele's assumption that group identity is always victimology. Kennedy characterizes society's major problems as collective difficulties and appropriates Steele's militaristic vocabulary for benign ends. Kennedy urges that poverty "just like war constitutes a collective challenge."[5]

For Stephen Dedalus and Shelby Steele, by contrast, the culture necessarily tyrannizes the intellectual. The young Dedalus proclaims, "My art will proceed from a free and noble source. It is too troublesome for me to adopt the manners of these slaves. I refuse to be terrorized into stupidity." Steele echoes, "Each race has its politics and its party line that impose a certain totalitarianism over the maverick thoughts of individuals." Whereas Joyce's authorial voice ironically and sympathetically undermines Stephen Dedalus's pretensions, Shelby Steele's view appears entirely in earnest. "Every jackass going the roads thinks he has ideas," comments young Dedalus's activist school friend in Joyce's book. Further discussion of Shelby Steele's cultural vision would be uninteresting and, at least since James Joyce, superfluous.

What remains interesting is the quiet audacity of Steele's project. When Steele's book offers *the* content of *our* character, we should not underestimate his descriptive ambitions. Steele presents his vision as fact, not a jackass idea. Steele assures us that while ideas generally come a dime a dozen, he has discovered the right fit of ideas and reality. How? Steele credits his wife's "specialized knowledge" as a clinical psychologist. With his wife's science, Steele is able to distinguish mere "hyperbolic correlatives" of oppression from "actual oppressive events." With his wife's science, Steele can see that in reality the civil rights movement is behind the times, like a person wearing a coat in the spring because she remembers being cold in the winter. With his wife's science, Steele parlays a personal schoolyard humiliation from his childhood into an anguished and universal black *antiself* (a solemn term of art that Steele italicizes in his own text). Steele summarizes the wisdom of his wife's science with this stern and opaque aphorism: "Denial and recomposition always deliver illusion and distortion." Dr. Spock has spoken.

Steele's indebtedness to his wife's scientific expertise and acknowledgment that without her help his ideas would have no fit with reality both increase the importance of an otherwise *utterly, utterly* irrelevant fact: Steele's wife is white. This is of central importance given Steele's own statement that she "helped immensely" in his search for "the human universals that explain the racial specifics." Steele's scientific diagnosis of the objective neuroses of African America is underpinned by his wife's specialized knowledge of psychology. *That* is the way Steele chooses to validate his wife's influence on his work, whereas there are other ways he might have done so. Steele, however, makes no claim that his wife's authority is based on any affinity with African American culture. Steele's wife's influence is, *declaredly,* based on her supposedly neutral scientific knowledge. Steele does not see the irony, in this context, of calling such knowledge "specialized." Steele is thus behind in his own literary studies, for it is nearly twenty years since Edward Said's *Orientalism* showed up the dangers of scientific-anthropological forays into alien cultures. Steele nevertheless immobilizes Negroes beneath an outsider's "specialized" microscope, then presents his vision as a vital corrective to the prattlings of deluded civil rights campaigners. And in what is surely his most ironic claim, Shelby Steele, the ferocious *uber*individualist and resident of a pleasant California suburb, accuses these sweaty campaigners of pursuing "escapist racial policy."[6]

4

# Tough Love Economist

Thomas Sowell, economist, has a straightforward faith in the ability of his methods to deliver untainted truth. His entire book on civil rights is a protest against what he sees as the displacement of fact by belief. That book, *Civil Rights: Rhetoric or Reality?* (1984), proceeds under headings that are sufficient to convey the truth-telling authority Sowell claims for himself: "Realities versus Perceptions"; "Civil Rights versus 'Civil Rights'"; "Beliefs versus Facts"; "Assumptions versus History"; "Effects versus Hopes." Sowell throughout laments that a "sense of economics" and of "underlying realities" is missing from the civil rights debate. He claims access to "unvarnished facts" that fearful others refuse to face. Sowell is not entirely blind to the influence of values on fact; he is not entirely unaware of the deficiencies of his economic methods. But his skepticism is unswervingly reserved for his opponents' investigations. Sowell's faith in his *own* ability to uncover the truth about the universe remains robust, not chastened: "The domination of civil rights discussions and decisions by lawyers and politicians—people who deal in plausibilities made by persuasive words—may help to explain the ignoring of systemic processes like the economic marketplace and the ignoring of underlying realities immune to words."

Sowell's entire oeuvre is built on a faith in the possibility of "systematic verification" of competing hypotheses: "The question, then, is whether assumptions are to be accepted for their plausibility and their conformity to a larger social vision, or whether even the most plausible and satisfying assumptions must nevertheless be forced to confront actual facts."

Sowell's confidence in his "observable factual evidence" leads him to some quite unsparing rebukes of civil rights activism. In his view, such activism trades on "the subordination of evidence to belief." Ever the economist, Sowell suggests that the civil rights activists depend, for their very employment and visibility, on manufacturing "an adequate flow of injustices." This is a familiar Tough Love theme. Clarence Thomas has denounced self-interested "government and civil rights groups who are adept at the art of generating self-perpetuating social ills."[1] The Toughs say their opponents mouth fake grievance.

Yet the Tough Crowd spends little time bolstering the claims of truth underneath their arguments. When Sowell attempts to criticize the legal doctrine that permits a plaintiff to use statistics to raise a prima facie case of discrimination, he inadvertently confesses that his own claims of truth are overblown. Sowell says that the relevant case law (which he discusses in zero detail) establishes an "automatic inference" of discrimination and turns statistical disparity into a "federal offense." That is an invented statement of law. Even under the most expansive reading of the landmark *Griggs* case, to which Sowell is presumably referring, there is no automatic federal offense. The employer is merely required to prove that the employment practices causing the disparate impact are supported by authentic "business necessity." This requirement is, if anything, a form of *deference to* economists, not flight from them. Sowell's objection is, if anything, a confession of the uselessness of economic analysis in solving legal issues. The *Griggs* test gives economic efficiency full sway while ensuring that managers do not discriminate under cover of business discretion. If management and its experts (Sowell, et al.) can show that their practices are rooted in the realities of economic efficiency, they will be left alone. *Griggs* prohibits only irrelevant "qualifications" that, *additionally,* have disparate impact (a Ph.D. for a car-wash job, a college degree for a cannery job, perhaps Rehnquist's as yet unlitigated requirement that his Supreme Court clerks play tennis). The problem is that Sowell, et al., cannot meet the test of justifying job requirements in terms of a science of economics. The businessmen cannot deliver the goods. Sowell concedes as much when he says that, in making civil rights determinations, "there is no 'objective' or 'scientific' way to decide at what level of aggregation to stop breaking the [employment] data down into finer categories." Once he has spotted this problem, Sowell's complaint changes subtly, crucially, and momentarily. For the moment the problem is no longer the displacement of authoritative method by civil rights mysticism. Rather, the "fundamental" problem suddenly becomes that "*the burden of proof is on the accused* to prove [her] innocence, once suspicious numbers have been found" (emphasis original). Sowell's objection is no longer the supposed displacement of economics by ideology, but rather the (for him) inappropriate placement of the burden of proof on the employer.

There are several problems with Sowell's urgent, italicized complaint about the burden of proof. How is it that competent executives are unable to justify their chosen business practices in terms of economic reality? More importantly, if they are unable to validate exclusionary practices by reference to economic reality, why are they so intent on keeping them? How do they know that changed practices would chill productivity? Moreover, if employers can't show that exclusionary practices are necessary because of efficiency, why should courts let them stay with old ways? *The answer to such questions is not reason, but faith: a secular doctrine of managerial infallibility.* That, not science or economics, is where Sowell sits despite all his rhetoric of "observable factual evidence."

Moreover, while Sowell chides civil rights activists for resorting to fake "morally charged scenarios" and not facing "mundane, commonsense facts," he is himself guilty of his own charge. Sowell's rhetoric of innocent-until-proven-guilty itself elevates demagoguery above legal analysis. The presumption of innocence is a hallowed part of a *criminal* proceeding. The allocation of burdens of production and of proof in *civil* proceedings is always a question for debate. Sowell seeks to evade this debate by talking like television. He invokes the civil procedure rules of *L.A. Law.* Without referring to a single court decision, Sowell announces that the "perversions of the [civil rights] law by federal judges appointed for life have been especially brazen." Elsewhere, Sowell offers about four pages of something that might be mistaken for a lawyerly review of the legislative history of the civil rights legislation of the 1960s. But whereas lawyers search for the meaning of legislative history, Sowell tells us up front what equal opportunity "is" and then "shows" how it was degraded into a quota system. Every assertion in Sowell's excursus in the civil rights law is tendentious. To take only the most obvious example, Sowell laments that the Supreme Court "simply rejected a literal interpretation of the words of the Civil Rights Act." Sowell thereby assumes that literal interpretations of legislation are possible, and that if they are they should unquestionably prevail over contrary indications of legislative intent, contrary norms of established legal usage, or contrary indications of statutory purpose—each highly debated among lawyers.

Thomas Sowell's amateur lawyering provokes a comparison with Shelby Steele. Steele assures us that the effect of unnamed Supreme Court decisions that Steele describes as moving away from racial preferences is "to protect the constitutional rights of everyone rather than take rights away from blacks." Steele's willingness to offer "legal" commentary of this sort is worthy of comment. Tough Stephen Carter has himself noted that civil rights law takes "years of careful study to master, no matter the contrary impression given by the sometimes simpleminded reporting of civil rights in the mass media." Shelby Steele's commentary is a model of the reporting that Carter disparages. Harvard law professor Randall Kennedy (who has studied, taught, and written about the relevant law) suggests that "the general public does not understand how far right the Supreme Court has swung on civil rights." It is the most wonderful of ironies that, in a book purportedly protesting the displacement of substance by racial stereotyping, Steele has no difficulty trading on the authority of pigmentation as a substitute for the hard work of legal analysis.

Ultimately, however, the feigned authority with which Steele and Sowell write on legal issues is of broader significance. Sowell's authority as an economist in debates about civil rights is itself not on firm ground. Sowell's conspicuous talk about underlying realities flounders upon his concession that statistics solve nothing. He urges us to face facts, then fails to generate the facts we ought to face. Tough Love economics is, in the end, a call for African America to wriggle more firmly within the grasp of the already formidable empire of unreviewable managerial expertise protected by what the courts call the "business judgment rule." In 1986 Clarence Thomas, nearing the end of his first term at the EEOC and hoping for reappointment, objected that the *Griggs* rule and related guidelines "force government to enter into the minutiae of business decisions." Yet Thomas himself, three years earlier—before questions of reappointment loomed large—actually defended *Griggs,* pointing out that it required merely that job tests fairly measure job performance.[2] Thomas's opportunism and Sowell's blind deference to managerial expertise are both, perhaps, not the same as pursuing racial justice. Indeed, it would be a misstatement to say that Sowell has chosen between the conflicting goals of racial justice and managerialism. There is, for him, no conflict. The goal of racial justice is, in Sowell's world, simply not a real goal: "The battle for civil rights was fought and won—at great cost—many years ago. . . . The right to vote is a civil right. The right to win is not. . . . Everything desirable is not a civil right."

When his books are stripped of their economist's paraphernalia, it is clear that Sowell simply thinks civil rights are the wave of the past. Yet no quadratic equation will ever establish that proposition. Sowell holds this view today; he held it in 1983, when he published the language last cited; and he held it in 1972, when he published *Black Education: Myths and Tragedies*. In fact, Thomas Sowell has never *not* held the view that civil rights (defined as anything more than removing the Whites Only and Juden Verboten signs) are unnecessary and ineffectual.

Sowell further argues that the supposed gains of the civil rights revolution were merely the predictable playing out of trends that predate the legislation of the 1960s. This further claim goes beyond the usual, already interminable, war of statistics about whether present-day disparities reflect racism, merit, or other things. Sowell here multiplies the uncertainties exponentially by casting a cumbersome backward glance (would the gains that happened have happened without the laws we passed?). Yet his expert's certainty is, he would have us believe, intact.

Thomas Sowell is certainly free to believe what he will, but he ought to spare us the rhetorics of reality and of expertise. And those who strongly disagree with his impressionistic hunch, that the civil rights battle was won yesterday, can legitimately describe him as treacherous. He is, *in his own words,* outside that civil rights battle.

# 5

# Tough Love Lawyers

One love. One heart. Let's join together and I'll feel all right.... [But yet] there is one question I'd really like to ask. Is there a place for the hopeless sinner who has hurt all mankind just to save his own soul?

—Robert Nesta Marley, "One Love"

Until there's no longer first class and second class citizens of any nation ... Everywhere is war.

—Robert Nesta Marley, "War"

## Will "One Love" Work Right Now?

Yale law professor Stephen Carter and Harvard law professor Randall Kennedy, unlike Shelby Steele, do not seek a somehow raceless culture. Unlike Sowell, they do not seek to displace race by a mock-scientific public policy. They generally believe that it is both futile and undesirable to make such attempts. They value what Carter calls racial solidarity. Carter and Kennedy believe, however, that race presents the intellectual with dilemmas. Carter finds aspects of racial identity potentially "inimical to the intellectual life" in which one ought, ideally, to be "a free thinker with ideas of [one's] own." Kennedy, too, shares this allegiance. He aims at "a commitment to truth above partisan social allegiances."

Can such notions conflict with commitments to racial justice? In one sense, Carter and Kennedy fully admit, even insist upon, such a conflict. They assume that sometimes the intellectual's allegiance to truth must legitimately lead her to voice politically awkward conclusions. However, thus framed, the issue is an easy one. Nobody, intellectual or otherwise, ought generally to tell deliberate lies (but certainly, lie to the KKK about where the fleeing Negroes are, to the German Nazis—past and present—about where the Jews and "Gypsies" are).

An unthinking refusal to criticize public figures on the sole basis of their race is positively harmful. It is easy to answer the question, Ought Clarence Thomas's race to exempt him from public criticism by blacks who disagree? Obviously not. Such automatic solidarity worked in favor of Thomas, and against important interests, in Thomas's confirmation hearings. Unthinking solidarity is hardly an ideal. The interesting debate is not over whether to disclose or to conceal criticisms of prominent African Americans.

We are on more interesting ground when Carter objects to the "ridiculous proposition that Clarence Thomas ought to have certain views." Contrary to Carter's unargued suggestion, everyone is surely equally entitled to have an opinion about what views Supreme Court justices ought to have on any issue of concern. And if lots of us dislike lots of Thomas's views, it is sensible, not ridiculous, to oppose him. Carter's view that blacks seeking *public office* have a "right" might seem dictated by his view that "open dissent is an act of loyalty." Although Carter states this view of "dissent" as a truism, it surely raises *a question. Is* dissent always loyalty? *Is* melanin really a carte blanche? *Is* Judas defunct in African America?

The debate surrounding Randall Kennedy's "Racial Critiques" article, in which he attacked Negro Crit writings, offers a good entry into this discussion. Richard Delgado, a Kennedy critic and himself a target of Kennedy's article, correctly *rejected* the view that Kennedy ought to withhold the article from publication simply because a group favored nonpublication. However, Delgado declined to join in the view that Kennedy shares common ground with Negro Crits. Delgado insisted that Kennedy and others are doing something very different from Negro Criticism. *That* suggestion raises the interesting debate about the political consequences of associating oneself with inherited ways of doing things. It allows discussion of whether Julien Benda's hold on contemporary thinking has political consequences. Perhaps progressives who do things in old ways advance something other than justice? This issue is lucidly defined by Edward Said, near the end of *Orientalism:* "The trouble sets in when the guild tradition . . . takes over a scholar who is not vigilant, whose individual consciousness as a scholar is not on guard against 'idees recues' all too readily handed down in the profession."

Carter objects that those who label him a "BLACK NEOCONSERVA-TIVE" (his capitalization) enforce a "denial of his right to think." Overabsorption in labels is certainly always unhelpful, hence my own emphasis on the different views even *within* the Tough Love Crowd. Nevertheless, Carter's objection is hard to understand. If some are heatedly resisting Julien Benda while others are shoring him up, we have at least two incompatible projects. Carter's right to think is not in question; why should anyone's right to censure be less secure? Randall Kennedy himself, ably debunking the invented specter of "political correctness" on university campuses, has defended every community's right to "mobilize opinion." Yet Kennedy, too, laments—when his own ox, the "Racial Critiques" article, stands to be gored—that "disagreement becomes attack and dissent becomes betrayal."

Kennedy's complaint here is hard to understand. Kennedy avowedly endorses an ideal of impersonal legal work that is irreconcilable with Negro Criticism. Unless one starts by assuming that legal dispute is a kind of gentleman's disagreement (what Delgado has called an "elaborate minuet"), it is hard to see how one reaches the conclusion, suggested by some, that respectful disagreement rather than ferocious ideological struggle is the ideal picture of scholarly engagement.

Those, then, are the stakes. On one side are the doubters of the guild, who insist that law schools update their ideals and gear up for justice in the world. On the other are unreconstructed scholars, hewing old wood in Benda's way. The deficiencies of Benda's guild are widely conceded. Writing in 1989 (the year that Kennedy's "Racial Critiques" piece appeared), Andrew Ross could take it as axiomatic that the "claim of disinterested loyalty to a higher, objective code of truth is, of course, the oldest and most expedient disguise for the interests of the powerful."[1] Yet Randall Kennedy endorses just such an ideal in the cause of racial justice. Similarly, Stephen Carter, quoting Kenneth Clark, endorses the view that, in weighty matters, the hordes must be kept at bay: " 'Literalistic egalitarianism, appropriate and relevant to problems of political and social life, cannot be permitted to invade and dominate the crucial areas of the intellect, aesthetics, and ethics.' "

Carter never pauses to consider whether social equality and elitist knowledge production might *conflict*. He entirely ignores what is arguably the single most influential strand of contemporary thought: the insistence that knowledge and power are inseparable. When Carter says that "a commitment to an inclusionary politics bears no necessary relation to a judgment about what is good and right and what is bad and wrong," he seems unaware that this is a tendentious and arguably absurd statement. Certainly, Carter is at best raising a *question* (*is* an inclusionary politics compatible with entrenched intellectual tastes?) rather than announcing a truth. To detect such issues, Carter need go no further than the epigraph of Michel Foucault's *Language, Counter-Memory, Practice:*

Thought is no longer theoretical. As soon as it functions it offends or reconciles, attracts or repels, breaks, dissociates, unites or reunites; it cannot help but liberate and enslave. Even before prescribing, suggesting a future, saying what must be done, even before exhorting or merely sounding an alarm, thought, at the level of its existence, in its very dawning, is itself an action—a perilous act.

When Carter calls for calm voices and common cause he is unaware (or pretends to be unaware) that to heed his call is to hand him victory. It is Carter who is uninterested in questions about the inherited mode of legal scholarship; it is critical race theorists who want to raise those questions. In one of the more significant of his law review articles, "The Right Questions in the Creation of Constitutional Meaning," Carter notes, with real or feigned perplexity, that "critical analysis without an accompanying denunciation is an art form that barely has a place any longer in legal scholarship." Carter objects to what he sees as an unfortunate tendency for constitutional theorists to castigate each other for addressing wrong questions. Carter argues that *every* question is in some sense a "right question," including the old questions that traditional lawyers have always asked. Carter here enters the tedious rhetoric of pluralism, which has reduced much of American critical practice to the exact opposite of a *critical* practice and has made so many American intellectuals unthreatening embellishers of the existing order. Carter's entire constitutional theory proceeds on the frank and debatable assumption that things will always "muddle on" pretty much as they are. Carter's call for the compatibility of everything, his call for common cause despite his own complacencies, is quietly oppressive.[2]

## Is Judas Defunct in Law?

The existing criticism of Carter and Kennedy mostly takes parts of their work in isolation. This grants the Toughs an unfair advantage. It sets the debate in narrow terms and allows them to pose as courageous dissenting truth tellers on particular single issues ("You mean a black man can't have doubts about affirmative action?"; "You mean a black man can't chase scholarly merit?"). Yet the specific problems with Kennedy's "Racial Critiques" and Carter's *Reflections* reflect broader, dispositional flaws in Kennedy's entire oeuvre, in all of Carter's writing. *Their progressive intentions fall flat in practice because they adhere to ideals of intellectual untetheredness.*

A good example is Kennedy's article on the death penalty case of *McClesky v. Kemp.*[3] This article is frequently cited as a work that emphasizes the American criminal justice system's systematic undervaluation of black victims of crime. That conventional reading is an important part of the message of Kennedy's *McClesky* piece, but it is not the whole story. Kennedy's article deserves closer attention because its ostensible progressivism is paper thin.

Kennedy's racial-justice concerns in *McCleskey* disappear in a mist of unfetteredness. Kennedy refuses to be bound by the "orthodox"-progressive view that the death penalty ought to be abolished. He instead announces that his analysis "does not proceed from abolitionist premises." Kennedy's rejection of abolitionism is much more than the usual lawyer's tactic, presenting arguments in the alternative. Kennedy presents his rejection of abolitionism as his considered opinion. He notes that "death penalty abolitionists have argued movingly that capital punishment is wrong in principle and vicious in practice inasmuch as its administration reflects the pervasive racial and economic injustices of American society."

He continues, "Although I concede the powers *[sic]* of these arguments, I am not an abolitionist. In my view, considerations of deterrence and retribution sometimes justify condemning criminals to death."

This is thus a "considered" opinion in the sense that Kennedy has adopted it as his own view, not simply for the sake of argument. Yet, in a more important sense, it is exactly *un*considered. Kennedy made not the slightest attempt to engage the arguments in favor of abolition. He entirely ignored the jesuitical standards of academic method that he elsewhere took up in order ostensibly to test Negro Crits. Far from assessing and rejecting the racial justice arguments for abolitionism, Kennedy simply asserted a peculiar and somehow "intellectual" freedom to adopt, as an act of raw power, the opposite view.

Kennedy proceeded in a similarly untethered fashion when he faced a specific and central tenet of abolitionism, the death-is-different distinction. Death-is-different advocates urge, first, that no political entity ever has the authority to take a citizen's life. In analogy with laws against suicide pacts, they argue that a citizen lacks the power ever to consent to a social contract in which her life is part of the bargain. Less abstractly, opponents of death argue that even if the state can, in theory, impose this ultimate sanction, death can nevertheless have no place in a world of racially skewed and fallible criminal justice systems, because death can never be undone. While one who is wrongly imprisoned can be superficially compensated by an award of money damages, a corpse cannot be revivified. We haven't yet institutionalized the fable of Lazarus.

Rejecting this distinction between death and other criminal sanctions, Kennedy simply announced, without explanation, that he "sees the death penalty as part of a continuum of punishments rather than a unique phenomenon occupying a wholly different moral plane." Yet this "seeing" does not easily resemble thinking. Kennedy's unfetteredness operates more like a backhoe than a ballerina.

With this bulldozered rejection of the death-is-different distinction, Kennedy apparently intends to clear a path for race-conscious administration of the death penalty. Aware that race consciousness is used in lots of contexts outside that of the death penalty, Kennedy realizes that if death is not different from those contexts, those contexts are precedents for a progressive race consciousness in death-penalty administration. This sounds like it might redeem Kennedy's argument, until one looks closer. Kennedy is not merely or at all concerned to avoid the fallible justice system's imposition of death sentences on black convicts. Kennedy instead announces that "the plight of convicted murderers" is not his priority. He instead advances a remarkable proposal that, he acknowledges, "might move some black criminals closer to the gas chamber." The remarkable proposal is meant to repair the undervaluation of black victims by the criminal justice system. "Undervaluation," in this context, means that convicted killers of blacks are less frequently sentenced to death, regardless of the race of the perpetrator. Kennedy proposes that this problem might be solved by the execution of more of those convicted of killing black victims. Since some of those accused of killing blacks are themselves black, full acknowledgment of the value of black victims might mean killing more blacks convicts.

The widely acknowledged fallibility of the criminal justice system simply disappears in Kennedy's analysis. Kennedy simply assumes that being a "convicted murderer" is the same as actually having murdered someone. In fact the Supreme Court has recently taken judicial notice that America has executed at least twenty-three demonstrably innocent persons during this century, the last as recently as 1984.[4] Kennedy's analysis is not tethered by such concerns.

But perhaps there is yet a way to salvage Kennedy's racial-justice credentials. Kennedy says he is disregarding the plight of accused Negroes the better to serve decent, law-abiding Negroes. Unfortunately, Kennedy's championing of Negro community interests itself collapses upon examination.

Kennedy chose to portray his antiabolitionism in a "community oriented fashion." Kennedy suggested that abolitionist influence within the NAACP Legal Defense Fund (LDF) may have diverted the LDF's energies from pursuing the true interests of the black community. He postures, then, as our hero. The racial-justice concern that captures Kennedy's attention is an "inequality in the provision of a public good." But the public good in question is an astonishing one. Kennedy elucidates: "Whereas other [equal protection] cases have involved the racially unequal provision of street lights, sidewalks and sewers, *McClesky* involves racial inequality in the provision of a peculiar sort of public good—capital sentencing."

Kennedy senses that in order to validate his peculiar public good he has finally to tether himself somewhere: "I recognize that in speaking in terms of group rights I am taking sides in a controversial debate over the legitimacy of group rights as distinct from the more familiar conception of individual rights."[5]

Yet, despite his awareness of the trickiness of this issue, Kennedy's discussion of why the death penalty is a public good to the black community consists of two baffling sentences suppressed in a footnote: "That a large sector of the population views capital punishment as a valuable public policy is beyond dispute. Thirty-seven states currently authorize capital punishment, and thirty-three have actually carried out death penalties since 1976."[6]

This breezy conclusion that the thing is good for Negroes simply because "a large sector" of the general population evidently enjoys it ought to unsettle even the most indolent of progressive minds. Yet the flaws in this argument not only escape Kennedy's energies but also survive Kennedy's explicit acknowledgment, in this very article, that "opposition to the death penalty is more prevalent among blacks than whites"; that "the disparity in views between blacks and whites on the death penalty has been increasing"; and that "a relatively large percentage of blacks favor abolishing the death penalty."[7] In his subsequent "Racial Critiques" piece, where his central (and reformulated) intention was to debunk what he had by then come to see as the excessive currency of group claims, Kennedy nevertheless felt obliged to give ground on this issue, conceding that "Negroes are more likely than whites to oppose capital punishment." Kennedy actually cited, in the *McClesky* article itself, a Harris poll showing that a majority of blacks (52 percent) want the thing abolished. The same poll, as cited by Kennedy, showed that a majority of whites (67 percent) want to keep the death penalty. Kennedy expressly referred, again in the *McClesky* piece itself, to the role that "majoritarian politics" and black political weakness play in death-penalty issues. *Yet Kennedy uncritically adopted the majoritarian evaluation of the death penalty as a "public good."* This is scary heroism. Indeed, if this is not an intellectual betrayal of black interests, it is unclear what could ever qualify as such. Derrick Bell's widely dismissed remark that "the cause of diversity is not served by someone who looks black and thinks white" here assumes renewed significance. The issue is not an inner ethnic tingling. Anthony Appiah's *In My Father's House* makes it very hard for opponents of Negro Criticism to paint its claims as crude forms of biological determinism. As Appiah argues, "The existence of racism does not require the existence of races." Likewise, the legitimacy and usefulness of remedies intended to address racism need not wait upon "proof" that race, somehow defined, somehow exists. The author of the book in your hands writes, for now, as a "Negro Crit," which hardly erases the Malayali heritage of his mother's house, in southern India. The book in your hands right now endorses one Frenchman (Michel Foucault) while resisting another (Julien Benda) who in turn has the Tough Love Crowd in his grip. The book invokes an Irishman (James Joyce) to answer a suburban Californian English professor (Shelby Steele). Moreover, following the simplistic biological compass that Appiah has attempted to discredit, many continue to call this West Coast professor black, despite his own advocacy and lifestyle of "passionate racelessness" and of a "deracinated" America.

The issue, then, is not some ethnic innateness, but rather tetheredness to interests outside law's walls. And this tetheredness, in turn, is not to some homogeneous and monocultural black constituency. Rather, tetheredness reflects itself in resistance to the quietly oppressive protocols within law's walls. One need not wait upon an authoritative account of African American interests in order to question the innumerable practices, within law schools, that serve the powerful rather than the dispossessed. This crucial tetheredness is *not* advanced by Negroes, steeped in Benda's school, who see law as a site of insular musing and intellectual diversion. And the latter is the choice Kennedy made. In *McClesky,* Kennedy's makeover of Negro abolitionism as its opposite permitted a number of snazzy analytical moves. Undoubtedly, analogizing the death penalty to street lights and to drains contains exactly the right balance of provocation and irrelevance to satisfy prevailing scholarly norms.

Despite quick mention of the complexity of claims of group interest,

Kennedy's analysis of that intractable issue never gets at all sophisticated, *despite the fact that his entire analysis depends on an asserted grounding in "community interests."* And this is no accident. Taking the problems of group interest seriously would have rendered Kennedy's analysis impossible. He would have been forced to write a very different article, with time spent establishing his premise (that death is a public good from a Negro community perspective) rather than arguing from it. Kennedy refused to do that kind of hard work.

There are, then, real limits to the idea that Negro Crits and the Tough Love lawyers share common goals of racial justice. The two schools differ vigorously over what the work of lawyers ought to be. This central difference over the nature of legal work was clear in the public debate over Kennedy's "Racial Critiques" piece. Kennedy proceeded as if in ignorance of Tray Ellis and the "New Black Aesthetic." This project, as summarized by Professor Henry Louis Gates, Jr., "takes the blackness of the culture for granted" and writes with a new self-assurance "by assuming [blackness] as a legitimate grounds for the creation of art."[8] While Negro Crit lawyers have set about rendering race in that new way, Kennedy would detain us with a pedantic dance of proofs and evidence. Ironically, in a supposed attack on stereotypes, Kennedy assumes that Negro Crits are attempting a "substantive definition of blackness" that would have to withstand some process of mock-scientific "testing." Conversely, in Patricia Williams's response to Kennedy, the centrality of the nonstereotypical new black aesthetic in Negro Crit law is unmissable:

[Kennedy's] article is a *representative* response from the academy to new black voices. He is saying, "Prove that racism exists." *I'm not going to do that.* I take American history as a given, and work with the results.[9] (Emphasis added)

The definition of legal work is thus at the heart of the debate, yet Kennedy's impersonal intellectual ideal is not presented as a debatable one. It is presented as a *given,* as is Carter's pursuit of universalized standards. The call for common cause with the Toughs is a call to abandon our refusals, while the Tough Love lawyers keep their own. The Tough rhetoric of common ground is a synonym for surrender.

## The Slipperiness of Common Ground

Despite their obviously strong political differences, Stephen Carter confesses, in his *Reflections,* to a "daydream" that one day Thomas Sowell and

Derrick Bell might shake hands across a conference table. This charmed aspiration is, ironically, a form of the same sin that Carter ostensibly addresses throughout *Reflections:* the sin of stereotyping. Profound disagreement is, in Carter's daydream, happily remedied by shared brownness. Carter's celebration of black diversity has room in its rainbow for every form of life except the black person who is bad for other black people. If melanin really works in this way, like teflon against claims of racism, then Ronald Reagan was surely right, as Stephen Carter reports, to seek Thomas Sowell's services after winning the 1980 election. And Reagan and Bush were both right to create Clarence Thomas. *In an enormous paradox, the Tough Love Crowd begins by posturing as heroic dissenters and ends by claiming nothing less than the right, single-handedly and assisted by the rhetoric of "common ground," to redefine African American political interests.* Stephen Carter, like Julien Benda, first declares that "just as I deny the right of the group (or any of its members) to tell me what to think, I deny the right of the group (or any of its members) to decide for me whether expressing my views will do harm or good."

Despite conceding that his opponents, too, reject group vetoes, Carter persists in calling those opponents "would-be silencers." Taken with his embrace of racial solidarity and with his express desire *not* to be considered a dissenter ("I don't even want to be known as a dissenter"), Carter's attack on the supposed silencers begins to look, paradoxically, like a power grab that would itself silence mass opposition to Toughs. Carter's plea for common ground suddenly resembles something with tentacles.

Carter's objection to the silencers, alarmingly, extends well beyond a defense of his right to hold his own views, unharassed. Carter objects, under the rubric of "silencing," to the group moving as a group to take political action against black political appointees who hold views that the group opposes. He laments the fact that "there was a moment when it appeared that Clarence Thomas, a black lawyer, might *lose a judgeship* because of his vigorous dissents from the mainstream civil rights program." (Carter, writing before the Supreme Court nomination, refers here to an earlier Thomas nomination to the Court of Appeals for the District of Columbia). Carter here attempts to transform, without argument, the very concept of "a judgeship." His language quietly recasts federal appeals court posts away from what they are (sites of political power) and toward what they are not: earned private or professional distinctions to which individual blacks have a career entitlement, properly beyond group interference. Carter's arguments that judges are ideally not political actors are dealt with below. What's interesting here is his attempt to get around the weakness of those arguments by appealing to an invented right of dissent. *Carter's "right to dissent" conjures a Tough entitlement to power, immune from those with the power to stop the Toughs in their tracks.*

Carter's model of judgeships as professional achievements is carried even further when he argues that for civil rights groups to have opposed Thomas more strongly than they did whites with similar political views would have been "reverse discrimination." In this new objection, overtly appealing to an employment law concept, a judge's power becomes Thomas's entitlement. Carter's "reverse discrimination" claim would be sufficiently distracting even within its usual labor law parameters. Outside those parameters, the difficulties multiply. We easily recognize, for instance, both that Justice Ginsberg is a talented individual *and* that she filled the Court's too-long-vacant "Jewish Seat" (as it was widely described in the press). Moreover, then-President Bush's claim that Thomas was chosen regardless of race was widely ridiculed. And we know Thomas filled Thurgood Marshall's seat. In this setting it is hardly fanciful to say that, but for Thomas's presence on the Court, the political pressure for an African American nominee would be irresistible. So the process Carter describes (more aggressive black collective opposition toward a black neocon than a white nominee like Souter) is entirely rational. Racial representation is already, in practice, a legitimate part of thinking about the Supreme Court.

Carter's unfortunate assumption that nominees are entitled to judgeships reappeared, writ large, in the Clarence Thomas Supreme Court nomination itself. During the hearings the Senate Judiciary Committee assumed that Thomas was "innocent until proven guilty" of Anita Hill's disclosures. Yet that legal standard is, as others have observed, irrelevant since the proceedings were not a criminal trial and the Senate's task was to assess whether Thomas had the exalted fitness for the Court, not whether he could sustain a plea of "not proven" in the face of Hill's disclosures.

Moreover, the Senate's adoption of an entitlement-based model (and Carter's lapse into such a model in defending Thomas as to the earlier hearings) contradicts Carter's own considered view of the appropriate confirmation process. Carter has himself written that Senate participation in the confirmation process ought to be more than a "resume review." The Senate ought also to reject the too-demanding role of inquiry into a nominee's judicial philosophy (which Carter thinks is beyond the senators' competence). The senators ought instead, Carter says, to confine themselves to

probing a nominee's "background moral vision and degree of moral reflec-
tiveness." Moreover, while a test of simple "moral vision" would be sufficiently unfathomable (its only determinate consequence is to deprive mass
Negro opposition of its legitimacy), Carter also wants to exclude what
he considers mere minor transgressions and mere personalization of the
confirmation process. Carter's test is designed to ensure that the right sort of
"moral philosophers" sit on the Court. Let's observe how Carter's test,
designed to sift mere trivialities from truly revelatory moral flaws, worked in
the Hill-Thomas affair.

Carter publicly spoke up for Anita Hill's integrity when her disclosures
hit the news. He said that, as her personal friend, he did not doubt that her
disclosures were accurate. He wrote an article defending Hill's integrity.
Surely, then, Thomas failed Carter's moral vision thing? Wrong. Carter's
public intervention, in the *Houston Chronicle,* was headlined "Both the Accuser
and the Accused Are Two Very Fine People." Carter never once argued that
Thomas ought to be denied confirmation (whether for want of credentials,
judicial philosophy, or failures of moral vision). Yet Carter credited Hill's
story. Carter faulted the attacks on Hill by Thomas and his supporters. And
Carter regretted that Thomas failed to come forth with "statesmanlike
words" of apology. All this notwithstanding, Carter did not oppose Thomas.
Rather, he praised Thomas as one of "two very fine people" ("fine" is surely
now the 1990s' least-coveted accolade). Carter's test is not only unpersuasive
legal scholarship and unworkable legal practice; it is also a cakewalk. This is
especially problematic since, on Carter's view, the only other possible check
(group mobilization against neocon nominees) is declared taboo as a form of
"silencing." Carter ritually invokes morally charged examples of people
subjected to hideous abuse and drummed out of academic settings. Far less
prominent in Carter's analysis, however, is the complete irrelevance of these
morally charged scenarios to ostensible dissenters like himself. *The Tough
Love Crowd is plightless.* They are the exact opposite of victims. Speaking as if
for an oppressed group, Carter opines, "Our need for these free-thinking
dissenters may prove to be greater than their need for us. The black conservatives ... are quite comfortable in their tenured academic positions and
other posts, which is, after all, what academic sinecures are for." [10] (Note, in
passing, Carter's Bendaresque formulation of what academic posts "are"
for.)

Carter's use of the inclusive pronoun ("our need") does not conceal the
fact that this veiled threat is his own. He may be besieged, but his bushels

are full, his powder is dry, and he will outlast us. "Silencing" nevertheless remains, despite its complete irrelevance to himself and the Tough Love Crowd, a conspicuous theme of Carter's *Reflections*. Of the book's nine chapters, one is called "Silencing Dissent," another "On Contenting Oneself with Silence," and a third "Silencing Doubt." Almost every page of Carter's book is shadowed by the imminent door knockings of an eerie thought police. The sympathetic reader might assume that Carter is on the verge of turning in his quill. But no: "Despite the name calling of their critics, they [i.e., the black conservatives] will not be silenced." Despite his use of a distancing pronoun ("they" won't be silenced) it's clearly Carter strutting here. And while he forever urges the rest of us to face up to Tough professional competition, Carter's rhetoric of silencing is itself a retreat from robust and legitimate debate of the differences that separate him and his critics. Continuing in this vein, Carter repeatedly warns us not to "alienate some of the best minds we have." [11] This new phrase ("best minds") now implies not only that there is a common cause (which itself needs argument, unless pigmentation is enough) but also that Carter and his Crowd have smart solutions that elude the rest of us. This argument is not only self-aggrandizing but—Carter seems unaware—also a political dead horse. The idea that "competence" solves political problems where "ideology" fails was the central plank of the unmemorable Democratic presidential campaign of 1988. Moreover, the Tough Love Crowd's insufficiently challenged declarations of analytical prowess are overblown.

## Just How Clever Is Tough Love Lawyering?

Stephen Carter, in his *Reflections* and elsewhere, speaks approvingly of Randall Kennedy's "Racial Critiques" piece, concurring in its substance and defending its author from what Carter thinks are *unjustified* and *unwise* betrayal claims. Assessment of the first complaint ("unjustified") is already underway in the form of the arguments against common ground. Time now to address Carter's new claim—that African America stands to lose through alienating fine minds. Carter and Kennedy have a shared agenda: stable standards of intellectual excellence. These standards, they say, are besieged by Negro Crits and other vulgarians who would abolish valuable notions of meritorious scholarship. So, let us test the stable excellences of Kennedy's own attempt to show the failed excellences of the Negro Crits in "Racial Critiques of Legal Academia."

At a pivotal turn in his controversial attack on Negro Crits Mari Matsuda, Derrick Bell, and Richard Delgado, Kennedy announces what is unquestionably the cornerstone of his critique. Without it, his entire meritocracy-based attack on the Negro Crits would be groundless. In this key passage, Kennedy states his allegiance to a

widely accepted ideal of scholarly procedure [that] reflects values at the heart of what Robert K. Merton describes as "the ethos of modern science." One of these values is universalism, which refers to "the canon that truth claims are to be subjected to *preestablished impersonal criteria.*" A related value is disinterestedness, meaning a commitment to truth above partisan social allegiances.[12] (Emphasis in Merton's original)

Robert Merton's *Social Theory and Social Structure* is a rather big book, evidently sometimes unwieldy. Merton carefully and separately discusses what he considers the very different pursuits of scientific and of nonscientific knowledge. In his discussion of knowledge outside the physical sciences, Merton *expressly* denies what Kennedy here takes him to assert: Merton denies both the possibility and the usefulness of seeking truth outside of partisan social allegiances. Merton explicitly debunks the idea that a disinterested or "Outsider" perspective "has monopolistic or privileged access to social truth." Merton instead insists, sounding rather like the Negro Crits Kennedy wants to attack, that both the Outsider and the Insider have "*distinctive* and interactive roles in the process of truth-seeking"[13] (emphasis added). Merton's argument is thus a ringing *endorsement of* the inclusion of "Outsiders"—Merton's word—in the legal academy. How else, indeed, could Merton's preferred interactive ideal unfold?

Furthermore, disastrously for Kennedy, Merton's argument is a resounding and *express* rejection of the idea that Insiders should strip bare of partisan social allegiances. Unfortunately for the unwary reader of "Racial Critiques," Kennedy missed all Merton's relevant thinking (summarized in the previous paragraph) and opened his copy of *Social Theory* at Merton's part 4, which is declaredly relevant to the physical sciences and declaredly irrelevant to law. The very first sentence of Merton's part 4 reads, "Part IV is composed of five papers in the sociology of science, a specialized field of research which can be regarded as a subdivision of the sociology of knowledge which springs from and returns to controlled experiment or controlled observation."[14]

This doesn't quite resemble the tax code. Moreover, had Merton's language that Kennedy quotes in support of universalistic ideals in legal scholarship been quoted in full, its irrelevance would have been manifest. Merton refers, in a sentence that Kennedy sliced in half, to "preestablished impersonal criteria: *consonant with observation and with previously confirmed knowledge.*[15] This, too, is not quite the tax code (the italicized language, my emphasis, is what Kennedy omitted). Moreover, on the very same page as the irrelevant language that Kennedy half-quotes, Merton *explicitly* distinguishes scientists (whom he is talking about) from lawyers (whom he, expressly, is not talking about). This distinction between scientists and lawyers is indeed one that philosophers of science habitually make. Thomas Kuhn, in *The Structure of Scientific Revolutions,* wrote that lawyers are different from scientists because scientists are accountable to a closed circle of professional peers whereas, in contrast, the "principal raison d'etre" of the law is "external social need."[16] This criterion of external social need is exactly the one to which Outsider theorists are trying to make law responsive as they push it away from science-based models.[17] *Robert Merton's work is an impetus, not a bar, to this effort.* Kennedy's reliance on Merton to the contrary is misplaced. Kennedy nevertheless insists that his "intellectual debt" to Robert Merton "can be seen in practically every aspect of ['Racial Critiques']." Kennedy's gaffe, at the heart of what sets out to be an exposé of the scholastic failings of law's foremost insurrectionaries, invites an unflattering comparison with Allan Bloom. Bloom's *Closing of the American Mind* undertook, too, an attack on various insurrectionary intellectual currents. Paul Bove, in an article entitled "Intellectual Arrogance and Scholarly Carelessness," has remarked that "it is a sign of the crisis under which Bloom writes that he so profoundly contradicts some of the deepest tenets of the position he claims to espouse."[18] Kennedy's "Racial Critiques" piece is mired in similar contradictions. Ostensibly a champion of careful and traditional scholarly method, he demonstrably misreads the central text on which he purports to rely.

Kennedy's adherence to scientistic ideals in legal scholarship is a second gaffe, independent of his misreliance on Merton: Kennedy proceeds as though legal realism never happened. If Kennedy made the slightest effort to pursue legal scholarship somehow based on observation and previously confirmed knowledge, it is difficult even to imagine what his work would look like (think of test tubes in contract class). Such work would probably be derided—even in an unreconstructed legal academy. It is perhaps unsurprising that Kennedy's actual practice of legal scholarship, outside of his convenient attack on Negro Crits, discloses no such narrow scientism. In an article published almost contemporaneously with the "Racial Critiques" piece, Kennedy evinced a more sensible (though still problematic) awareness of "the ways in which politics inescapably affects scholarship." No longer needing an instrument with which to attack Negro Crits, Kennedy shifted gears to a questionable, but at least not facially absurd, allegiance to the prevailing Bendaresque model of disinterested inquiry. Kennedy rejected, as Benda would, the approach of those who have opted "to fashion their scholarship into ideological weaponry serving immediate political ends." He favored those who attempt "the difficult, but far more fruitful, task of expressing their politics without forsaking the *independent* claims of their intellectual craft" (emphasis added). This is, precisely, Benda's call for the elimination of the passions from the clerkish sphere. In this article, "Reconstruction and the Politics of Scholarship," Kennedy offered a favorable book review of Eric Foner's work on the Reconstruction. He praised Foner for pursuing his work in a mindset unfettered by political baggage.

Yet there are several problems, brushed aside by Kennedy, with the idea that political values can be held in check for the supposed benefit of intellectual craft. (No view of Foner's work is implied here; my concern is only with the logic of Kennedy's account of that work.) First, Kennedy suggests that, through adherence to "intellectual craft," scholars may approach nearer to a "reality" that is sometimes "intractably complicated."[19] Kennedy's demon is thus the blinkered zealot who distorts truth because of unmoderated politics. Yet, moderating one's politics under the supposed demands of craft is merely to be *differently* blinkered, not *un*blinkered. Kennedy evinces a stereotypical notion of what counts as political scholarship. For him, as for Julien Benda, politics resembles disarray. Yet, others have asked, "Must it be assumed that only that is politics which is preparation for an insurrection?"[20]

Moreover, there is a troubled twist in Kennedy's allegiance to Julien Benda's way of thinking. Many writers have shown that dispassionate ideals oppress. Audre Lorde has objected that

men avoid women's observations by accusing us of being too "visceral." . . . Pain is very visceral, particularly to the people who are hurting. . . . Pain teaches us to take our fingers OUT the fucking fire.[21] (Capitalization original)

Kennedy advocates disinterest, yet ostensibly favors mass voices. He praises Foner's work—in terms that echo Noam Chomsky—because of its attention to "the masses that are often rendered invisible by elitist historical studies." Yet Kennedy never seriously faces the question of methodology *as a question*. One might expect Kennedy's intellectual ideals to reflect his desire to give voice to the dispossessed. Yet Kennedy entirely fails to address the straightforwardly elitist agenda that underlay the successful attempt, at the turn of the century, to cast legal study as a science. Kennedy treats the received ideal of disinterest as a fixed truth rather than an unfortunate legacy of a questionable past.

The uneasiness between Kennedy's allegiance to impersonal ideals and his allegiance to the dispossessed is striking when one sets his "Racial Critiques" piece alongside his article, published three years earlier, called "Race Relations Law and the Tradition of Celebration: The Case of Professor Schmidt." In this earlier article Kennedy straightforwardly championed the dispossessed. Kennedy criticized the methods by which legal scholars maintain the idea that "the United States Supreme Court has served the nation well and furthered human freedom." Kennedy argued that legal scholars have cultivated hyperbole about the moral rectitude of the Court and of its various justices. He argued that this celebratory scholarship assists patterns of racial subjugation by heaping disproportionate praise on morally ambiguous decisions. In a powerful analysis, Kennedy commented that such scholarly celebrants underestimate "the degree to which radicals on the margins define the ambit of possibilities open to persons acting in any given historical moment." Kennedy's underlying complaint was that the celebratory scholars slighted black interests and belittled black suffering. Kennedy ended with a manifesto:

Analyzing the Supreme Court's race-relations jurisprudence from a point of view which adequately assimilates the feelings and interests of black victims will require the cultivation of new sources of information, the revision of established views, and perhaps most daunting, an empathetic imagination of the suffering inflicted by racial offense. . . . *whatever the difficulties, few things pose more of a moral and intellectual imperative.*[22] (Emphasis added)

This early manifesto is far from Kennedy's later conversion to *impersonal* scholarship and disinterestedness above partisan social allegiances—which he suddenly adopted, three years later, to attack critical race theory in the months before Harvard Law School's vote on his tenure. The passage above reads like a critical race theory document in its insistence on the place of the personal in law. The "Racial Critiques" piece, three years later, discarded this manifesto and rejected "race, nationality, religion, class and personal qualities [as] irrelevant" to good scholarship.

Why the change? One need not leave this question to gossip or speculation. In the 1989 "Racial Critiques" article Kennedy acknowledged that the "impersonal" model is a "widely accepted ideal of scholarly procedure." In the 1986 manifesto, Kennedy, seeking a "fundamental explanation" for the tradition of celebration of the Supreme Court, suggested that the explanation for such "apologetics" (Kennedy's choice of word) is "the relationship of scholarship to power." Kennedy continued:

Nations exert the political equivalent of gravitational pressure on the thinking of their intellectuals, frequently pushing scholars toward various modes of nationalistic self-congratulation. Despite their pretensions to independence, scholars are subject, like others, to the blandishments and intimidations that power can mobilize. . . . [The legal] community, like every community, has created a politics that governs its actions and, in particular, the conventions that bestow intellectual legitimacy. Although deference to such conventions may well be unconscious, a consequence of the very socialization we call "education," it is nonetheless real.[23]

Three years after writing this, Kennedy mysteriously converted to the creed of Julien Benda, to a widely accepted ideal of scholarly procedure: disinterestedness. In 1989, in the "Racial Critiques" piece, this paradoxical ideal—both lucrative and disinterested—became the linchpin of Kennedy's attack on a genre of scholarship advancing the highly personal aims with which he earlier seemed to align himself. In "Reconstruction and the Politics of Scholarship" (also published in 1989) this prevalent ideal was, again, his starting point.

Kennedy's confirmation conversion, as Harvard Law School's tenure decision loomed in 1989, was, moreover, a broad-based affair going beyond the works already discussed. In 1986, in "Persuasion and Distrust: A Comment on the Affirmative Action Debate,"[24] Kennedy scathingly and specifically rejected the view that all the players in the affirmative action debate had a common abhorrence of racial injustice. He openly disparaged the idea that Benjamin Hooks and William Bradford Reynolds could be considered "ideological brethren." And he went further, explicitly rejecting the view that the "realm of scholarly discourse and the creation of public policy" could be considered untainted by prejudice. He rejected the view that prejudice was confined to the "workaday world of ordinary citizens." He explicitly considered and rejected the arguments against "scrutinizing the motives of policymakers and fellow commentators." In 1989, Kennedy converted as tenure day loomed. Racial prejudice in legal academia was now a mere "plausible hypothes[is]." Its status as a "persuasive theory" had suddenly to wait upon a procedure of "testing." Far from providing the new sources of information that Kennedy urged in his 1986 critique of conventional legal scholars, Negro

Crits suddenly "distort[ed] reality" and offered "deficient diagnosis." Citing a Shelby Steele article, Kennedy concluded, in 1989, that Negro Crits were merely playing "the race game." Far from infusing law with valuable insight, Negro Crits were really employing a "stratagem" of misrepresentation in a cynical attempt to manipulate white guilt.[25] Kennedy repeated, in the press, the misrepresentation that Negro Crits "are engaged in interest group ethnic politics."[26] In 1986 it was naive to believe that "the realm of scholarly discourse" is free of prejudice. In 1986 Kennedy further asserted that the "portrait of conflict-within-consensus is all too genial." But in 1989, Kennedy was "tired of it."[27] As of 1989 critical race theory is to blame for frustrating "fruitful collegial exchange" and is responsible for creating an "us" and "them" atmosphere and a "conception of academia as battleground."[28] In 1986 Benno Schmidt was faulted for his "apologist" invocation of too-accommodating moral standards in evaluating Supreme Court justices. Yet in 1989, in "Martin Luther King's Constitution: A Legal History of the Montgomery Bus Boycott,"[29] Kennedy is suddenly concerned "to respect segregationists in the sense of taking their ideas seriously" and to reject the view that "the side supporting de jure segregation ... was wholly bereft of morality or reason." This is either trite (who's ever *wholly* bereft of anything?) or itself a form of apologetics (resembling the more recent media rehabilitation of repentant Alabama segregationist governor George Wallace).

Kennedy's 1989 volte-face turned farce at the end of the "Racial Critiques" piece, written slightly before the fall of the Berlin Wall. In explaining how he came to write that article rather than something else, Kennedy's language echoed the hyperbolic Cold War project of containing the enemy in our midst. Kennedy wrote, he said, to contain the spread of a dangerous Negro Crit tendency. Kennedy worried that "left unchallenged, this tendency will seep into the culture at large."

With this apocalyptic challenge of the American Left, Kennedy joins other culturally comfortable critics, such as Allan Bloom, Walter Jackson Bate, and Roland Picard, in their nostalgic resistance to intellectual ferment. The late Roland Barthes, for instance, insisted that the inherited language of French literary criticism itself be placed in question, much as the new Negro Crits insist that the inherited manner of legal scholarship itself be part of the discussion. Barthes was subjected to a familiar, hyperbolic, and public attack by a member of the postwar French establishment (Raymond Picard) who said Barthes was a dangerous leveler. Picard argued that Barthes would deprive French criticism of its ability to distinguish between pebbles and diamonds. Barthes, in response, emphasized Picard's place within the tradition of Julien Benda and made a comment that deserves to be read unexpurgated:

When a word like dangerous is applied to ideas, to language or art, it immediately signals a desire to return to the past. It means the speaker is fearful. . . . The speaker fears all innovation which he denounces on each occasion as "empty" (in general that is all that can be found to be said about what is new). *However this traditional fear is complicated today by the contrary fear of appearing anachronistic.* . . . Regression [read "racism"] today [1967] appears shameful, just like capitalism. Whence come the remarkable jerks and abrupt halts: there is a pretence for a while of accepting modern works, which one ought to discuss since they are being discussed; then, suddenly, a sort of limit having been reached, people proceed to a joint execution. (Emphasis added) [30]

What is remarkable, returning to Randall Kennedy, is that while Picard was declaredly a scion of the establishment and was acknowledged as such by a laudatory mainstream press, Kennedy's analogous work continues to be feted as heroic dissent—even though life tenure on Harvard's law faculty followed smartly upon his intervention. The *New York Times* suggestively reported the controversy caused by Kennedy's article under the headline, "Minority Critic Stirs Debate on Minority Writing." Kennedy claimed that he was struggling to "break down a confining etiquette." He certainly achieved that, though perhaps not in the manner he meant to suggest. Kennedy liberated conservative columnist George Will to dispatch a widely syndicated column attacking Negro Crits and amplifying, exponentially, Kennedy's own considerable oversimplifications. Will praised Kennedy for "74 pages of temperate arguments against the balkanizing of the academic mind." Kennedy also partially liberated some of his own colleagues. The *Times* article quoted "a white law professor, *speaking on condition of anonymity,*" who protested that "there was a sort of 'lynch Randy Kennedy' mind-set." Derrick Bell's letter in response to that faceless colleague's remark made the point (not a novel one) that there is in America a healthy market for blacks who wish "to achieve eminence by serving as racial apologists." [31] Was Bell raising an invented issue? The misplaced lynching metaphor, for instance, has a familiar ring, having been deployed for the benefit of a Tough Love judge. To mention intellectual independence, in this context and on Kennedy's record, defiles language.

## Stephen Carter's Tough Stuff

The tone of Stephen Carter's work differs from Randall Kennedy's in a crucial and deceptive sense. Carter is entirely the opposite of an appointed executioner. He appears impeccably liberal and humane. Conversely, Kennedy is more overt in enforcing his preferences. Kennedy was not, for instance, content to rest with his correctly scathing review of Houston Baker's perplexing book *Black Studies, Rap, and the Academy*. Kennedy's first order of business in reviewing Baker's book was to attack the author's publisher for printing it. The issue here is neither the quality of Baker's book nor Kennedy's right to criticize it. Nor has Kennedy transgressed a taboo against attacking publishers. *Rather:* it has become hard, now, to tell the silencer from the silenced. Kennedy's misreading of Robert Merton's work, and his invented rendering of the work of those he sets himself to criticize, certainly occasion firm views about the status of "Racial Critiques" as serious scholarship. Yet it is far from hard to believe that the *Harvard Law Review* published it anyway.

Kennedy's enforcement of his intellectual tastes is even more effective where he is no mere petitioner in a book review (as in opposing Baker), but actually the man in charge. As editor of *Reconstruction,* a journal that he founded with philanthropic funding, Kennedy again created controversy. In an article entitled "Pulling Punches on Thomas: Journal of Opinion Finds Some Topics Too Hot to Handle," the *New York Times* discussed Kennedy's rejection of an article critical of Clarence Thomas. Its author was a former Rehnquist law clerk who supported Rehnquist's elevation to chief justice (no radical law clerk, he). Kennedy announced that the article violated his tastes because it contained a "hint of smarminess." Therefore, Kennedy said, "I didn't want to be a part of it." Given the enormous place of claims of silencing in Tough Love complaining, this is an odd way to edit a journal. Kennedy's implicit assertion that he considers himself *part of* everything that he allows to pass into the pages of the journal is sufficiently alarming. Even more so is the impressionistic manner of his decisionmaking. Kennedy initially accepted the piece but then rejected it, citing two points of detail and a piece of whimsy. The details: a reference to Thomas's penchant for pornography and a reference to what Kennedy called "the infamous Coke can." (Both these details featured prominently in a subsequent article on Thomas in the *New Yorker* magazine, itself hardly a racy news organ.) To these details Kennedy added this whimsy: "Perhaps I am being unduly skittish, but so be it."[32] SO BE IT.

Stephen Carter looks warm and cuddly by contrast. Carter can appear to be America's most tolerant lawyer. The *New York Times Book Review*, assessing Carter's *Culture of Disbelief*, suggested that Carter's work might reawaken a disappearing "middle ground of civility and reasonability *[sic]*"[33] in American politics. Carter's apparent tolerance is, again, clear in his response to Negro Crits themselves. One reporter observed that although Carter's *Reflections* had been attacked by Negro Crits, Carter nevertheless had encouraging words for the group. "As time has gone by, my sympathy and admiration for their work has increased,"[34] said Carter. Carter's unsolicited benediction asserts, yet again, that he shares common ground with Negro Crits. Carter's assertion of a sweeping "right to dissent," and his manipulation of the rhetorics of dissent and of silencing in order to implement a redefinition of group interests, were each remarked upon earlier. It is now time to face, frontally, the systematic problems with Carter's ostensibly humane allegiance to an impeccable liberalism.

Carter's unsolicited encouraging words are themselves the first clue. Carter instinctively asserts the *authority* of the patient mentor. This charming self-aggrandizement pervades *Reflections* itself. Carter, like the other Toughs, repeatedly portrays his opponents as still gripped by a school-day idealism beyond which he has himself matured. He patronizes his students: "I fear that a weakly conceived ideology may be clouding their analytical faculties, and that is when I begin to worry a little."[35] What is clearest in remarks like these is surely not what Carter intends. He wants to seem a wise overseer. Instead, he comes across as an anxious aspirant for membership in what Liza Featherstone has called the "elite of the self-styled well adjusted."[36] And this elitism works both ways. Carter has a consistent neo-Confucian deference to his own elders: "My more mature and far wiser colleagues tell me that . . . the occasional upsurge in student activism is natural." This infantilization of himself and of others becomes a concrete part of Carter's constitutional law scholarship itself, in his overt defense of "ancestor worship" as a principle of constitutional interpretation. In constitutional law, ancestor worship refers to the theory that the views of relevant Wise Elders (in America, the Founding Fathers) ought to be given automatic obedience. Thus Carter: "They were the Founders who laid down the rules; we are the inheritors who follow the rules that the Founders laid down."[37]

This is an odd philosophy for a black racial-justice progressive, give that our own ancestors were in chains at the relevant time and, perhaps understandably, played hooky from the Philadelphia Convention. Such facts prompt Carter to the occasional, but always temporary, renunciation of personal reverence for the Founders. Yet in these interregnums, Carter merely erects a more mystical constitutional theory of "intertemporal identity" in which "we" are all, today, at one with a select band of privileged ancestors.[38] Carter presumably envisages everyone's ancestors in immaculate and metaphorical ancestral couplings, so as not to offend the antimiscegenation laws, some of which survived nearly until the 1970s. Hard to see why anything so ethereal should detain a serious scholar—except that in this respect Carter enjoys significant company among law professors. Carter ultimately concedes that this constitutional "mythos" is just that—a myth. "Nothing in the argument turns on the *truth* of this assumption," says Carter, and the emphasis is his own. Yet, instead of making the most of this room for creative progressivism, Carter, remarkably, turns to resurrect old chains. Carter slides away from his unstable renunciation of ancestor worship and insists anew that

the irrelevance of the Founder's political science to our era is a proposition to be argued not assumed; and even should the wisdom of the Founders turn out to be nonsense when translated to our era, the question of who should hold the power to abandon it sits uneasily and unanswered on the interpreter's shoulder.

Furthermore, when Carter does remember to renounce worship of the Philadelphia men, his task becomes choosing a preferable Founding Event, the values of which should guide constitutional interpretation. In this new task, Carter again takes the most conservative path available, opting anew for the felt immanent values of the 1787 Philadelphia Convention itself. Others have argued, for instance, that the upheaval surrounding the New Deal constitutes a far more relevant founding event than does Philadelphia, 1787. This argument would transform talk about "America" into talk about the New Deal, at least for legal-constitutional purposes. Such a transformation has arguably strong benefits, from a progressive point of view, over an "America" frozen at 1787.

Carter, faced with this argument, becomes both a dinosaur and a scientist. Carter the dinosaur admits that contemporary theorists reject his own preference for the 1787 Founding Event. Carter concedes, as is habitual, that his own argument "has about it a somewhat musty, antiquated, even shabby air, like a quaintly decorated table." While antiquated, Carter is nevertheless a scientist because he shifts into a finely tuned factual inquiry in order to reject the New Deal as the relevant Founding Event. Carter rejects it because of his empirical hunch that the "public veneration" attaching to the New Deal doesn't quite match the "awe" that attaches to Philadelphia, 1787. Carter further rejects a range of contemporary arguments against his position with the triumphant assertion that his own conceded "muddle" is better than the opposing arguments because "none of [the contemporaries] can trump the arguments for judicial enforcement of the science of the Founding Generation."[39] Here we have dinosaur, scientist, and ancestor worshiper, in one large and single gush. Carter announces, "The Spirit of the Constitution is the spirit of 1787." This proclamation occurs in a 1990 article, in the course of Carter's harsh criticism of *Olsen,* the case that upheld the congressionally created office of independent counsel that led to Lawrence Walsh's Iran-Contra investigation. If Carter's analysis by now sounds less like dispassionate investigation than like Madison Avenue hype, the point has been made. Carter is a cheerleader, with shrewdly concealed pom-poms—and for the wrong crowd.

Less amusing is Carter's omission. Entirely absent from Carter's search for the nation's Founding Event is the single period in American history in which blacks achieved significant political influence in parts of the country; a period that followed a bloody war in which the status of the Negro was a central issue; and a period that saw Negro equality enshrined (albeit hesitantly and partially) in law for the first time in American history. The idea of the Reconstruction era as the relevant constitutional mythos is, moreover, not a novel one. *Reconstruction* is the name that Tough Love lawyer Randall Kennedy chose for the journal that he founded. And that choice was no accident. Kennedy himself has written of the extent to which a powerful pejorative tradition of Reconstruction historiography has unduly suppressed the relevance of Reconstruction-era jurisprudence to present-day issues. Kennedy has referred to Reconstruction as "the second founding of the nation" and has agreed that "rarely has a community invested so many hopes in politics as did blacks during the Reconstruction."[40] Eric Foner's book, the subject of Kennedy's article, is itself suggestively entitled *Reconstruction: America's Unfinished Revolution.* Yet we search Carter's ruminations on Founding Events in vain for any reference to this rich vein of inquiry. Furthermore Kennedy, like many others, calls the civil rights revolution of the 1960s a "Second Reconstruction," which might logically suggest a third Founding Event (or fourth, if we include the New Deal) that Carter might have pursued. Carter chose to ignore all these in favor of the spirit of 1787.

Still, Carter's preference for 1787, his preference for the legal theory of originalism, and his erasure of Reconstruction need not have any absolute significance. What matters, after all, is not the theory one adopts but where one takes it. And it is here that Carter's counterprogressive values reveal themselves in the raw. Carter readily concedes that originalism "privileges one set of values over another." [41] *Carter actually chooses to privilege liberal legal theory as an end in itself and ahead of the distinct value of racial justice.* Carter might retort that liberal legal theory and racial justice are not competing, nor merely compatible, but actually complementary. He might claim that he is not choosing between legal liberalism and racial justice. He might claim that the best way to advance racial justice is to advance the cause of legal liberalism. But upon a closer look, it is clear that Carter repeatedly and actively suppresses racial-justice concerns for the specific benefit of something called liberalism, and in deference to a presupposed original balance of power within the federal government.

Carter's allegiance to liberal theory as a distinct end in itself is obvious in his broad pronouncements as well as in his detailed arguments. Carter's main constitutional law article is subtitled "A Preliminary Defense of an Imperfect Muddle." In this article Carter is passionately and frankly concerned to "repulse the assault" of those who argue that law does not bind judges. He is concerned to preserve mainstream liberal constitutional discourse. Carter's work is "confessedly reformist." [42] His project is entirely premised on a piece of fine calibration, another empirical hunch: "Most Americans probably consider their government—their society—essentially just, and my empirical hunch is that most Americans consider the laws promulgated by their government presumptively entitled to respect." [43]

This hunch ignores *exactly* those people, the culturally dispossessed, whom Carter claims ought to accord him the status of loyal dissenter. Carter here duplicates the blind spot that turned Randall Kennedy's ostensible championing of Negro community good into something else on the death penalty issue. When Carter speaks, it is avowedly in the name of "we the people (or many of us anyway)." [44] The question is, Who's left out? He, moreover, openly defends the interests of the state over the lesser pesterings of morality. Defending a distinction between law and morality, Carter insists that "if the liberal state is to function we can't invoke morality too often." [45] Finally, Carter's renunciation of morality in liberal politics is itself dramatically unstable. Carter's *Culture of Disbelief* is an extended *criticism* of liberalism's exclusionary rhetoric of neutrality and of the fact that it requires

America's religious to recast themselves before they enter the public square. Yet what remains firmly excluded from the public square, in Carter's constitutional theory, is the expression of passionate views about America's fundamentally unjust racial caste system. Carter excludes such views by his empirical hunch that everyone thinks the opposite; by his manipulation of the rhetorics of loyal dissent and of silencing to hush a race; and—a new point—also by silencing these voices in his adherence to what, ironically, sets out to be a "dialogic" model of constitutional law.

To facilitate his ideal constitutional model of a society in orderly dialogue, Carter produces a series of new empirical hunches. To his previously disclosed hunch that everyone who matters thinks society is essentially just, he adds a hunch that Americans are all "essentially decent people"; a hunch that "judges are essentially conservative creatures"; and a hunch that civil disobedients are "essentially" not radicals.[46]

The central problem with these eminently convenient hunches is that they hinge on a violently narrow yet pleasant-sounding concept of reasonableness. When Carter explains, in the *Wall Street Journal,* his "partial estrangement from the civil rights establishment of which [Thurgood Marshall] has always been a hero," he attributes this estrangement partly to his preference for an ideal of a "rule of law" as enforced by justices "amenable to reason."[47] Faced with compelling moral arguments in favor of political egalitarianism, Carter endorses a sharp separation between moral preferences and constitutional analysis. This separation is a relentless Carter theme wherever the issue is social justice (his tune changes, arbitrarily, where the issue is religious rather than political morality). An "ideal of justice beyond politics" recurs in all of Carter's relevant law review articles. Carter's charmed hopes for the separation of principle from politics flounder on the impossibility of the suggested ideal, as Carter himself tirelessly concedes. Carter's life's work in constitutional theory has so far been an attempt to preserve the viability of American constitutional legal practice, despite its own glaring failure to deliver on claims central to its legitimacy. Carter gamely calls his own constitutional theory "a tool of legitimacy." Carter's passion to prop up a nonexistent impartial system cannot be overstated. He admits that his arguments do not meet the challenge of his opponents. But he doesn't therefore abandon the old kinds of oppressive theorizing. Rather, he confesses that his argument requires "a leap of faith,"[48] and he continues as before. Carter thus averts the collapse of his preferred system of constitutional law through a simple refusal to face the arguments that would enforce that collapse. Such arbitrary deliverance of a system from a crisis it would otherwise face is, of course, the central function of the apologist. Whether or not Carter's leaps of faith are *loyal* to African America is hardly self-evident, but rather depends on which complications he suppresses in order to preserve his preferred system. The important question is, Who becomes, in Carter's ideal model of rational dialogue, the culturally dispossessed? Sadly, Stephen Carter, like so many lawyers, politicians, and theorists before him, chooses to suppress America's Negro Question. What first seemed an affable, even courtly, parenthetical remark—"We the people *(or many of us anyway)*"—becomes the site of a moral and political atrocity. Carter elsewhere explicitly argues that "if 'the law' is 'our law,' the reason must be that 'we' are the elite without whose consent no one could govern."[49] Carter's point is that "the elite" in a successful democracy such as Carter believes America to be must be broad enough so that the great mass of people identify with it. Clearly Carter is alluding to the great American middle class. Yet they are an elite *relative to whom?* None other than the Negro faces at the bottom of the well. Carter here unknowingly recites exactly the same story Derrick Bell tells, except that he does it in smiley face. He overtly places himself (and his hopes for the survival of what he calls democracy) with the self-styled elitist middle rather than the peripheral dispossessed. How then is he *loyal* to the latter?

Carter's abandonment of the dispossessed is further evident when he resists those who emphasize law's unbindingness in order to open a space for social change. Many have argued, powerfully, that law does not bind judges, and many believe that such arguments open a space for ethical choice and progressive politics within legal practice. Carter deletes this space:

Sometimes, the principles the courts would need to embrace [to reach a politically preferable result] are simply too outlandish, too unconnected to anything resembling "law." Recent efforts to avoid this *truth* by treating law as mere arbitrary power and bounds on judicial discretion as illusory often read less like serious analysis than like sour grapes. (Emphasis added)

The compelling argument that law does not bind judges is detailed below. Here, the interesting point is that although Carter has himself created a self-described muddle culminating in an ignominious leap of faith in his attempt to address this very argument, he now suddenly opines that it is not serious. This way of proceeding is an act of raw power rather than of intellect. He asserts that his opponents are avoiding something called "truth," and this assertion evidently dispenses with any need for further argument. This recurs in those rare moments when Negro Crit arguments confront Carter's own. In the course of Carter's championing a dialogic model of constitutional law, Derrick Bell makes a forlorn but devastating appearance. Carter notes that dialogic theorists (himself included) offer "no solace for those troubled by Derrick Bell's provocative challenge to mainstream theorists to show why those the Constitution was designed to oppress should now be bound by it."

Carter's talk of solace is a pale response to an unanswerable question. Moreover, Carter is himself, declaredly, not a solace seeker of the kind he takes Bell to be. When Carter calls Bell's argument "provocative," it is as though Bell's effort were an adolescent trick rather than a successful attempt to throw Carter's entire enterprise into question. Carter concedes the success of Bell's argument, redefines Bell as a solace seeker, exempts himself from such solace seeking, and simply continues with what, in another self-immolating confession, he calls his "justification project." Carter persists in the questionable project despite admitting "shuddering contradictions" of which he is "not proud." He acknowledges that the "republican revival" that is at the heart of the dialogic tradition he follows is rooted in a heritage that "was horribly oppressive, at least for those who were not white male property owners." He concedes that the dialogic model has numerous other problems too ("the difficulties are legion"). But he presses on: "The dialogic metaphor still has much to recommend it."

Carter's frank admissions of the priority he places on preserving liberal theory, and his equally frank dismissals of racial-justice priorities as solace seeking, are so frequent that it takes a certain stamina to match his self-accusations with one's own protests. Carter is declaredly concerned to find *"happy proposition[s] for liberal theory."* Carter elsewhere devotes an entire article to something called the "Theory of Democratic Prosperity," according to which majoritarian democracy must be organized so as never overly to offend the wealthy elite. If that elite should ever feel genuinely threatened, Carter reasons, it will be forced to resort to extrademocratic means of protecting itself. So, the canny progressive judge ought always to make "partly empirical, partly instinctual determination[s]" as to whether particular populist decisions would too-threaten the elite. A court within this picture would, Carter points out, "be engaged in a pragmatic enterprise, one in which *the highest value is the preservation of the institutions of constitutional government*" (emphasis added). Looked at this way, Carter assures us, "seemingly odious" nineteenth-century decisions can really be explained as good-faith attempts to preserve democracy from "democratic excess of the kind that could end the constitutional experiment."

While others have criticized First Amendment doctrine to the extent that it facilitates the whims of the wealthy and tramples upon the dispossessed, Carter insists that "constitutional restrictions on the ability of the majority to strip the powerful of their resources (including speech resources) are hardly evidence that the document is undemocratic." Carter's contrary hunch is that since money is a necessary counterweight to an overweening state, the First Amendment's responsiveness to monied interests is perhaps really a guarantor of democracy. If the unpropertied rabble could influence the government, it might try to gouge the rich—and the rich would respond with undemocratic repression, so we ought to be grateful that the First Amendment doctrine empowers the rich in advance, and saves us all that unpleasantness. Under Carter's Theory of Democratic Prosperity,

The anti-majoritarian protections of property, for example, become not the safe-guards of the propertied class, but rather the preservatives of democracy itself; by limiting the scope of societal changes that the masses can demand, the Constitution lessens the likelihood that those with the greatest private power will dismantle the democratic institutions. *The Theory is also able to justify the exclusion of slaves, and to a large extent, the poor from suffrage for the first century of the nation's existence.* Before the massive economic expansion of the past century, there simply was not enough wealth to share with all these potential voters. (Emphasis added)

When Carter says his theory can justify the exclusion of slaves and the poor, the question is, Justify *to whom?* And the answer is, to some audience *other than* the slaves and the poor themselves. To the wealthy, certainly. And to some disembodied entity known as the "American experiment," which, at all costs, Carter feels must be preserved. One could hardly ask for a clearer clash of *racial justice versus something else* (in this case, Lockean liberal theory with a dash of Hobbes and a paradoxically weak stomach for a fight). Carter includes a wan disclaimer in the midst of indulging this analysis. He says that "without endorsing a judicial review based on the Theory of Democratic Prosperity, it is a matter of more than passing interest to try to work out what its method might entail." Yet Carter makes no serious attempt to illuminate the ethical atrocity of the theory. His uncritical and "more than passing interest" in the theory is itself *already* an endorsement. Certainly, Carter hasn't spent anything near as much energy or ink on Derrick Bell's work. Moreover, the theory is eminently consistent with Carter's views generally, such as his oft-repeated opinion that society will pretty much muddle on as it is. Carter's affinity for the Theory of Democratic Prosperity is unmistakable upon the most cursory reading of the article.

In summary, Carter's allegiance to an avuncular yet oppressive liberalism, his recognition that liberalism obliterates difference, his patronizing attitude toward his students, and his anticipated patronizing attitude toward his own children are all explicit here:

> I am reasonably sanguine—not to say cynical—about the future. Capitalism will co-opt most of the current activists, because that is what capitalism does best. Liberalism will learn from them, absorbing what is valuable in their ideas and discarding what is not, because that is what liberalism does best. And, God willing, something over a decade from now, my own children, rebelling angrily on college campuses, will be lamenting the demise of "real" student radicalism—you know, the kind they had back in the 1980s and 1990s.

Carter's statement that liberalism is, after all, a kind of ultimate arbiter, having final say over what to keep and what to discard, is a straightforward admission of Edward Said's claim that liberal cultural idealism is a "forceful and tyrannical"—not pluralistic and accommodating—values system. Carter here affirms that liberalism, discarding the supposedly valueless, creates Said's culturally disenfranchised.

In *The Culture of Disbelief,* Carter appears to resist the violent exclusions enforced by U.S. liberalism. Carter's *Culture* advances a plea for the inclusion of religion within rational liberal dialogue. He appeals to liberalism's vaunted tolerance. It would certainly be entertaining to parse the collapse of Carter's *Culture* into a condemnation of both religion (for "Faustian" political pacts such as tax exemption) and liberalism (for enforcing an arbitrary model of rationality), but that would be a diversion. More interesting is the *absence* of any such contradiction and collapse in Carter's work in the areas of constitutional theory and civil disobedience. *In Carter's constitutional theory, racial-justice concerns (unlike religious ones) are eviscerated. While Carter has an empirical hunch that all Americans view their society as fundamentally just, he has no such hunch that Americans view their society as fundamentally sufficiently religious.* In Carter's theory, "rational" liberal reason has its way wherever racial-justice passions, rather than religious ones, are the issue. The result is a rout of racial justice in Carter's constitutional world. While Carter laments, in *Culture,* that religious devotees are violently forced to dress themselves in secularism before engaging in public debate, Carter's own writings breezily require exactly such cross-dressing on the part of those who view American society as fundamentally tainted by racial injustice. So, Carter's allegiance to a patrician liberalism is the opposite of the harmless, apolitical, and inherently humane pursuit that he fancies it to be. Carter's affable sensibility is like a scary kind of Mister Magoo in its somnambulant violence. Telling of his young daughter's exposure to an offensive slogan emblazoned on a Confederate flag, Carter gratuitously informs us that his wife is wiser than he in matters of childrearing. This gracious and back-handed tribute to natural female wisdom exactly captures the simultaneous charm and violence of Carter's high liberalism.

And Carter carries this genial and oppressive disposition even into legal interpretation. In law, which has been described as a field of pain and death, Carter's humane liberalism quickly becomes an affable sadism. Evidence Carter's championing of what he concedes is a quaint relic in legal theory: the prima facie obligation to obey the law. Carter begins by invoking—over Derrick Bell's admittedly unanswerable dissent—his empirical hunch that America is fundamentally just. Carter then announces a requirement that all laws are presumptively entitled to obedience. Next, invoking a highly debatable interpretation of the legacy of Martin Luther King, Jr., Carter prescribes what can, *with precision,* be described as legal-theoretical sadism. Carter asserts that King, driven primarily by a relentless optimism and by a belief in the essential good faith of the American people, counseled not only nonviolence but also willing submission to the punishment of unjust laws. In fact, as Tough Randall Kennedy has pointed out, King's campaign was premised not on a naive rule-of-law idealism but on "a keen appreciation for *both* the power and the limits of the law" (emphasis added). Carter's King is thus as much an uninteresting icon as is Spike Lee's Malcolm X.

Driven by this icon and by rule-of-law rhetoric, Carter's ostensible commitment to racial justice soon disappears in favor of a peculiar "ideal of the just law." Under Carter's ideal, citizens should submit to punishment under laws that are entirely unjust in those citizens' views. Submission to such punishment will, Carter says, spur dialogue among America's essentially decent polity, and will appeal to the conscience of the ideal citizens who will then be moved to amend the law. Were this accepted by Negro Crits, here's what Carter would have in store for Audre Lorde, Patricia Williams, Mari Matsuda, and Kimberle Crenshaw. Of each he would say that "she can show no greater love for the ideal of just law and no greater faith in the capacity of just societies to change than by submitting herself to punishment under the law that is unjust."

The female pronoun is Carter's, and this is Tough stuff. It is the law-and-order mirror image of certain ostensibly progressive excesses of the 1960s. The Black Panther party's Elaine Brown has written of brutal beatings, with a bullwhip, that she suffered at the hands of David Hilliard, also a prominent figure in the Black Panther movement. Alice Walker's criticism of Hilliard's bullwhip affection triggered this perplexing response from Brown: "Yes, I was beaten, as [Walker] pounds home. . . . [But] David, who never laid a hand on me but to heal, whose touch was revolutionary love, David does not deserve so much venom."

If Carter recoils from this bullwhip vision (and I make that charitable assumption), how come he adopts some analogue thereof in his own work? The answer is that Carter's "dialogic" theorizing is so untethered from any real person's body that the specter of sadism he proffers is intended as some kind of metaphor or something (again this is a charitable reading: Carter relies, in his analysis, on the real spectacle of pain as a trigger of the polity's conscience). Yet law is not a metaphor, but rather a field of pain and death. So Hilliard's bullwhip is apropos, and Carter's suggestion is terrifying.[50]

As always, it is useful to contrast Carter's Tough commandments for Negroes with his leniency toward others. In criticizing the case of *Morrison v. Olsen,* which upheld the office of the independent counsel (think of Lawrence Walsh, Iran-Contra), Carter performed a wonderful turnabout regarding the meticulous punishment of wrongs. Carter suddenly opposed "overly literal enforcement of the law" as "profoundly unfair" to potential defendants, and he suddenly berated "fans of criminal punishment who want to see every wrongdoer in jail."

Carter's Tough scheme for social progress through mass submission to the punishment of unjust laws is, finally, built on a number of his own "empirical hunches," all of which might prove faulty. His main idea—that the spectacle of pain will yield results in law reform—depends wholly on an intriguing idea of an American polity governed by rational dialogue about morality and about policy. We would, in Carter's intriguing model, pay in pain *now,* without any assurance that Carter's utopia has arrived. Indeed, on Carter's iconographic reading of the Martin Luther King years, the American utopia had then arrived, and so has either subsequently been lost, or else is still here and therefore decades old.

Finally, the unreliability of Carter's empirical hunches is compounded by a general deficiency in models of constitutional law as dialogue. Stanley Cavell's *Claim of Reason* is easily the most thoughtful work we have on conversation in culture. Stephen Carter's work, in contrast, is strong evidence that Cavell's worst fears have materialized. Cavell cautions, "It does not appear unthinkable that the bulk of the entire culture, call it the public discourse of the culture, the culture thinking aloud about itself, hence be-lieving itself to be talking philosophy, should become ungovernably inane."

Need one mention the Guinier affair to press this point? Tough Randall Kennedy himself called the Guinier affair "one of the most vivid examples of the dumbing down of American politics I've ever seen."[51] Stephen Carter's offering of Negro bodies to an idealized and speculative dialogue is, more than dumb, *immoral.*

# III

# Negro Crit Law

# 6

# Is Law Like a Friar's Roast?

I have tried to do my part towards making the teaching and the study of law in that school worthy of a university.... To accomplish these objects, so far as they depended upon the law school, it was indispensable to establish at least two things—that law is a science, and that all the available materials of that science are contained in printed books.
—Christopher C. Langdell, *Harvard Celebration Speeches,* 1887

Have you not noticed what a false and unreal sound abstract terms have on the lips of those ancients in the college?... The toy life which the Jesuits permit these young men to live is what I call the stationary march. The marionette life which the Jesuit himself lives as a dispenser of illumination and rectitude is yet another variety of the stationary march.
—James Joyce, *Stephen Hero,* 1944

## Is Law School a Friar's Roast?

A Friar's Roast is a no-holds-barred escape from accountability in which, according to actress Whoopi Goldberg, anyone familiar with the club's tradition knows that "jokes about sex, gender, bodily functions, religion and race are the rule rather than the exception."[1] And lawyers have traditions that, while less spectacular, appear equally immune to serious questioning. Julien Benda's tradition of disinterested truth seeking remains the way of business for intellectuals in America. The landmark Declaration of the American Association of University Professors (AAUP) endorsed in 1915 the tradition that Benda, in 1927, would fortify with his powerful voice: that of the university as a nonpartisan forum detached from the conflicts of the outside world.

This detached ideal continues to dominate popular debate about the role of universities, even though few deny that the ideal is outdated. Derek Bok, former dean of Harvard Law School and former president of Harvard College, entered the debate over the role of the contemporary university with a book called *Beyond the Ivory Tower*. Bok's title might suggest a move beyond the transcendent ideals of Julien Benda, but the opposite is the case. Bok concedes that the image of the ivory tower university grew obsolete after World War II because of the universities' increasing immersion in, and reliance on, society beyond their walls. Yet Bok does not abandon old transcendent ideals, but rather addresses himself to "the constant tensions that result from embracing transcendent goals and ideals while having to exist and be of service to a practical, imperfect world."[2] Bok thus admits the obsolescence of the ivory tower image without conceding the irrelevance of transcendent goals. He sets himself to achieve a balance between old goals and new conditions. He ignores the possibility that new conditions might require new goals.

This debate, which Bok discusses in relation to universities generally, is also raging in America's law schools. Contemporary legal scholars are all now vaguely aware of the connections between legal knowledge and power. Stephen Carter himself has recently served up a good example of this connection. Carter has long opposed "litmus tests" for judges. In *The Culture of Disbelief*, Carter advanced a mildly prochoice position but also urged that religion ought to have an expanded role in public debate and that the antichoice religiously based argument, that a fetus is a person, ought to be a legitimate part of American jurisprudence. Carter made this suggestion in *Culture* while being well aware, as he states elsewhere, that "it will obviously be easier for pro-life forces to enact abortion restrictions if they can convince legislators (and the public) of the personhood of the fetus."[3] Within days of *Culture*'s appearance, President Clinton personally urged Americans of all political and religious stripes to read it. Days after that, the White House announced that it would not eliminate candidates for appointment to lower federal courts because of their opposition to abortion. This caused predictable and robust *political* protest. A *New York Times* editorial characterized the Clinton action as "a political sellout of incalculable dimensions." It is of course unlikely that Carter's book *caused* this White House action. Clinton was probably expressing a long-held or somehow expedient view. Unquestionably, however, Carter's book *facilitated* the announcement by supplying Clinton with a veneer of intellectual respectability.

Less dramatically, law teachers shape their students' visions of what it is possible for a lawyer to do. Law teachers thus play a role in deploying the energies of many of America's talented. Additionally, law professors directly participate in the political process on many issues (congressional testimony on proposed legislation, judicial confirmations, etc.) in which Congress listens precisely because of a professor's authority as a legal "expert."

In this politically charged setting, some scholars have sensibly suggested that new goals ought to displace the "transcendent" priorities that have held sway for so long. The Tough Love lawyers, in contrast, tell us that impartiality, disinterest, and neutrality keep us nearest truth. Law is the last bastion of such old rhetorics. Despite the legal realist movement of the 1930s, Herbert Wechsler's 1959 article, bearing the self-explanatory title "Toward Neutral Principles of Constitutional Law," could become influential among American lawyers. Stephen Carter, even today, insists that the legitimacy of judicial review hinges on justifying the process of judicial decisionmaking rather than on the decisions of individual judges. And in 1993, a lawyer who has himself launched vituperative attacks on transcendentalism in law could plausibly ignore the entire tilt of his own career in order to attack Negro Crits in the name of the supposedly inherent general rules of persuasive argument. Someone else has argued that lawyers are now engaged in an "idolatrous practice," in a religious enterprise, because lawyers proceed on an unacknowledged assumption that their habits carry transcendent authority. He added that the law school (not the supposedly untutored public) is the "leading temple" devoted to this idolatrous practice. His conclusion? This state of affairs may be "an illusion too precious to be relinquished."[4] Precious *to whom* is the question he neglects to answer.

Given the unfortunate state of legal commentary itself, it is not surprising that even the most thoughtful contributors, outside of law, assume that law has a certainty that eludes other disciplines. Literary theorist Stanley Fish, turning his energies to legal theory, defers to "competent" practitioners of something called "adjudication." Likewise, philosopher Stanley Cavell assumes that parties before a court are in competition for a stable standard called "the favorable or unfavorable response of *the law*" (emphasis added).[5]

Lawyers who reject the transcendent assumption that such stable legal standards exist are roundly attacked for degrading the law and for intolerably departing from what are said to be the settled rules of legal truth production. Work that questions these ostensibly settled rules is dismissed as fiction. It has, for instance, been suggested that Patricia Williams's *Alchemy of Race and Rights* is clearly not a factual work and ought therefore to have been presented as a novel. Meanwhile, Randall Kennedy's "Racial Critiques" article, notwithstanding its serious flaws, continues to be cited as evidence that Negro Crits, whom Kennedy criticizes, neglect an indispensable ideal: the production of empirical evidence and real proof.[6] Moreover, allegiance to these illusory standards of legal-scientific truth production is not confined to opponents of Negro Criticism. A relatively friendly *Harvard Law Review* Book Note on *Alchemy* treated the book as bifurcated between literary and scientific claims. The reviewer praised the supposed literary aspects of the book but commented that "when the text crosses back from art to science ...Williams's argument becomes as partial and contradictory as that of her adversaries." It is, however, news that Negro Crit texts participate in scientific ambitions at all. A passage in *Alchemy* where reference is made to statistics on crime prompts the reviewer to suggest that Williams "masquerades a partial picture ... as objective truth." Yet Williams's resort to statistics always intends to throw up their indeterminacy and further a principal Negro Crit theme: frequently in America "truth like a fad takes on a life of its own, independent of action and limited only by the imagination of self-proclaimed visionaries." Williams's point is that the crucial irresolvability of episodes like the Tawana Brawley affair is usually solved, simplistically, by a regime of truth that elevates an arbitrary truth from among a multitude of competitors. Even this friendly reviewer thus manages to overemphasize the semantic posture of the chapter in question (asserting a *competing* truth). The reviewer neglects that competing truth's arbitrary erasure by the prevailing regime of truth, and therefore misses Williams's central theme: given the failure of objectivism, power makes truth.[7]

In another assault by friendly fire, Edward Rubin has offered an attempt (entitled "On beyond Truth") to address the crisis of stable standards within legal academia. Rubin begins promisingly, noting that in law "the entire field crackles with normativity," so that the scientific concepts of validity are unhelpful. Yet Rubin himself proposes the spectacularly unhelpful alternatives of "normative clarity" and "persuasiveness," limited by a principle of "bizarreness." Who is to apply these new tests of truth? Rubin means to be reassuring when he says that this task will be handled by "a large sample of distinguished reviewers" guided by a belief that something called "theory" provides something called "altitude" and thereby guards against mere opinion and bias.[8] Rubin thus reenters the quest to escape the crackling normativity of the field by employing a spurious metaphor of flight.

In yet more friendly fire, Daniel Farber and Suzanna Sherry also begin in a promising fashion. They specifically note that since Negro Crits have challenged prevailing standards, "A constructive response . . . cannot simply reassert those traditional standards." Yet the epigraph of their article prefigures their own failure: "To have crafted . . . something true and truly put— whatever the devil else legal scholarship is, is from, or is for, it's for the joy of that too." Seemingly unaware of the enormous and foredoomed audacity of such truth seeking, Farber and Sherry set themselves the old task of elaborating "*methods* of judging truthfulness" (emphasis added). Farber and Sherry are aware that "the meaning of 'truth' itself is contested," but they simply assert, "We do not believe it necessary to explore the philosophical disputes over the nature of truth in order to resolve the standards for assessing nonfictional stories." Farber and Sherry admit the unattainability of truth (or at least decline the question) even as they retain the legitimizing rhetoric of truth. While Negro Crits insist on unswerving allegiance to communities outside of law school walls, Farber and Sherry would block that project with this dogma: "Community building may be valuable, but it is an enterprise quite distinct from increasing understanding of the law."[9] No further argument, apparently, is necessary.

This, then, is the Friar's Roast that legal scholarship has become. Legal scholars, right now, are playing a game of make believe. Right now they are operating on the *explicit* assumption that questions about the nature of truth are not central to legal practice. They assume it's fine to continue in rhetorical allegiance to Benda's mission of disinterested truth seeking, even while admitting that Benda's model is unattainable in practice. Yet, as Ernest Gellner has put the point in criticizing the undeserved dominance of Julien Benda's ideals in contemporary intellectual practices,

The tacit deployment of a model which fails to do justice to the seriousness of [the] difficulties is itself a kind of intellectual treason. The strident denunciation of the treason of the clerics, which pretends that our situation is far clearer and unambiguous than it in fact is, is itself a form of infidelity to the truth.[10]

Law needs new unsparing satirical critics. Perhaps Negro Crits are new Jonathan Swifts.[11]

## People Enact Truth

Contrary to a myth whose history and functions would repay further study, truth isn't the reward of free spirits, the child of protracted solitude, nor the privilege of those who have succeeded in liberating themselves. Truth is a thing of this world.
—Michel Foucault, *Truth and Power*

Negro Crit responses to the mock-scientific attacks and assorted misunderstandings canvassed in the previous section have persuasively emphasized that, in law, the issue of truth versus fiction is not "out there" to be picked up like pebbles off a beach. Law isn't like manna from heaven. Judges, law clerks, Court TV, messengers, lawyers, paralegals, Federal Express couriers, secretaries, and interactions among all of the above enact much of society's legal "regime of truth." The courts participate in big and small ways.

*Small ways:* the court's evidentiary rules decide what evidence is admissible in any dispute, and then the judge decides what among the admissible evidence is persuasive. Even in the relatively rare cases where there is a jury, so that the judge doesn't have the final say on the persuasiveness of the evidence, the judge still guides the jury's deliberations. And trial jurors are themselves hardly infallible arbiters of truth. What was previously a malcontent's complaint has become, since the Rodney King verdict, a part of popular lore: juries can and do flunk the truth test.

*Big ways:* conservative and progressive lawyers alike agree that courts generally, and the United States Supreme Court in particular, contribute to the country's "vision" of itself. Their job is either to drag everyone back to an imagined traditional America (conservatives) or to push everyone forward to an imagined best America (progressives). It is easy to show that this vision-announcing function always and necessarily involves contestable values rather than simple truth. Those who oppose the courts' inevitable visionary role claim that judges are and ought to be confined to a distinctly professional, legal, or rule-of-law vision. Making the case for *that* peculiar idea is an uphill battle indeed.

On June 28, 1993, the U.S. Supreme Court rejected the claim that the orthodox scientific community has a monopoly on scientific truth. The Supreme Court refused to give automatic deference to the dominant scientific community. In *Daubert v. Merrell Dow Pharmaceuticals, Inc.,* the justices held that courts of law have to accept scientific evidence as expert evidence even if the scientific method followed by the particular expert is not generally accepted in the scientific community. After *Daubert,* in each case even the most well-credentialed scientist must convince the courts afresh as to the merits of the particular contested scientific claim. The judge or jury, not the scientists, thus have the final say on what constitutes scientific truth for legal purposes. This is potentially important in product liability cases like *Daubert* itself, where well-funded drug companies and other corporate defendants often bankroll much of the scientific community's research.

Law's truth-making role can help America's dispossessed enormously if lawyers relentlessly question the things law does every day. But only Negro Crits sustain this questioning. Superficially similar lawyers group within a strand of feminism known as "difference theory." But difference theorists call for each lawyer to pursue plural values individually and believe that these values can be harmonized through our openness to each other. While this sort of thing might perhaps serve well in a Himalayan ashram, it is less well suited to the American legal system, which imposes pain and death every day.

The difference school is built around a new-age "plea for judges to engage with perspectives that challenge their own." Yet their underlying desire, to approach nearer other people's truths, might be better advanced if the dispossessed spend energy on uncompromising expression of previously excluded truths rather than on trying to empathize with their oppressors. We might expect difference theorists' ideal of the judicial role to take account of the difference with which they are so concerned. Yet, in outlining the appropriate judicial role, a leading difference theorist, Martha Minow, slips away from her own best insights. Minow begins with the laudable suggestion that the plea for openness to difference is not a mere "call for sympathy or empathy, nor a hope that judges will be 'good people.' Sympathy, the human emotion, must be distinguished from respect, the legal command."

This good insight does not, however, last very long. Minow approvingly cites the view that

whereas sympathy involves an imaginative extension of our own person, our beliefs and perspective, respect heeds the distinctness of persons. . . . We can respect [another's] views without sympathizing with them. We can find them justified from his perspective, without believing that they would be ours in that situation.[12]

But how can we find another's view "justified" if we would, *even in her situation,* have a different one? Minow's distinction between sympathy and justification is nonexistent. The distinction trades on a diluted sense of justification. Justification in a strong sense just *is* what we think right. It provides us with reasons for action. In a diluted sense, justification might mean something like, "I can see what you're saying but . . ." In this weaker case, justification simply might not provide us with a reason to act in accord with the other person's view. Moreover, this weaker sense of justification will be especially useless where controversy is especially intense. Minow neglects Stanley Fish's useful first law of tolerance dynamics: *toleration is exercised in an inverse proportion to there being anything at stake.* Anyone with strong views in a heated controversy would probably, if it were her choice to make, withhold the legal command her opponent wants. And if she does not withhold her opponents' preferred command, it will be because she doesn't really feel strongly about the issue, or because she feels strongly that exactly where one feels strongly about an issue, one ought to defer to one's opponents in certain circumstances. This latter view—that one *ought* to defer to one's opponents—represents a perfectly respectable ideology called liberalism. The action it compels—award the legal command to one's opponent in certain circumstances—is not manifestly absurd, but neither is it universally desirable. There are times when we *ought not* to turn the other cheek. Minow's model only works among persons who are *already* unseparated by urgent moral and political differences—or among those who feel so secure in their own position that permitting their opponent a victory on a single particular occasion resembles philanthropy more than self-abnegation. If this is this case we are, alas, thrown back upon the toothless empathy that Minow thinks she has overcome by importing the notions of respect without sympathy and of justification without belief. This is an important point because empathy, while perhaps cathartic for the empathizer, is not a good political strategy for the dispossessed:

For blacks, describing needs has been a dismal failure as a political activity. It has succeeded only as a literary achievement. The history of our need is certainly moving enough to have been called poetry, oratory, epic entertainment—but it has never been treated by white institutions as the statement of a political priority. . . . Some of our greatest politicians have been forced to become ministers or blues singers. Even white descriptions of "the blues" tend to remove the daily hunger and hurt from need and abstract it into a mood. And whoever would legislate against depression? Particularly something as rich, soulful, and sonorously productive as black depression.[13]

The astuteness of this observation is difficult to overstate. Negro Crit scholarship has been alternately praised as "eloquent" and dismissed as fiction. Thus, even where blacks enter political institutions, as lawyers, judges, or otherwise, their views stoke emotion more often than set agendas. During the mass eulogy that followed Justice Thurgood Marshall's death, a *New York Times* headline referred to the "plain-spoken, gut-wrenching eloquence of the Justice's real voice." The *Times* described Marshall's voice as a "sonorous instrument." And the text of the article, consistent with this cathartic hype, referred to Justice O'Connor's remark that Marshall had "influenced her most as a raconteur."[14] Yet, whatever this influence was, it did not resemble a consistent pattern of concurrence with Marshall's opinions. O'Connor's transmutation of Marshall's priorities into some kind of raconteur's recital allowed her to strike an enlightened posture. She could praise the man even while withholding concurrence in his pattern of values — even while withholding the legal command. Empathy, thus, is bullshit. It does more for the self-righteousness of the empathizer than for the well-being of the dispossessed.

# 7

# Can We Judge Judges?

Who did you bury to become enforcer of the law?
— Audre Lorde, *The Marvelous Arithmetics of Distance*

Justice Thomas is at the start of a term that could easily exceed forty years. The following discussion will bypass numerous opportunities to prove Thomas wrong on specific points of legal doctrine in order to provide an enduring critique, beyond ephemeral doctrinal skirmishes. Additionally, this approach reflects the important argument presented in the next section: *doctrinal debate does not determine the results of Supreme Court cases.* In every interesting case, there are various views that Thomas might competently adopt. Thomas's chosen doctrinal paths will frequently seem quite wrong, but the moral complaint will be based on the very availability of the other doctrinal line of reasoning. Wherever Thomas, ostensibly unhappy, follows controversial doctrine to results he avowedly laments, he drops the ball.

There are lots of objections to judging judges in this way. *First,* this approach may seem to violate the idea that law is a scientific, technical, or professional skill ideally separate from moral concerns. Judges are known to have moral and political beliefs, but, the argument goes, they shouldn't allow these beliefs to influence their performance as professionals. This rhetoric of judicial restraint as a professional ideal is still powerful in talk about law. *Yet we ought to oppose the ideal of judicial restraint, not because it is inherently undesirable in principle, but because it is admittedly unattainable in practice and FOR THAT REASON undesirable in practice.* The conventional wisdom that urges us to strive for all sorts of abstract ideals (in law and elsewhere) while in the same breath admitting that those ideals are unattainable is positively harmful. Such foredoomed striving obscures injustices that less grandiose ideals might remedy. *Every principle that is admittedly unattainable in practice is also immediately suspect IN PRINCIPLE since it is likely to be a distraction from meaningfully improving our practices.*[1] At the very least, admittedly unattainable ideals ought to receive extremely close scrutiny. And judicial restraint, it turns out, cannot bear the weight of such a careful examination.

*Second,* passing moral judgment on anyone may itself seem presumptuous and even oppressive. Thomas himself has raised this objection throughout his career, and has continued to raise it since joining the Court. In a speech prominently published in the *Wall Street Journal* at the height of the Guinier affair and entitled "The New Intolerance," Thomas criticized a perceived black orthodoxy: "Is it really more laudable to make a man afraid to express his beliefs than it is to make him ashamed for the color of his skin?" While the idea that this book might make Thomas quake is flattering, even encouraging, it is unlikely. Moreover, Thomas's underlying reasoning (the sanctity of self-expression) equally protects everyone's right to censure the conduct of others. It is the judges who have the power, and Justice Thomas has more than most.

*Third,* the present argument might wrongly be thought to single out black judges. A white judge, however, might have rhetorical civil rights commitments more conspicuous than her black colleagues. This rhetoric would then set the benchmark for our assessment of her. The cornerstone of evaluation is thus commitment, not pigmentation. Yet this does not mean that black judges have no special obligations. It is, in theory, conceivable that American black judges without a conspicuous commitment to American racial justice exist, or might exist. Such judges would be beyond the present criticism (though probably criticizable on broader humanitarian grounds). I, however, know of no such judge. Certainly, Clarence Thomas is not such a judge. Thomas consistently voices a sense of America's unjust racial past and subscribes to a conspicuous rhetoric of redress. His rhetoric, not his pigmentation, is the basis for moral criticism. This answers the following objection: "Why are you holding Justice Thomas to a higher standard than the other, white Justices? The other Justices can choose to be liberal or conservative, average or great, pro-business or pro-people. So what if Justice Thomas chooses to be conservative, average, pro-business?"[2]

The response is that Thomas has made no such choice. He has not chosen conservative ideology as an end in itself regardless of its impact on racial justice. He has not chosen pro-business over pro-people. His point is always ostensibly that racial justice is better served by his agenda.

In a sense other than the sense that it intends, however, this last objection ("why a higher standard?") contains an important insight. The objection assumes that Justice Thomas is *not* committed to racial justice. It assumes that the contours of Justice Thomas's jurisprudence reflect the contours of a pro-business agenda. If this is accurate, Justice Thomas must either persuade us that the interests underlying a pro-business agenda are actually identical with racial justice, properly understood, or else he must admit that his rhetoric of racial justice has been conquered in practice—that he has been led to mistake the prerogatives of other interests for the imperatives of racial justice.

## Thomas and the Rule of Law

There are seemingly lots of problems with holding judges morally account-able for their decisions. *First,* Thomas, like all Supreme Court justices, will often depend on the research and writing of law clerks. Can he be held responsible for his decisions? Easy answer: he supervises and is responsible for decisions that he signs. Authoring Supreme Court (or other judicial) opinions is an extremely self-conscious exercise. The justices review opin-ions very closely and where they disagree with even the smallest details, they indicate that disagreement. If they agree with the result of the case but not with the underlying reasoning—or vice versa—they say so. They may join all but the objectionable parts of the decision, or may write a separate concurring opinion. If they disagree with the result they dissent, again with or without an opinion. Where other justices also dissent, the whole range of choices (joining a dissenting opinion in full, in part, writing separately) repeats itself. In this manner Supreme Court opinions reflect extremely nuanced coalition-building exercises. No one ever signs anything by ac-cident. In *Conroy v. Askinoff* Thomas joined the entire majority opinion with the exception of a single footnote. In another case Justice O'Connor joined all of Souter's opinion except "the sentence to which n. 29 is attached." When a justice sits out a case, we hear about it: "Justice Thomas and Justice Ginsberg took no part in the consideration or decision."[3] Supreme Court justices are thus firmly bound for purposes of moral assessment by every-thing to which they lend their name.

*Second,* law is found, not made. A Supreme Court justice is only a funnel through which law expresses itself. The claim that Thomas is responsible for law would be both inaccurate and improper, because law is a science in which correct answers are compelled by technical rules. A justice's job is to set aside her personal ethics and to provide professional readings of those rules. Any ethical critique of a sitting judge must reckon with this influential idea that judges follow legal rules, not personal morality. This idea is the flip side of the ideal of judicial restraint. Judicial restraint urges that judges *ought* ideally to follow rules, not morality. The present point urges that *since* judges follow rules, not morality, ethical assessment of judges, including Justice Thomas, is misplaced. However, popular ways of talking about law exaggerate the hurdle posed by this argument. Much that passes under the banner of the rule of law rests not on impartial law but on value judgments, judicial acquiescence, and sloppy scholarship. This objection nevertheless raises law's liveliest controversy and requires extensive discussion. It would disallow moral assessment of a Supreme Court justice.

## Why Law Absolutely Must Bind Judges

The peculiar constraint called "law" is essential to justify the everyday work that courts do. If judges are only politicians, we have no reason to pay them any more attention than we would pay the average congressional windbag acting in her personal capacity. When judges talk, people listen, and controversy ends in a crucial sense, even as it continues in other senses. Law happens. Judges settle what action the state will permit or demand in heated disputes. The loser listens not because she comes to see the moral soundness of her opponent's case, but often simply to avoid punishment. This punishment, or threat of punishment, would be easy to justify if judges speak a peculiar impartial ("legal") truth that is free of the moral, political, and opportunistic differences that separate the plaintiff and the defendant. Such impartial decisionmaking would in turn make it acceptable for other officials to use force in inflicting the judges' decisions on the parties. *That*, ideally, is law's special leverage. Underneath the classical ideal of the rule of law is a desire to escape, in the words of landmark constitutionalist A. W. Dicey, "the rule of men." If we haven't escaped the rule of persons, the traditional enterprise of law collapses in a crucial sense. Law loses its ability to command automatic and universal obedience. It loses its claim to flow from neutral principle. Law loses its peculiar leverage. *Most importantly, Thomas loses the scapegoat that law's leverage would provide.* He loses a moral alibi. He can't claim that law automatically dictates the results of cases without any action by him. There might still be numerous reasons why Thomas follows a rule, but these reasons would now be of the same political, strategic, or personal sort that the rule of law was supposed to move us beyond. If law's leverage has collapsed, Thomas is brought into the fray and is open to ethical assessment, just like the rest of us.

## Law Doesn't Bind Judges

Law's leverage has collapsed. The neutral view of legal process has been thrown into serious question. Most lawyers now accept that legal doctrine is manipulable; that legal concepts frequently do not dictate particular results in actual cases; and that legal rules are "indeterminate" and therefore do not bind judges in the peculiar way that would shield them against ordinary moral criticism. The claim that law doesn't bind judges is, however, complex. It is frequently misunderstood by its opponents and its meaning is hotly contested even among its adherents. The key question, for the present analysis of judges as moral actors, is how much *choice* judges have. Is Thomas ever blocked by a thing called "law"? Perhaps not.

Judges may be blocked by many considerations, but a thing called law is never one of them. Much that we call law is merely an ordinary combination of strategic reasoning and value judgments. This kind of reckoning is certainly a constraint; but it is not the peculiar constraint that the thing called law needs to be. It is, rather, the same sort of thing that congressional windbags deal with every day. This kind of reckoning lacks the special leverage law needs in order to wall its empire off from the rule of men. It fails to give a judge the scapegoat she needs in order to escape ordinary moral criticism. If legal rules don't bind judges, then legal disputes are like our other disputes. If legal disputes are like our other disputes—if judges are like the rest of us—then we can advance ordinary moral criticism of the work they do.

## Why Some Lawyers Still Think Law Binds Judges

[The Constitution] is made for people of fundamentally differing views, and the accident of our finding certain opinions natural and familiar, or novel and even shocking, ought not to conclude our judgment.
                    —Justice Holmes, Dissenting, *Lochner v. New York*

The *Lochner* case gave its name to an entire era of what is commonly called judicial activism. The Supreme Court struck down minimum-wage legislation in the name of freedom of contract, and the case is fodder for both the Right and the Left. To the left *Lochner* shows that judicial neutrality is a myth. To the right, *Lochner* shows that judicial restraint (the idea that rules bind and ought to bind judges) is everybody's friend, not just a reactionary fetish. What gets lost in such arguments is that both judicial restraint and judicial activism derive their meaning from some preexisting judicial culture. Abstract argument over the desirability, in principle, of one or the other judicial posture is thus useless. A more useful way of looking at the issue is to ask about the legitimacy of particular judicial cultures. The rhetoric of reasonableness and rationality is, for instance, prominent in the *Lochner* decision. If judges, today and in the *Lochner* era, are drawn from a relatively narrow band of society's privileged, how do we justify giving them control over the concepts of reasonableness and rationality that are so central to the law that governs everyone? And if we can't justify their control, what is the binding force of what they think law is?

The fact that legal decisions, even in areas of intense political controversy, can frequently be predicted by those in the legal community is often assumed to enhance the legitimacy of judicial decisionmaking. But it should have the opposite effect. It should trigger alarm bells and make us wonder about oversimplification. It should give us pause, not speed us to accept "legal" results.

Most lawyers admit that legal rules have fringes ("penumbra") of uncertainty within which judicial discretion and personal values come into play. But they argue that legal rules also have core meanings and that there are clear cases in which judges have no meaningful discretion. They often assume that fringe cases are rare, and that even in fringe cases there are other constraints (such as legislative intent) limiting a judge's room for maneuver. Such arguments reawaken the idea that law is relatively apolitical and essentially binds judges. Such arguments reawaken the idea that the intrusion of politics in legal practice is regrettable and, fortunately, containable.

Such arguments, however, confuse the claim that legal rules don't determine legal results with the claim (which nobody need make) that legal outcomes are random. Those who argue this way assume that to say that law doesn't bind judges is to say that judicial decisions are *random* (e.g., depend on a judge's breakfast), and so they think they can prove that law binds judges by pointing out that the results of cases are frequently *predictable*.[4] But this predictability can be explained by the prevalence of a conventional wisdom. And this prevalence doesn't in itself recover law's lost leverage, doesn't restore the judge's scapegoat, doesn't establish that law binds judges in the lost, traditional sense. All it does is shift attention to the *legitimacy* of the prevalent legal culture. Who cares, for instance, if it was predictable in Munich in 1938 that the legal culture would expect expropriation of Jewish property whenever the issue arose before a court? If law bound judges in the peculiar mechanical sense, such expropriation would follow automatically without meaningful space for individual reflection by a judge. Legal doctrine, however, always requires judges to *work* toward legal conclusions. "The official who feels 'bound' reasons from nonexistent 'grounds' and hides from herself the fact that she is exercising power."[5] If laws don't bind, judges make choices *even in* reaching the expected or predictable result. Our ordinary moral reasoning may then seize on such acts of choice in a way that would not be available were it true that rules dictate results. If, in practice, the law appears simpler than ordinary moral reasoning outside of law, something funny is happening.

## Something Funny Is Happening

That all valuations of law are moral judgments, that legal philosophy is a branch of ethics, that the problem which the judge faces is, in the strictest sense, a moral problem, and that the law has no valid end or purpose other than the maintenance of the good life are propositions which jurists are apt to resent with some acerbity.... It is submitted that [the contrary] tenets of current juristic faith spring from an indefensible view of the nature and scope of ethics and tinge current legal criticism with a peculiar confusion.

—Felix Cohen, *The Ethical Basis of Legal Criticism,* 1931

It is nearly seventy-five years since Felix Cohen, a central figure in American legal realism, wrote these words. Nevertheless, thoughtful lawyers continue to enforce increasingly baroque separations of law and morality. Cohen's *ethical* legal-realist message has largely disappeared in modern legal academia. In today's legal community, ethics is a charming and diluted embellishment on the practice of law, rather than its governing impetus. Today ethics is corralled into a series of bar association "canons" that provide a set of protocols or a kind of etiquette to be consulted only when the practitioner wishes to resolve minor questions of lawyerly propriety. In Felix Cohen's picture, by contrast, moral evaluation would be the very engine room of the law, its primary animating force. Today, this aspect of Cohen's thought has been effectively muted.

Sometimes this silencing of ethics is accomplished by straightforward revisions of history. One commentator reports, for instance, that Felix Cohen advocated a "new objectivism based on the facts of social science" and that he "essentially silenced" the "idea that facts are contingent on one's interpretive framework." Wrong. As in the epigraph above, Cohen was *emphatic* that ethical evaluation was the only way to escape "a horrible wilderness of data" because "we shall never understand the facts as they are." Cohen was *emphatic* that "the postponement of the problem of values is equivalent to its repudiation."[6]

Such revisionism is, moreover, central to some funny happenings among lawyers today. A bunch of progressive lawyers, presenting themselves as savvy theorists, work hard to demonstrate that they have learned the lessons of legal realism. Yet they ultimately suppress realism's most attractive insights. These lawyers venture into debates outside law and return with the news that arguments about law's nonbindingness are not really a problem for current practices of law. They suggest that the individual lawyer's "situatedness" in the practice of law rebuffs many of the arguments about law's unbindingness. Although the effect of their arguments is to dampen the prospects for political change, these lawyers claim to be progressives. They view law's unbindingness as a problem because it seems to condemn us to endless rounds of meaningless and politically quiescent critique about whether and what kind of legal activism to support. However, their response compounds, rather than solves, this problem. A problem with the legal system, posed sharply by Drucilla Cornell, is "*the erasure of its own mystical foundation of authority so that the system can dress itself up as justice*" (emphasis added). Rather than exposing these mystical foundations, this bunch of lawyers lapses into a tidy project of legal reform. Their project sometimes bears a far greater resemblance to the nineteenth-century legal positivism of Jeremy Bentham than they seem willing to admit. They say that fancy arguments about law's unbindingness overstate the implications of skepticism. Their researches outside law convince them that the current state of philosophical debates outside of law provides a basis for greater certainty and bindingness within law. They ultimately argue that despite law's unbindingness, judicial decisionmaking is *legitimately* constrained. They admit that law does not constrain judges in the sense that would render law apolitical or unproblematically legitimate. Rather, they claim to find legitimate constraint in a value-generating culture, an authoritative science, the nature of the experience of judging, or the brute factual existence of a practice called "adjudication." These several sources of legitimacy for law all understate the degree of controversy within the practice of law, and all proceed upon the unexamined assumption that *legitimate* consensus about the meaning of legal rules exists within legal practice. This imagined consensus oppresses the dispossessed whose voices are often, by definition, beyond its scope. The following sections criticize this bunch of lawyers. They are a cultural tyrant, a quack scientist, a café crit, and an English professor who enjoys legal debates (a fish out of water). Their work, despite their progressive intentions, shores up the mystical foundations of law's authority.

## A Cultural Tyrant?

I feel: These people are in a great hurry to separate out lunatics.
— Stanley Cavell, *The Claim of Reason*

It's a good thing I don't allow myself to be influenced.
— Ludwig Wittgenstein, *Culture and Value*

Professor Joan Williams, in her article "Critical Legal Studies: The Death of Transcendence and the Rise of the New Langdells,"[7] distances herself from the unsophistication of previous attacks on those who argue that law does not bind judges. Her effort, ostensibly based on Wittgenstein, is to furnish the sophisticated defense of law's bindingness that those others have failed to provide. Proponents of law's unbindingness are described, in her account, as "irrationalists." Yet Williams's Wittgensteinian defense of law's bindingness renders Wittgenstein entirely unrecognizable.[8] Williams sums up her critique of the irrationalists:

The irrationalists, girded with Derridaen [*sic*] learning, jump from the long-established tenet that law does not function by internal logic to the conclusion that law is therefore radically indeterminate, and can[9] be argued for any given position. This rhetorical structure sets up a false dichotomy between two alternative conclusions: Either one believes the liberals' [objectivity] analysis or one adopts the irrationalists' view of law as radically indeterminate.

Joan Williams's third way would reject both these extremes in favor of a Wittgensteinian approach that uses "the concept of culture to explain the human experience of certainty." She urges that Wittgensteinian forms of life provide "our" law with a degree of certainty sufficient to ward off irrationalist attack. She says that law's doctrinal discourse is "an integral part" of Wittgensteinian "forms of life." Her aim, then, is to bring certainty in law. Citing, without specific references, Roberto Unger's *Passion* and his *Law in Modern Society,* she writes, "The point that doctrine in particular, and law in general, sharply constrain the scope of choices defined as 'thinkable' has been developed by some critical legal scholars."[10]

This casual and baffling[11] reference to Roberto Unger's work is, however, not the main basis of Williams's claim that culture gives law certainty.[12] Williams places principal reliance on Stanley Cavell's work, *The Claim of Reason,* mistakenly assuming that Cavell's Wittgenstein helps her to resist the argument that law is unbinding. Williams correctly says that Cavell has "aptly stressed how deep and unconscious the agreements are that ground" *human communication.* But Williams takes this to mean that *law* is, after all, binding. This step wholly misreads both the substance and spirit of Cavell's work. Cavell *expressly* argues that legal criteria and the Wittgensteinian criteria on which Williams seeks to rely are different ("disanalogous") in a crucial sense.[13]

Williams's conclusion that a shared culture helps law bind is, moreover, wholly inconsistent with the spirit of Cavell's enterprise. Williams's view suggests that culture disciplines deviants, and Williams throughout refers to her opponents as "irrationalists." Her criticism is, unmistakably, a call for cultural conformity within the legal profession. Worse, she simply *posits* such conformity and makes it the *basis* for law's bindingness. Wittgenstein's work, in contrast, is preoccupied with the fragility of human communication, with how easily such communication might simply not exist. Ironically, Cavell's book is, in large measure, a *defense* of Wittgenstein against the cultural tyranny that Williams would attribute to Wittgenstein.

Moreover, even if Cavell's Wittgensteinian criteria were relevant to law (which, expressly, they are not), they would certainly not solve the disagreements that Williams takes them to solve. Cavell is clear that when deep, instinctual mutual attunement is absent between persons, the only recourse is a disappointed withdrawal, an acknowledgment that communication has failed: "I am thrown back upon myself; I as it were turn my palms outward, as if to exhibit the kind of creature I am, and declare my ground occupied, only mine, ceding yours."[14] Ceding ground once instinctive agreement fails is an unlikely prescription for a practice of deciding court cases. It is wonderfully anarchist rather than, as Williams takes it to be, restorative of order. And where Williams understands Wittgensteinian criteria as solving the problem of skepticism in law, Cavell emphasizes that "*since criteria and skepticism are one another's possibility, criteria cannot be meant to refute skepticism; on the contrary they show skepticism's power, even something one might call its truth. I sometimes think of this theme as our disappointment with our criteria.*"[15] Thus, Williams is only halfway correct when she says, "The ultimate message of the new epistemology is not ethical relativism, but that ethical choices are ours to make [yes], and that we must accept responsibility for the constraints and choices we have embodied in our law [no]."

Name a single slave who must accept responsibility for the embodiment, in the 1787 Constitution, of the three-fifths rule! Joan Williams's "we" is ethnocentric. Blameworthiness waits upon the power to choose. There can be no responsibility without representation. Where there are injustices embedded in the forms of life that, Williams says, rescue a concept from indeterminacy, the subjects of those injustices *precisely deny* the apparent sharedness of the concept. Given Williams's progressive rhetoric, our differences are, in abstract terms, dwarfed by common concerns. But when this view is expressed in the only relevant terms—the identification of law in particular cases—we inhabit different universes. For Williams, "Since our choices about [legal] doctrine constrain the scope of our conversations about vital issues, and *delimit future sense and nonsense,* they are important choices indeed" (emphasis added).

Williams's critique here lurches toward traditional legal positivism, in which legal rules somehow *exist* (as determined by purportedly shared current practices) and the reformer's role is to subject this found law to moral criticism. For Williams, the reformer's criticism, while desirable, remains essentially separate from what law *is* for the time being. Yet mightn't one rather transgress Williams's comfortable line between sense and nonsense? Such transgression is especially tempting and entirely viable since Williams's distinction between sense and nonsense is learned through a renounceable process:

If you break the rules consistently enough, you have ceased to play the old game and you have invented a new one. For me this describes the series of sensations one experiences when studying the history of legal doctrine. Initially the rule patterns seem foreign, the connections bizarre, and the lines drawn quite maddeningly arbitrary. Gradually, arduously, things fall into place, until at last one greets a new case without the initial, wrenching sense of disorientation and surprise.

This confessional moment provides nothing less than a glimpse of cultural indoctrination. Anxiety and disorientation give way, as if by epiphany, to a reassuring sense of inclusion in "legal" discourse. While Williams sneers at her opponents as "irrationalists," Stanley Cavell, on whom Williams purportedly relies, asks, "Who is crazy? I do not say no one is, but must somebody be, when people's reactions are at variance with ours? . . . *If I say 'They are crazy' or 'incomprehensible' then that is not a fact but my fate for them*"[16] (emphasis added).

What gets entirely lost in Williams's work is the need to justify, to *legitimize* prevailing legal culture (if such exists), given its impact on others. As it stands, Williams's resort to ostensibly shared legal culture in order to solve intractable moral controversy elevates violence over ethics. Legal interpretation deals always in the currency of violence. Important ethical questions are effectively suppressed in Williams's project, despite her good intentions. Joan Williams's cultural fiat abuses extremely useful Wittgensteinian metaethics and harnesses them in an anomalous attempt to squelch skepticism.

### A Quack Scientist?

The competence of the general public could be vastly improved by an education that exposes expert fallibility instead of acting as if it did not exist.

—Paul Feyerabend, *Against Method*

Another doubter of law's unbindingness, Steven Winter, is inspired not by Wittgenstein but by the work of two impressive lawyers, and by something called "cognitive science." Winter expressly presents his project as homage to both Felix Cohen and Robert Cover. Yet Winter ends by suppressing the prominent ethical strand of Cohen's work, and by suggesting that Robert Cover is excessively antistatist. Something funny, then, is happening.

Winter would subordinate Robert Cover's relentless focus on state violence, and Felix Cohen's relentless emphasis on ethical choice, to a discipline called "cognitive science." Winter's effort has in turn given new hope to those, like Stephen Carter, Margaret Radin, and Frank Michelman, who would justify the legal system through a pleasant-sounding but quietly oppressive myth of orderly societal dialogue ostensibly open to all voices. These dialogists think that Winter has usefully outlined the "prereflective cognitive structures" that might provide a basis for the shared vocabulary they need to launch their own theory of society in conversation.[17] While these dialogists have been persuasively criticized for ignoring dispossessed voices, Winter's work has given them new hope.

Winter's work, like that of Joan Williams, presents itself as theoretically savvy. Winter carefully disavows any argument that the cognitive process he outlines is objective in the sense that it represents transcendental truth. He nevertheless suggests that language and cognition are "empirical constructs" that can be investigated in a manner meaningful for legal practice. He thinks that a "competent model of human knowledge" can be developed. And this competent model would, usefully, govern all our activism:

> These are not merely academic issues of only epistemological concern. For many, the absence of grounding or foundations is a liberating phenomena, a momentary opening for other ways of being or other forms of life. They think they see a plasticity in the constructed nature of our cultural forms that permits dramatic, unconstrained social transformation. For those of us who perceive the injustice of the current social order, this is a seductive vision because it suggests a clear shot at effective social change. *But it is mistaken, doomed to failure because it does not understand or take into account the constraints of the cognitive process, dependent on experience for the raw materials of the models by which it constructs the world.* Because many (maybe even most) idealized cognitive models are grounded in social experience, these "raw materials" are often themselves cultural constructions shaped by normative social processes. In this way, our very ability to construct a world is already constrained by the cultural structures in which we are enmeshed. (Emphasis added)

This is an extraordinary grab for the mantle of expertise. Winter would discipline utopian enthusiasts with his reliable scientist's eye. He sneers at "the vogue misidentification of the arbitrary with the socially contingent" and at the mistaken assumption "that the lack of objective foundations means that there are no constraints." His project is to map these constraints and to deliver untutored activists from their misguided urges for dramatic change. Winter will guide us safely through the "sedimented meanings" and "stabilized matrices" that comprise the legal landscape. His knowledge will help activists be shrewd strategists because "in the end, the effective practice of constitutional politics cannot rely on purely interpretive efforts. For the ultimate persuasiveness of these interpretations will depend on their ability to take root in the actual experiences and institutions of the culture."[18]

At one level this is a laudable call to broad-based social activism and a useful recognition that law is written not merely in ink, but in the currency of blood. Winter might be read, innocuously enough, as reminding us of the limits of formal and institutional initiatives in effecting profound social transformation. But Winter is in fact more ambitious. He thinks his theory can guide our actual practices both of advocacy and of judging.

Winter repeatedly trumpets his own legal expertise, to which, it is clear, unbridled activism would best defer. Winter's task is "to explore the 'magic chasm,' to characterize the nuances and contingencies in ways that are *usefully predictive and that enable more considered action*" (emphasis added). Winter, struck by the intricate role of "interaction, imagination, and self-reflection" in law as in other human activity, is concerned to provide "an understanding of these complex phenomena [that] will be *instrumentally useful to advocates interested in effectuating change*" (emphasis added). He boasts that "as a lawyer, I have happily consulted theory and self-consciously constructed arguments calculated to increase my chances [of prevailing in a case]." Winter withholds specific examples of his courtroom prowess only "for fear that the reader might crack under the weight of yet another immodesty." Winter's theory promises to lead us to good arguments, away from bad ones, *in particular cases*.[19] In the courtroom, science is invoked to sort among available, coherent, already intelligible arguments and weed out the wrong (i.e., unpersuasive) ones:

Within any given stabilized matrix, there will be *intelligible counterarguments that are not persuasive*. In that case, it will be possible to challenge the dominant position without seeming to violate the rules of the game. It can nevertheless be predicted that the challenge will be unsuccessful.[20]

This passage reflects the extent of Winter's commitment to the notion that *legal* decisions are those that will not unsettle (his version of) the legal community. Winter's alleged predictive ability remains trite once his predictions are uncontroversial, so the interesting point is that where lawyers disagree, Winter thinks he has a special tool. *Winter would transform familiar clashes of "professional judgment" into clashes of "Intuition versus Knowledge," in which his knowledge wins.* One might easily, in such a case of disagreement, ensnare Winter in an interminable argument over the accuracy of any particular prediction of his that an intelligible counterargument would necessarily fail. One easily sees analogies with self-censorship, self-deselection, failures of confidence. Winter's science might easily blind advocates to the possibility of spectacular and unanticipatable success. We have no startling 1803 Supreme Court decision holding slavery unconstitutional. Perhaps we *ought* to have had one.

It is even more revealing to set aside advocates for judges. Winter concedes that predictably unpersuasive legal arguments will yet be linguistically and doctrinally coherent (will not seem "to violate the rules of the game"). This concession—that unpersuasive argument isn't always gibberish—crucially undermines Winter's claim that something called a "stabilized matrix" constrains a judge and so constrains what law is. A judge might well choose a counterintuitive ("improbable") but conceptually coherent outcome. This freedom is, indeed, at the heart of the argument that law does not bind judges:

If someone's considered judgment is that an existing rule or a prevailing interpretation of current law is bad (inefficient, unjust, immoral or bad policy), she can almost always construct a plausible, conventional legal argument supporting her interpretation of the law.[21]

Moreover, Winter's clinical language of "cognitive science" and its attendant "topographic map of the sedimented social field" obscures questions of ethics and of legitimacy. He reassures us, "Sedimentation, however, is not stasis. Sedimentation is simultaneously conservative of past experience and an invitation to a sequel."[22] But if this past experience was heinous, a judge might rather not conserve it. In Winter's preferred mode of constitutional change (spectacularly labeled "trimorphic constitutionalism"), judges may not ever proceed faster than with all deliberate speed:

The relentless processes of social and cultural construction produce new sedimentations that are *first* institutionalized in social practice and *then* concretized as constitutional rules. In its highest form, trimorphic jurisgenesis is marked by a moment of conscious, situated reflection in which the Court probes the development of and experience with these social norms before transmitting them into constitutional commands.[23] (Emphasis added)

One is startled that, on Winter's account, a judge's resort to a felt legitimate, conceptually coherent, ethically preferable interpretation of law must wait until Winter's cognitivist paraphernalia detects her cultural truth as institutionalized (in some unspecified fashion other than enactment as law) in social practice. Winter, like Joan Williams, sees the conversation about societal values as separate from, and prior to, the conversation about what law "is." Yet, Winter's "stabilized matrices" are not a constraint on *a judge,* once she can conceptualize an ethical outcome (because a judge may disregard the advocate's probabilistic reckonings and reach a surprising result). Winter thus has no legitimate means, scientific, theoretical, or otherwise, by which to constrain a surprising or improbable decision to which a judge is committed. At best, Winter must resort to a form of unreliable strategist's prophesy: if the judge outruns society's shared cognitive forms, Winter might counsel, her attempt to change law will be undermined in fact and fail in the end. Even if such prophecy is potentially accurate, a judge may have nothing to lose by enacting legitimate improbable law. At worst, her decision will dissolve into conformity with the governing stabilized matrices. At best, Winter is wrong and an ethical and legitimate ruling spawns progeny.

Alternatively, Winter might appeal to the notion that his approach is democratically superior. But isn't it often precisely the job of the Court, on constitutional questions, to decide the limits of majoritarianism? And anyway, the question of what *really* is the majority will at the moment of judicial decision is as unbinding as the legal-doctrinal questions themselves.

Bereft of jargon, Winter's scientific descriptive legal theory is premised on an arational and prescriptive commitment to a peculiar ideal. Winter starts out determined to "describe the underlying, unconscious structure of how we think about law" and to show that "awareness of this structure can help us think about the normative questions that confront us." Winter says the "central insight" of his approach is "that human knowledge is grounded in our direct physical and social experience with the world, but is elaborated indirectly, largely by means of metaphor and the extension of idealized cognitive models."

Setting aside the problematic assumption that there's a common grounding for the various forms of human knowledge; the further problematic assumption that everyone shares a unitary direct physical and social experience; and the problematic distinction between direct and indirect experience, the cornerstone of Winter's research into human knowledge is something called an idealized cognitive model (ICM). Human cognition is, Winter says, embodied, not arbitrary, and therefore (a further non sequitur) attention to ICMs will yield "a sense of knowledge and meaning as neither arbitrary nor determinate, but rather as systematic and imaginative." The ICM is

a "folk" theory or cultural model that we create and use to organize our knowledge. It relates many concepts that are inferentially connected by means of a single conceptual structure that is meaningful as a whole. For example, our understanding of the words "buy," "sell," "cost," "goods," "advertise," "credit," and the like, are made meaningful by an ICM of a commercial transaction that relates them together as a structured activity. The use of any of these words individually evokes the entire picture or model, the ICM—a sort of holistic, standardized account.

Winter then claims that, within law, our ICMs structure our experiences of the core bindingness and peripheral unbindingness of legal rules. One could, in response, illustrate that this notion of shared ICMs merely adds another level of controversy (what *is* "our" ICM?) to sufficiently interminable legal debates (do rules have core instances?). But, even if one charitably assumes the cogency and sharedness of ICMs, the question of *allegiance* to the ICM must be separately answered. Winter admits that the conclusion ICM = LAW is neither an instinctual or preconscious attunement (like Cavell's Wittgensteinian criteria) nor a logical and necessary entailment (like algebra). Allegiance to ICMs is, ultimately, a matter of conscious and deliberative commitment. Winter says,

When the facts of a case display a good fit with the particular ICM motivating the precedent or legal principle, most legally trained observers *committed to applying the rule* will experience the rule as having sufficient structure to constrain decision. (Emphasis added)

He continues,

The reader will note that I deliberately refrain from making any claim of determinacy. . . . *No matter what one's jurisprudential stance, it should be common ground that people, not rules, decide cases.* The question is only about the degree of meaningful structure that the rules provide. Even where decisionmaking is understood as highly structured, it is a human process involving human agents, human will, and human commitment to an ideal called Law.[24] (Capitalization original, emphasis added)

This important confession is suppressed in a footnote and Winter does not seem to grasp how far his concession (people, not rules, decide cases) destabilizes his assertion (rules provide meaningful structure). To illustrate: a judge wants what she thinks is a just result, and must reach it by using a conceptually coherent legal argument. Given unbindingness of rules, such an argument is usually discoverable. The just result may, however, violate expectations (the ICM) and may violate any commitment to the peculiar ideal called Law. The judge reflects on the illegitimacy of the ICM, of the sedimented meanings it reflects, and of the legal conclusion it prescribes. She has a commitment, say, to an ideal called Justice. Assume she has a second commitment, to the ideal called Law (setting aside, for now, its fatal peculiarity). She faces these conflicting commitments and makes an ethical choice to reach the just result. She then structures her decision in the required legal language. The ICM has only provided "meaningful" structure on some definition of meaningfulness other than: that which determines the result of the case. One is thus forced to conclude that, for Winter, meaningful constraint based on an ICM requires not merely a commitment to an ideal called Law, but a commitment to that peculiar ideal above any and all competitors.

Indeed, one can go further. An ethical judge need not conceptualize her decision as a choice between an ideal called Law and one called Justice. She may wish to retain the semantic prize (the designation Law) for herself. Her decision, she says, reflects the authentic commitment to the ideal called Law. At this point Winter is out in the cold. He cannot resist this view without treating the ICM as legally sacred. What he dressed up as an allegiance to an ideal called Law reduces to an allegiance to the ICM, to the notion that options the ICM renders thinkable are the *truly* legal options.

Winter's allegiance to ICMs might, even now, appear somehow more rational than our judge's ethical choice. Indeed, Winter will probably claim that if his cognitive stuff is ignored in the cause of supposedly moral decisionmaking, our judge's efforts will be self-defeating. We must, therefore, reveal Winter's expertise as unsalvageable quackery.

## Cognitive Quackery

[1.] Within a legal/cultural community or subculture that shares the same contextual non-neutral assumptions, a system of meaning like constitutional law will work. [2.] Judges, no less than others, are situated in and dependent upon the structures of social meaning that make communication possible. [3.] Although this situatedness will not yield anything like determinacy, the stabilized matrices within which the judges operate will have already demarcated the arguments and counterarguments they will recognize as persuasive. [4.] And this means that, in a conservative era, the stabilized matrix will already be legally secure from penetration by the very arguments and positions that those on the liberal-to-left of the political spectrum would want to urge on the Court. [5.] Hence, the quandary of constitutional theory in a conservative era.[25]

This passage adequately summarizes the background assumptions that must hold if Winter is to sustain his predictions that, sometimes, morally preferable arguments are precluded by the stabilized structures of legal thought.

Yet sentence 1 assumes inconceivable consensus—and its mildly hypothetical tone has entirely disappeared by the time Winter announces, in his last sentence, a real-life "quandary." Alternatively, this sentence envisages plural subcultures but conveniently assumes that each constitutes its own judicial system.

Sentence 2 clearly assumes a uniform and monolithic society ("*the* structures of social meaning"). Moreover, it makes an assertion (judges rely on a broader context for communicative intelligibility) that, *even if accurate,* is irrelevant to legal controversy. In court, the question is, Which among the already intelligible arguments before the court ought to prevail? Intelligible communication, in general, may thus be conceded without damaging the argument that law, in court, is unbinding. Sentence 2 is thus wholly logically independent of sentence 3—although Winter appears to think otherwise.

Sentence 3 itself illustrates the familiar slippage from a concession of law's unbindingness to a contradictory assertion of surviving, demarcated constraint. There is no constraint if the legitimacy of the alleged demarcations is denied by the judge. Sentence 3 implausibly assumes that all judges share a uniform view of which arguments are persuasive.

Sentence 4 suggests an implausibly homogeneous conservative era that determines our stabilized matrices and excludes liberal-left legal arguments. This radically understates controversy among judges. It also assumes an extraordinarily tight link between political eras and persuasive legal argument (did the "Reagan era" really influence Thurgood Marshall's conception of a persuasive legal argument?). Finally, this sentence overindulges the journalese of "political eras." Do such "eras" exist? Or do politicians (the presidents who appoint the justices) win and lose elections because of imponderables like "the economy" or irrelevances like personal charm or strategic acumen? Noam Chomsky, writing in the very year (1988) in which Winter's "Cognitive Stakes" piece appeared, admonished a student interviewer for assuming that conservatism was prevalent:

[Conservatism] is by no means prevalent. It might be prevalent among the elite groups, but that's not too surprising because it is an ideology that favors the transfer of the resources from the poor to the rich, power for the privileged and so on. Among the general public it has never been particularly popular. In fact, Reagan's popularity has by no means been unusually high, judging from the polls. Furthermore, the public has been strongly opposed to every major element of the Reaganite program with very rare exception. Through the 1980s for example, the polls have shown the public has been strongly in favor of social rather than military spending. In general, the public has continued in a long slow drift towards a New Deal-style, welfare kind of social democracy.[26]

Winter seems to have succumbed to a jurisprudential version of Susan Faludi's *Backlash*, in which ill-researched trend journalism and other cultural flotsam persuaded some activists that the price of feminism was too high, and that the feminist agenda had alienated mainstream female America.

Sentence 5 thus introduces a fake quandary.

This litany of misdescription is not something Winter can easily disavow. The stable "cognitive baseline" (Winter's phrase) furnished by this picture enables Winter's misreliance on the work of Thomas Kuhn. Winter urges that law functions like Kuhn's picture of "normal science." Kuhn's normal science is a mopping-up operation in which normative controversy is absent because the scientific community has (arationally but firmly) converged on shared norms. Whether or not this alleged consensus legitimately exists within the practice of physical science, law is undoubtedly different. Law minus controversy is bullshit. Paul Feyerabend has commented that the casual appropriation of key terms from Thomas Kuhn's work has spawned "various forms of pseudoscience" and "encouraged a lot of trash." Numerous of Winter's turns of phrase, together with the uninhibited way in which he invokes Kuhn's terms—such as "normal science" and "paradigm shifts"—in manifestly controversial contexts, suggest that Winter's work belongs in this category. Thomas Kuhn criticized naive "textbook presentation[s]" of scientific progress in which "one by one, in a process often compared to the addition of bricks to a building, scientists have added another fact, concept, law, or theory" to our knowledge. Winter, in contrast, ultimately sees cognitive science as exactly the incremental, cumulative, and teleological process of knowledge accumulation that Kuhn set out to debunk. Winter sets out to "reconceptualize law in light of what we are learning about the human mind." Winter assures us that "*recent developments* in cognitive theory make it possible to describe the underlying, unconscious structure of how we think about law" (emphasis added). Winter refers to the alleged progress of cognitive research from 1970 to 1980 through its culmination in the late 1980s—exactly when, happily, he decided to write his own article. Moreover, *even if* this alleged progress in the field of cognitive science is admitted, *even if* it is granted that the cognitive research resembles Kuhn's picture of normal science, *it hardly follows that the practice of law, too, resembles normal science.* Winter ultimately concedes,

In the postscript to the second edition [of *The Structure of Scientific Revolutions*], Kuhn expresses some surprise over the application of his theory beyond science. He thinks that his account makes science more like other disciplines, but that science is still significantly different from other disciplines.

Clearly it is time for Winter to sit up straight and deal decisively with this direct hit from the very source on which he so heavily relies. Kuhn's idea of normal science has itself been criticized for understating controversy in the physical sciences. Kuhn's critics deny that the alleged normalcy exists. Whether those critics are correct or not, Kuhn himself doubts that other disciplines share science's uncontroversial normal periods. And of all the extrascientific disciplines that might be said to resemble Kuhn's normalcy, law is perhaps the least likely candidate. Yet instead of vigorous argument in favor of an analogy of law and normal science, Winter leaves us this hunch (relegated to a footnote):

My own sense is that the legal community, especially the legal academy, bears significant parallels to the scientific community as Kuhn describes it. Both rely on standardized textbooks for initiation into the profession; both enjoy substantial insulation from the laity; both concern day-to-day puzzle solving; and both display quite similar internal communal structure.

Winter would here describe a legal academy governed by standardized textbooks. Yet is the *Alchemy of Race and Rights* such a standardized textbook? Moreover, isn't the Bendaresque "insulation from the laity"—which Winter would dignify as a defining trait of legal academia—arguably the legal academy's biggest *problem?* Kuhn himself *explicitly* argued that law is different from the physical sciences because law's primary raison d'etre is external social need. Winter's announcement that legal practice is, factually or ideally, insulated from the laity reflects a disquieting comfort level with unfortunate and reformable features of some law schools. Winter would erase questions about the legal practice and the legal academy that others are struggling to place on the agenda.

Moreover, Winter has by this stage of his argument abandoned the production of topographic contraptions to guide legal advocates through sedimented social fields. He has momentarily fled advocacy to focus on the legal academy. Even there, his language of normal science vastly understates controversy over the nature of legal education—a subject that currently generates frequent and heated debates and symposia. "Quackery" is thus no overstatement. Winter's invocation of Thomas Kuhn's normal science in legal practice is counterprogressive hocus pocus.[27]

## Cognitive Science in Law Is Wrongheaded

Beyond the particular problems with Winter's effort, cognitive science is unlikely ever to solve the question of what law *is,* or to dictate one legal strategy over another. Winter throughout asserts that his theory is based on "empirical evidence from the cognitive sciences." Winter urges that language is an empirical phenomenon that can be usefully studied by a (cognitive or other) science. Such assertions are not necessarily wrong, but they might be. It might be that the mind is inherently unstudiable (can it adequately study itself?). And this *possibility* deprives Winter of the mantle of expertise that he needs. Moreover, even granting the questionable assumption that language and cognition are available to descriptive inquiry in some sense, it does not follow that they can be meaningfully studied with available analytical tools. Moreover, even if language is empirical, cognition might not be. And even if cognition is empirical, language might be the wrong path to it. Winter overlooks such stuff. Winter, additionally, shows no sustained awareness of the arguments that might foredoom his project:

Granted the form of our sensibilities supplies the conditions of the possibility of knowledge; why not give an empirical basis to all empirical science by investigating the specific structure of our senses? *There have been endless variations of this naturalist-reductionist dream. Each would ground all knowledge in an empirical theory of perception.*[28] (Emphasis added)

Even if Winter were to discover a persuasive picture of human cognition, we would not be bound by his conclusions if we didn't like their political or ethical implications. As Michel Foucault has said,

The analysis of actual experience is a discourse of mixed nature: it is directed to a specific yet ambiguous structure, concrete enough for it to be possible to apply to it a meticulous and descriptive language, yet sufficiently removed from the positivity of things for it to be possible, from that starting-point, to escape from that naiveté, to contest it and seek foundations for it.

Thus, while a somehow rectified version of Winter's effort might perhaps excavate a *plausible* picture of the nature of human cognition, it can never arrive at a *binding* picture: "What is given in experience and what renders experience possible correspond to one another in an endless oscillation."[29] The effort to give law authority by seeking shared whirrings within the skull is inherently wrongheaded.

## A Café Crit?

In a tremendous feat of legal scholarship called "Roll Over Beethoven," Duncan Kennedy and Peter Gabel, prominent Café Crits, debate the place of grand theory in progressive legal activism. Gabel champions a general theory of life that he thinks will help activists and permit a more authentic politics. Kennedy rejects this as "abstract bullshit." The men, it appears, disagree. But upon closer examination Kennedy, too, emerges as a disciplinarian. Both men claim the right to tutor the movement. Both claim that they can discern what makes law and society tick. This Café Crit claim, if believed, would demoralize those who lack these men's tutelage. Those without their wise guidance might believe themselves to lack some special insight. Café Crit vanguardism, taken seriously, might paralyze the rest of us.

Kennedy appears to renounce such a vanguardist role when he dismisses Gabel's "fantasies of controlling the world by thinking about it." Yet Kennedy's objection is ultimately not to Gabel's taste for authoritative investigation, but merely to the level of abstraction at which Gabel would conduct it. Kennedy's quest is not to abandon authoritative description, but to abandon Gabel's hyperabstraction because, Kennedy believes, it precludes accurate description. Kennedy instead pursues a "locked-down" and "concrete" version of Gabel's descriptive project. Yet Kennedy's concrete truth seeking remains very like Gabel's bullshit, as Gabel himself remarks.[30]

Kennedy remains a vanguardist because his concern with concrete description is itself not a simple task of neutral investigation. Kennedy's concrete description is itself mired in values and in interpretation. Kennedy claims to deliver concrete experience, not mere impression. Yet his every account of concrete legal experience is already freighted with his debatable value judgments, and these might offend an ethical judge.

The flaws in Kennedy's concrete descriptive effort are clear in a judicial discretion discussion that he published two years after "Roll Over Beethoven." In the later article, "Freedom and Constraint in Adjudication: A Critical Phenomenology," Kennedy set out to describe the process of legal reasoning, again emphasizing his distaste for abstraction. However, Kennedy's ostensibly concrete examination of law's unbindingness itself proceeds on a meager abstraction: an invented judge. Through this nameless judge Kennedy sets out to describe the nature of the constraint that law exerts. Let's call Kennedy's protagonist Judge Winthrop.

Judge Winthrop is a Café Crit jurist from Boston. He has what Kennedy calls a vocation of social transformation, and this guides his decisionmaking. But Winthrop's is a patrician activism. He cannot shake the idea that law binds judges, even if only pseudo-objectively.[31] These limitations undermine his progressive intentions.

## The Moral Force of Law?

Judge Winthrop's patrician sensibility binds him with certain reverences that make Negro Crits giggle—kind of like barristers in horsehair wigs. Kennedy refers to "the elemental normative power of any outcome reached by people I identify with. Because I think they were up to the same thing I am up to, whatever they came up with has in its favor my initial sense that it's probably what I would have come up with too."

Kennedy doesn't square this reverence with Judge Winthrop's belief that the rules in force were simply imposed in the self-interest of those in power. Others might not think the dead greyhairs were "up to the same thing" as them. Like Audre Lorde, others might instead embrace the heretical actions that so many old ideas disparage. Kennedy's Judge Winthrop is different: "I identify with these ought-speakers. I respect them. I honor them. When they speak, I listen. I even tremble if I think I am going against their collective wisdom. They are members of the same community working on the same problems. They are old; they are many."

Kennedy quickly adds that it's no good telling Judge Winthrop that this stuff is irrational. Reverence just *is* Judge Winthrop's response to his forefathers in the law. Kennedy starts out emphasizing that meaningful talk about judging requires some "grounding in a specific imagined situation," and he sets out to describe the processes of an imaginary judge's mind. Yet Kennedy doesn't expressly present Winthrop as his own ideal jurist. It is reasonably clear that "Kennedy" is not identical with "Judge Winthrop." This gives Kennedy apparent wiggle room in tight spots. Kennedy's project is "descriptive," but his judge is not real; Kennedy's judge is imaginary, but Kennedy's project is ostensibly not "prescriptive." Kennedy may thus personally disavow Winthrop's foibles and claim that through Winthrop he is merely providing a descriptive account of the typical, not ideal, judge's way of being in the world.

Kennedy concedes that the law will not necessarily have the power to persuade everyone. It may sometimes seem odd (even, perhaps, to Winthrop), like "yesterday's newspaper." Yet Winthrop's reverence is unperturbed. Kennedy neglects that to endow his fictional typical judge with arbitrary reverences under the banner of a "fact" is already to endorse those reverences. "Fact" is an honorific label. Whatever it attaches to is removed from controversy and fixed as a ground rule. Kennedy's descriptive effort thus grants Winthrop's reverence leverage in law, and ignores the need for him to justify each violence he inflicts.

Despite the generally nongrandiose and colloquial tone of Kennedy's "phenomenology" of judging, his descriptive ambitions resemble Steven Winter's more baroque quackery. When Kennedy calls Winthrop's forefather reverence part of the "normative power of the field," he is playing moot court. When Kennedy talks about the moral force of law, someone giggles.

When lawyers pronounce Kennedy a progressive, Jonathon Swift giggles, too.

## The Physical Constraint of Law?

Reverence for the forefathers aside, Kennedy's Judge Winthrop is also constrained by the fact that law is like "a physical medium." When Kennedy argues that law is like potter's clay, he wants to resist the view that " 'law' is one thing or another and can be treated as a kind of block contributing to a larger edifice." Equally, however, Kennedy argues that what the judge's project can be (what her pot can look like) is limited by the legal medium (the clay):

Law constrains as a physical medium constrains—you can't do absolutely anything you want with pile of bricks, and what you can do depends on how many you have as well as on your other circumstances. In this sense, that you are building something out of a given set of bricks constrains you, controls you, deprives you of freedom.

Kennedy argues that infinite judges may fashion infinite pots, but they'll never make one you can smoke—because the material they work with just isn't combustible. Kennedy then accurately identifies the "absolutely basic question": "whether there are some outcomes that you just can't reach so long as you obey the internal rules of the game of legal reasoning . . . 'things you just can't make with bricks' or silk purses you can't make with this particular sow's ear."

Kennedy answers that indeed there are some outcomes you just can't reach with a thing called law. He asserts that one must abide by certain constraints if one wishes to "legalize" one's position. What makes Kennedy's argument interesting is its disarming denial that there is anything *inevitable* about moments of constraint. Kennedy emphatically denies that the legal materials themselves uniformly (or at all) dictate the outcomes of cases. On another day, in another mood, with his adrenal glands fired up instead of opting out, Judge Winthrop might have happened upon the line of reasoning he needs. Just not today.

The problem with this is that, if we take it seriously, any constraint on a judge becomes a matter of personal energy, not of the medium of law. Of course the personal energy is applied in the area of law, so any personal failure will also be in that medium. But this is identical with constraint on personal effort in any arena. Perhaps Tolstoy had bad days in the "medium" of Russian language. To say that the constraint of law is as much a property of the medium as it is a product of individual exhaustion, talent, etc., is thus both accurate and uninteresting. It is uninteresting because what the rule-of-law ideal requires is a peculiar constraint that enables it to claim that judges are above the fray. Tolstoy hasn't a police force at his disposal. Winthrop does. If the only constraints on Winthrop are his mood and his materials, why do his materials, rather than Tolstoy's, get to tell the police what to do?

Most basically, Kennedy's assertion that there are things you "just can't do with bricks" implicitly assumes that the prevailing range of tricks with bricks is a legitimate range of tricks. He doesn't consistently question the "internal rules of the game of legal reasoning." This is a strange failure given Judge Winthrop's own insistence that the rules often were set down in the narrow and illegitimate self-interest of those in power. Winthrop and Kennedy slide into the assumption that particular acts within the game are justified by the very existence of the game. This would be the case if law were the automatic and impartial set of rules that Café Crits have shown it not to be. Café Crit work generally deprives law of its leverage. Yet Kennedy, via Winthrop, gives it back, gratis. Winthrop ultimately behaves as though "law" provides judges with reasons to act in ways that would be excluded by their overall moral calculus but for "the law." Others might, rather, refuse to ignore the *legal-ethical* observation that Winthrop's bricks are built of blood and flesh. Others might prefer the following criteria of the good legal brick: "The stone that the builder refused / Shall always be the head cornerstone" (Bob Marley, "Cornerstone," in *Songs of Freedom*, Disc 2, track 6[a] [Island Records, 1993]). "Our forefathers" are a more motley bunch than Kennedy's Winthrop assumes. Judges must justify each pain, each death—or else decline to inflict them.

### A Fish out of Water?

Stanley Fish would like to be known simply as an expert on John Milton. He has nevertheless been an instructive and long-serving participant in debates about law's unbindingness. Yet Fish's distance from legal practice repeatedly leads him to understate the legitimate place of controversy in legal practice and repeatedly leads him away from a potentially powerful argument in favor of ethical law: the argument that a presiding judge's moral conclusions are always, almost inherently, rendered in the language of the law. Fish always stops short of that argument.

*Über*activist judges might claim that the legal rules and the legislative history are bad and that judges are free to ignore those bad building blocks and instead follow their own unfettered moral preferences. Such judges juxtapose (bad) law against (good) preferences and choose the latter. Such judges unnecessarily undercut their own *legal* position by declining to claim that their ethical view of the appropriate outcome is legitimate *as law*. A better argument might be that a Supreme Court justice's opinion in deciding a case is always and inherently law. Stanley Fish has come close to arguing that this is indeed the case. He has argued that the *uber*activist is an invented evil.

Fish makes the general point, that the *uber*interpreter is an invented evil, in a variety of contexts, including an extended exchange with Ronald Dworkin. Dworkin argues that the enterprise of law resembles the authoring of a chain novel by successive generations of authors. For Dworkin, each new author is free to take the enterprise in new directions but is also constrained, by what has gone before, from enacting her own arbitrary preferences. Fish replies that since the question what *is* the enterprise of law? can itself only be answered by the individual judge's interpretation, the constraint Dworkin envisages is nonexistent. If the new author is constrained at all it must be by something other than the evident nature of the legal enterprise, since that nature is far from evident and is itself a product of the new author's interpretation.

But, Fish continues, the new author's ruminations are not unfettered in the dangerous sense Dworkin imagines. Dworkin's analysis depends upon a conflict between a judge's mere subjective preferences on the one hand and allegiance to the ongoing enterprise of law on the other. Dworkin wants to ensure that a judge is bound by the ongoing enterprise of law and so unable to head off in maverick directions. Fish responds that those who envisage this evil of unfetteredness must imagine that a judge might somehow decide a case in a way that had no relationship to the prior decisions. And Fish doubts that such feats of *uber*activism are possible, since any decision by a judge would have to be made in recognizably judicial terms.

Fish thus argues that any novel outcomes a judge reaches as a judge, once they are expressed in intelligible legal language, remain always and already "law." Much hinges, however, on the meaning of Fish's caveat ("intelligible legal language"). For an ideal judge, that caveat means that she will use law's concepts as rhetorical gestures reflecting her ethics. She will welcome decisions that might startle certain members of the onlooking legal community. This places the ideal judge at loggerheads with Fish. Fish has no stomach for startling the legal community. Fish believes that something called legal competence can be acquired through professional training, and that the legal community shares this training and is united in its competence. He believes that, once acquired, competence reduces controversy in rule applying. He therefore assumes a degree of consensus in rule applying among lawyers that, it turns out, is hard to defend.

In support of this assumed consensus, Fish offers only the unargued assertion that the essence of law is stability. Fish would hardly claim that this model of law as stability is politically (or otherwise) neutral, but he does claim that it *is* the prevailing practice of law. And that is an incorrect assertion. Detailed analysis of the Supreme Court case law of Justice Thomas and his colleagues demonstrates just how self-conscious and deliberate the pursuit of conflicting values is on the nation's most esteemed tribunal.

Fish's undue deference to claims of legal competence is clearest in his discussion of the work of Owen Fiss, a long-time denier of law's unbinding-ness. Fish effectively criticizes—in a manner that replicates his analysis of Dworkin—Fiss's faith that law constrains judges. Having thus Dworkined Fiss, Fish nevertheless asserts, in what is an odd move for him, that there is strong empirical evidence that a process called "adjudication" is possible. Yet Fish isn't terribly clear about what adjudication is. Is it the sheer fact of decision rendered? Or is it the myth of uncontroversial decision rendered? Is it, rather, the myth of self-applying rules? Fish is clear, however, that gaining competence within this practice of adjudication is a learned process: the result of professional initiation into legal practice.

Ironically, Fish's own distance from legal practice leads him to understate how much diversity there is within legal practice, including controversy over what it means to be a legal professional. Fish repeatedly assumes, always without sustained analysis, that the law-applying function of judges and the law-divining function of attorneys is both shared and near-instinctual. When Fish refers to the legal community's "interpretive preunderstanding" of legal practice he is always, without argument, asserting *shared* interpretive preunderstanding. If lawyers' rule applying were as reflexive and shared as Fish assumes, controversy could not be a pervasive feature of rule application. Yet it is.

Fish persuasively objects that Dworkin, Fiss, and others implicitly assume that one branch of any given legal-judicial controversy just *is* (or potentially is) consistent with the enterprise of law, whereas other branches reflect illegitimate extralegal influences. Fish is most persuasive when arguing against this distinction between arguments internal to law and those external to it.[32] Yet this pole of Fish's analysis does not jibe well with his other idea—that there could be (and is), for the time being, a uniform practice of law of which one might somehow be a competent practitioner. In deferring to ostensible legal competence Fish indeed seems, as several critics have suggested, to assert that practices are monolithic—that the legal community is a homogeneous interpretive community. Fish is at his least persuasive when slithering away from this accusation. He collapses into dogmatic assertions about the supposedly essential nature of legal practice: "the very point of the legal enterprise requires that its practitioners see continuity where others, with less of a stake in the enterprise, might feel free to see change."[33]

This is an unfortunate slide into the doctrinaire Dworkinian rhetoric of "the legal enterprise" that Fish himself has previously debunked. And it trades on a stereotypical legal practitioner—the kind who has a large stake in the continuity of the enterprise as an end in itself. Doubtless this nicely trades on the vogue vilification of the Wall Street lawyer. But what of Cornel West, whose vision of a progressive legal practice is one designed to facilitate threats to the social order? Fish is forced to argue that you can't *both* be a legal decisionmaker and have a primary stake in change:

The judge who has learned to read in a way that avoids crisis is a judge who has learned what it means to be a judge, and has learned that the maintenance of continuity is a prime judicial obligation because without continuity the rule of law cannot claim to be stable and rooted in durable principles. It is not simply that crisis would be disruptive of the process, but that *crisis and disruption are precisely what the process is supposed to forestall.*[34] (Emphasis added)

Fish's description of the practice of law as the pursuit of stability is not only dogmatic but flatly wrong. Much everyday corporate litigation practice aims to create uncertainty and instability where the law initially seems straightforwardly against one's client. It is ironic that Fish—certain that practice is everything, and not himself a legal practitioner—nevertheless feels comfortable expounding, authoritatively, on "what it means" to practice law. Fish's view that stability is the essence of legal practice is *theoretical* in exactly the sense that he so frequently disparages. It is an abstract speculation about a practice in which he is not immersed. Fish's distance from the turbulence of legal practice, his view that stability is the essence of legal practice, and the actual importance of *in*stability in legal practice are all reflected in the following passage from his work:

As things now stand in our culture, a person embedded in the legal world reads in a way designed to resolve interpretive crises (although as Walter Michals reminds me, after he was reminded of it by a practicing lawyer, at some stages in the preparation and even the arguing of cases, the proliferating of interpretive crises is just the skill called for).[35]

That parenthetical irruption devastates Fish's nonparenthetical claims about the practice of law. The next chapter will show that the proliferation of uncertainty is a pervasive feature of legal practice, not only in the preparation and arguing of cases but also often in the judging of them. Supreme Court majority opinions in controversial cases are frequently deliberately vague, so as to keep a majority aboard for a desired result. When Justice White, retiring in 1993, wished the Supreme Court good luck in providing clear and crisp guidance to lower courts, he was speaking tongue in cheek and the legal community knew it. Law is splashy, not becalmed. Legal scholars have even put the inherent turbulence of law on a *prescriptive* footing, arguing (unattractively) that the ambiguity of law ought to be preserved because it enables multiple views to coexist within a single system of law.[36] Fish understates the place of controversy in legal practice and therefore *overstates* the usefulness of ostensible legal competence in settling contested legal questions. In entering debates over legal practice, Fish may be out of his depth.

## Judges Must Justify Pain and Death

Legal interpretation takes place in a field of pain and death. . . . *The relationship between legal interpretation and the infliction of pain remains operative even in the most routine of legal acts.* . . . The judges deal pain and death. . . . As long as death and pain are part of our political world, it is essential that they be at the center of our law.
—Robert Cover, *Violence and the Word*

Law happens. Legal decisions, often predictable, are arrived at every day even on issues about which few people agree. Law is, in practice, simpler than the political and moral complexity in which it is enmeshed. Judges settle, every day and with violence, issues that you and I admit are reasonably open to question. How come they can do this?

Given the collapse of law's leverage, the possibility of a general or systemic justification for the acts of violence ordered by judges has disappeared. Each judge must now justify, individually, each pain she imposes and each death she orders. Each judge is a moral actor. Yet many people forget this insight in their debates about what law "is." Right now, progressive lawyers are playing moot court. What passes as progressive scholarship turns out to be cultural tyranny, cognitive quackery, café criticism, fishy business, or, worse, Tough Love lawyering: more complacent than the rest.

IV

Tough Love Judge

# 8

# Justice Thomas's Sins

### How to Nail Thomas

This is what Clarence Thomas wanted. He wanted to be evaluated on the fucking merits. We said fine, we'll take a look.

—NAACP board member, 1991

This comment was made in the process of explaining the NAACP's decision to commission a study of Thomas's record before taking a stance on his nomination. Clarence Thomas, protégé of Republican Senator Danforth, appointed by Reagan to head the EEOC, appointed by Bush to the Supreme Court, has likewise met with hostility from those even mildly concerned with the well-being of America's dispossessed. The *New York Times,* for instance, reviewing Justice Thomas's first term, headlined its editorial "The Cruellest Justice." Weeks later, commenting on Thomas's opinions in three death penalty cases, the *Times* editorial headline was "Cruel Injustice." Such labels are entirely fair characterizations of particular Thomas decisions. Still, to characterize Thomas as a knowing perpetrator of what he recognizes to be injustice is unhelpful in several ways.

*First,* demonization is simplistic psychology. Thomas probably doesn't view himself as an evil person. He probably thinks he is impeccable. *Second,* such demonization obscures Thomas's probable self-righteous belief that, because he has access to truth, he is pursuing the authentic benefit of those he cares about. He probably believes not only that he is impeccable because of his inherent qualities (the first point of this paragraph) but also that he is ably serving the true interests of the subjugated. *Third,* demonization of Thomas obscures a more general problem that may well be the root of

Thomas's self-righteousness: his reliance on the ideal of disinterested truth. A pillar of Thomas's self-righteousness is the idea that he has the expert's eye for reality or, as he himself has put it, that he stands "a few humble feet above the maddening crowd." *Fourth,* most importantly, to demonize Thomas is, paradoxically, to place him beyond our criticism. If our complaint is that he is simply evil and we are simply good, he might retort that we simply inhabit different moral universes. This would place him beyond a binding moral criticism from within our own moral universe. For every voice that calls him callous and uncaring another might call us paternalistic and self-pitying. Relativism might ride to his rescue. When we say that Thomas denies American Blacks due reparations for undeniable historical injustice, he might reply that he detests handouts and reveres self-sufficiency above all else, including the welfare of America's dispossessed. This is a conceivable moral choice. I would criticize it, and so might many others, but our criticism would proceed from our own values, which would precisely *not* be shared by Thomas. Our criticism would be reduced to spinning its wheels, would lack traction in Thomas's own moral mind. An appeal to the values of racial justice will not mobilize Thomas if he has duly considered those values and determined that they are subordinate to others (the Klansman attitude).

It is crucial, for meaningful criticism, that Justice Thomas is not such a person. Responding to far-right arguments that EEOC enforcement policies, however diluted, remain immoral in principle, Thomas had this to say:

What is more immoral than the enslavement of an entire race—what is more immoral than the vicious cancer of racial discrimination—what is more immoral than the fabrication of a legal and political syste[m] which excludes, demeans and degrades an entire race[?] Those who seek to invoke morality today, must first address the pervasive and persistent immorality of yesterday.[1]

Thomas is emphatically aboard the moral project of racial justice. Self-reliance, for example, is not for him a preferred value to which racial justice is secondary. He contends that the death penalty and racial justice are complementary. He contends that his approach to EEOC enforcement advances racial justice. This is, no doubt, intuitively odd (could it really be that Pat Buchanan was right all along?). But the important point is that Justice Thomas's allegiance to racial justice as a value gives us an important ethical foothold from which to criticize him. Hitler did not value racial justice, and should have. His barbarism is vulnerable to powerful criticisms on humanitarian grounds. Yet it is often more difficult—beyond clear cases like Pol Pot and Henry Kissinger—to decide what is factually evil and what is not. Because of this last difficulty, the present argument advances a second basis of ethical criticism—criticism internal to the project of racial justice. This second kind of criticism does not address unique cases like Hitler, or rare cases like Pol Pot and Kissinger. It is the kind of criticism that might (dubiously) berate Hitler as a bungling advocate of Jewish welfare. In Hitler's case, his crimes being as hideous as they were, the unavailability of this second ground of criticism is obviously insignificant. But once we shift to a liberal ethos in which the rhetoric of tolerance smooths over clashes of values, where racial oppression is often perceived as spontaneous rather than a matter of formal governmental policy, where race-based injustice hides behind neutral terminology, the importance of this second source of obligation increases. In this liberal setting, any attempt to analogize Thomas with Hitler will obviously and appropriately fail. And Thomas will assume that he is home free on the high ground.

The present argument shakes Thomas and his supporters from this moral high ground. It takes seriously his rhetoric of concern and examines his performance in light of this rhetoric. Certainly, objective facts (is it raining? is there a brick on the freeway?) must be acknowledged. But beyond the very small range of such facts (if any), Thomas advances a harsh agenda under the alibis of truth and the rule of law. If truth and the rule of law don't give him an alibi, the basis for his self-righteousness disappears and a basis for moral criticism takes its place.

The following discussion will pursue three main themes. *First,* in his role as a policymaker and bureaucrat, Thomas's rhetoric reveals a strong commitment to abstract ideals of racial justice. *Second,* Thomas also has an allegiance to ideals of disinterest in policymaking; he considers politics an unwelcome intrusion on expertise. He thinks that the disinterested, rational pursuit of truth in policymaking is not only possible but essential. *Third,* Thomas thinks that allegiance to disinterested ideals is even more important for judges than for policymakers. Thomas's ostensible allegiance to disinterest, however, turns out to be an allegiance to other interests. His truth-driven claim to be aboard the progressive project repeatedly fails.

## *Thomas's Partisanship*

Clarence Thomas has consistently spoken not only of an abstract commitment to racial justice but also of his own deeply personal indebtedness to those who struggled before him, and of the enduring racism of American society. Such statements are a pervasive feature of Thomas's writings and speeches, but his commencement address at Savannah State College on June 9, 1985, stands out:

I grew up here in Savannah. I was born not far from here (in Pinpoint). I am a child of those marshes, a son of this soil. I am a descendant of the slaves whose labors made the dark soil of the South productive. I am the great-great-grandson of a freed slave, whose enslavement continued after my birth. I am the product of hatred and love—the hatred of the social and political structure which dominated the segregated hate-filled city of my youth, and the love of some people—my mother, my grandparents, my neighbors and relatives. . . . That mean, callous world out there is still very much filled with discrimination. It still holds out a different life for those who do not happen to be the right race or the right sex. It is a world in which the "haves" continue to reap more dividends than the "have nots."

This speech could hardly have come from David Duke. A churlish researcher might prefer to emphasize Thomas's equivocations, as when he says that race-conscious remedial policies are "merely some form of retribution." Yet Thomas has conceded his indebtedness to civil rights forebears like Thurgood Marshall and Martin Luther King, Jr. ("Only by standing on their shoulders could I be here. At each fork in the road . . . someone came along to help."). And he does not deny his debt, in the abstract, to legal principles (somehow defined) intended to remedy racial injustice ("But for them, God only knows where I would be today").[2]

It is important to note that this and similar rhetoric was exhumed and prominently broadcast by the media within days of the announcement of the Thomas nomination. This and similar Thomas rhetoric clearly played a role in hobbling his opposition. Still, the Savannah speech was made more than six years before the hearings, and it is so representative of Thomas's pronouncements that it cannot be dismissed as straightforward dishonesty or opportunism. We needn't dismiss such statements in that summary fashion. We need only look closer.

Thomas pursues this rhetoric of concern as follows. *First*, his concern does not extend to gender egalitarianism. Thomas is straightforwardly hostile on women's issues. This is clearest in a District of Columbia opinion that he authored shortly before joining the Supreme Court. In that case Thomas expressly concluded that preference programs that can legitimately be based on racial factors cannot legitimately be based on gender because of the alleged failure of certain statistical connections where gender is concerned. This Thomas opinion is excellent evidence that the Tough judge is straightforwardly hostile to female America. *Second,* Thomas pursues his allegiance to African America through a frankly utopian brand of conservative politics. This is especially ironic given that Thomas habitually accuses everyone else of refusing to face harsh realities. *Third,* Thomas purports to serve African America through the belief that, from his perch slightly above the swirling world of passions, he can divine what is really in that constituency's best interests.

## Thomas's Indifference to Women

There is a difference between Thomas's partisanship on racial issues and his position on gender issues. Thomas is always very concerned to announce his allegiance to racial justice—and his rhetoric of concern is shallow once his practice of judging is observed. On gender issues, a slightly different claim can be maintained: Thomas is straightforwardly hostile. Thomas's conspicuous rhetoric favoring racial egalitarianism is not matched by any conspicuous rhetoric favoring gender egalitarianism. It is much easier to establish Thomas's rhetorical allegiance to racial justice than it is to establish a like record on gender issues.

Before Thomas was appointed to the EEOC in the early 1980s, he wrote a memorandum to Jay Parker, fellow black conservative and long-time lobbyist for the unreconstructed South African regime, attacking the EEOC's freshly minted Carter administration guidelines on sexual harassment. The Carter guidelines encouraged employers to take sexual harassment issues seriously by holding them responsible for harassment occurring under their supervision. The Thomas memorandum recommended diluting this incentive. Thomas suggested that liability be limited only to bosses who condoned or participated in the harassment. This stance suggests an outright unconcern with sexual harassment issues (an employer who participated or condoned sounds very likely to be guilty as a principal offender; Thomas's ostensible reform thus would not significantly have enhanced liability).

Subsequently, as EEOC chairman, Thomas actively campaigned *against* parental leave laws, claiming that the alleged expenses the legislation would impose on small businesses violated the "freedoms" of those businesses.[3] When he moved on from the EEOC and joined the Court of Appeals for the District of Columbia Circuit, Thomas authored an opinion in *Lamprecht v. FCC*[4] that is an important further piece of the argument that he is straightforwardly hostile to gender egalitarianism. Thomas's opinion in *Lamprecht* turned largely on a distinction between gender injustice and racial injustice.

Thomas concluded that while race was a sufficient basis for preference programs, gender was not. Thomas reasoned that while there was a proven link between racially diverse ownership of broadcasting licenses and the congressionally endorsed goal of broadcast diversity, no similar connection between female ownership and broadcast diversity had been proven. Thomas thus presented his decision as though it hinged on empirical questions of statistical proof. A close reading of his opinion, however, reveals that the fate of the FCC's gender preference programs was sealed by Thomas's overt and straightforward value judgment, suppressed in a footnote of the opinion. (Thomas's reasoning in *Lamprecht* is discussed more fully in another section.)

Thomas's outright hostility to gender egalitarianism is further evidenced by his tactics during his Supreme Court confirmation hearings. Thomas's explicit and implied attacks (and those of his supporters) on Anita Hill's character, honesty, even sanity, played into well-worn preconceptions in which female credibility is an easy target.

Thomas carried his indifference to women onto the Supreme Court itself, as evidenced by his support for antichoice positions. In *Planned Parenthood v. Casey*[5] the Supreme Court's majority upheld measures restrictive of a woman's right to choose. Justice Thomas joined Scalia and went even further than the heavily criticized majority opinion. Thomas would have overturned *Roe v. Wade* outright, on the basis that a woman's right to choose simply is not a constitutionally protected liberty.

### Swimming with the Barracuda: Thomas's Utopian Conservatism

In June 1987, twelve years after Jimmy Carter's ethnic purity campaign, eight years after Ronald Reagan's Welfare Queen campaign, one year before George Bush's Willie Horton campaign, and five years before Bill Clinton's Sister Souljah campaign, Clarence Thomas had this to say to Lee Atwater, Jesse Helms, Patrick Buchanan, William Bradford Reynolds, and the rest of the Republican party faithful:

Blacks just happened to represent [to the Republicans in the 1986 congressional elections] an interest group not worth going after. Polls rather than principles appeared to control. We must offer a vision, not vexation. . . . We must start by articulating principles of government and standards of goodness. I suggest that we begin . . . with the self-evident truths of the Declaration of Independence.

Who mentioned Don Quixote? Thomas's earnest lecture was, to say the least, optimistic, especially given Thomas's own views on the permanence of racism in American society. Derrick Bell's book, *Faces at the Bottom of the Well,* was widely and inaccurately reviewed as despairing, pessimistic, and even separatist for its conclusion that American racism is permanent. Less broadcast is the fact that Clarence Thomas shares that view. Thomas said as much in an interview, nearly ten years before the appearance of Bell's recent book:

QUESTION: Will discrimination ever disappear?
THOMAS: I'm not one who believes that it will.

Thomas has repeatedly denounced the "hypocrisy and irony of repeated calls for color-blind legal remedies in a country which has tolerated color-conscious violations of the law for so much of its history." Indeed, despite Thomas's adherence to Republican party politics and Reagan-Bush policies, he has never denied the racism of America's conservatives, and its Republican party in particular. He objected, for instance, that Reagan civil rights policy was "unnecessarily negative." Given this double acknowledgment— of the permanence of American racism and the prevalence of Republican distaste for blacks—Thomas's advocacy of conservative policies is a straightforwardly utopian exercise. Thomas urges an admittedly flawed, racist, American right wing to live up to a true self that Thomas has invented on its behalf: "I am of the view that black Americans will move inexorably and naturally toward conservatism when we stop discouraging them ... when conservatives stand up for what they really believe in rather than stand against blacks."

Thomas, throughout the eighties, untiringly urged his political allies to abandon the false conservatism of their racist ways and adopt, instead, the path of his imagined real conservatism. He urged a "principled approach" that would

make clear to blacks that conservatives are not hostile but aggressively supportive. ... This is particularly true to the extent that conservatives are now perceived as anti-civil rights. Unless it is clear that conservative principles protect all, there are no programs or arguments that will attract blacks to conservative ranks.

Thomas found his role as head of the EEOC compromised by his conservative fellow travelers, by the rhetoric of the Reagan administration, and by that administration's specific initiatives (and lack thereof):

Some employers have seen certain actions of this administration over the past two years as reason to cool their heels in reducing job discrimination. ... We made some mistakes in this administration that may have fostered the perception that attacking discrimination is not a top priority. One is the Bob Jones University fiasco, in which the administration argued that the Internal Revenue Service does not have the power to revoke that institution's tax exempt status, despite the school's ban on interracial dating. The controversy surrounding that issue overshadowed some of the good things this administration has done.

Thomas's political allies set him a task of damage control. He was forced to campaign against the impression that the EEOC was asleep at the wheel. Thomas lectured that, contrary appearances notwithstanding, employers "should not [cool their heels], because enforcement actions will be swift and very aggressive in cases where we can prove discrimination."

When Thomas publicly championed an affirmative action plan for the New Orleans Police Department, he was derailed by William Bradford Reynolds, who had him called to the White House and told to toe the party line. Again, on the Voting Rights Act, Thomas criticized his Republican brethren for "failing to get out early and positively in front of the effort" and he found it "intriguing that we consistently claimed credit for extending it." Nor did Thomas personally escape the conservatives' own stereotyping and their open demands that he serve as the mouthpiece for their antiblack agenda: "For (conservative) blacks, the litmus test was clear. You must be against affirmative action and welfare. Your opposition had to be adamant and constant or you would be suspected of being a closet liberal. . . . But what is done is done."

Despite being thus beleaguered, Thomas advocated the prevailing conservative policies and lent himself to promotion of the prevailing conservative agenda. He forgave his fellow Republicans ("what is done is done"), revealing a generosity of spirit that, sadly, did not extend to his sister.[6] All the while accusing others of ignoring reality, Thomas has been relentless in his own utopian conservatism.

This is clearest in Thomas's frequent references to the fact that the government could never do for people what his family did for him ("Those who attempt to capture the daily counseling, oversight, common sense and vision of my grandparents in a governmental program are engaging in sheer folly."). Perhaps the government and one's grandparents have dissimilar roles? The thought doesn't dawn on him. Thomas advocates "Family Policy, Not Social Policy," and boasts that in his youth, "Unlike today, we debated no one about our way of life—we lived it." Ironically, Thomas's frequently invoked grandfather himself apparently broke with Thomas over what he saw as Thomas's self-absorption and problematic pro-Reagan politics.[7]

Thomas's pride in his upbringing is, nevertheless, such that he occasionally appears to slide from a (justified) admiration for the endurance his ancestors showed in adverse conditions to a (strange) suggestion that such feats of endurance are worthwhile as ends in themselves. Thomas, overexuberantly, proclaims that he was "raised to survive under the totalitarianism of segregation, not only without the active assistance of government but with its active opposition." Despite these obstacles that the policymakers of his youth were able to place in his way, Thomas, in his own policymaking role, usually disavows the idea that policymakers have the ability to shape social landscapes. Instead he falls into a paralyzed nostalgia: "[The correct road] is the road—the old-fashioned road—traveled by those who endured slavery, who endured Jim Crowism, who endured hatred. It is the road that might reward hard work and discipline, that might reward intelligence, that might be fair and provide equal opportunity. But there are no guarantees."

Thomas's tendency to make policy as though a wished-for tomorrow had already arrived, or as though a painfully endured yesterday were an end in itself, is a serious deficiency in his attempts to serve the ends of racial justice. This utopian streak is the linchpin of his adherence to Ronald Reagan's small-government rhetoric: "Why do you need a Department of Labor, why do you need a Department of Agriculture, why do you need a Department of Commerce? You can go down the whole list—you don't need any of them really."

Yet Thomas, lifetime public servant that he is, does not think government ought to be entirely dismantled. It ought to exist, but just do little:

Not everything that the EEOC or the federal government has done has been correct, but we're going to need the EEOC for a very long time to come. Protecting the civil rights of citizens, in my view, is a prime responsibility of government. States, historically, have not done a particularly good job in this area, and until they show they can, the federal government will have to play the lead role in seeing that discrimination is stamped out.

If the parental path to virtue is the only workable one, and the government is a no-good parent, then it follows that the government, in fulfilling its prime responsibility, ought to confine itself to unshackling individuals rather than implementing broad remedial measures. How to go about this unshackling exercise remains vague: "It had been my hope and continues to be my hope that we would espouse principles and policies which by their sheer force would preempt welfare and race-conscious policies." But what are these forceful policies? Thomas, adrift for such alternatives, comments that "the most compassionate thing [my family] did for [me] was to teach [me] to fend for [myself] and to do that in an openly hostile environment." Eureka!: "Government cannot develop individual responsibility, but it certainly can refrain from preventing or hindering the development of this responsibility."

Predictably, the line Thomas appears to draw between nonhindrance (appropriate) and affirmative assistance (ineffectual and dangerous) is inconsistently applied. In 1983, early in his EEOC tenure, Thomas recognized that the EEOC's job was "to *shape* the law" and to be at the "forefront of defining the parameters of discrimination" (emphasis original). Thomas here acknowledges that policy can affect the social landscape and assist individuals.

Yet, as his first EEOC term expired and the issue of renomination loomed large between late 1985 and mid-1986, Thomas suddenly discovered a *tension* between shaping the law and fighting hard for those discriminated against under the current state of the law. The bottom line is, of course, that Thomas adopted the view that broad impact strategies—whether numerical goals and timetables, test cases, or disparate impact relief—are a bad remedy, that only actions short of those are acceptable remedies. Instead of arguing this point directly, Thomas at the EEOC often found it convenient to claim that "the statute" (Title VII) says nothing about broad impact strategies like timetables and goals, and so precludes them. This rationale ran into trouble where Thomas conceded that "even though the statute mentions nothing about quotas *[sic]*, courts as a remedy for discrimination have sometimes ruled that certain individuals be hired according to specific goals, timetables and, in some instances, quotas." Thus the barrier to race-conscious remedies (misnomer, "quotas") is, for Thomas, some sense of "the statute" *other than* that which some courts have announced. As a policymaker Thomas obviously agrees with some courts and not with others. His job is to advocate, yet he thinks he "can" ("the statute" binds him) only do *less* than "some courts" have granted. He gets behind the courts that take a restrictive approach to the statute he's meant to enforce, rather than the courts that would enable him to do more. In contrast, when William Bradford Reynolds championed an expansive reading of a Supreme Court case hostile to affirmative action goals, Thomas had no problem pushing that case to the edge of the envelope.[8]

That zig-zag (restrictive reading of progressive Court precedent; expansive reading of regressive precedent) reflects Thomas's truth. Thomas's truth is that the small state is best. The way his grandparents raised him "was not their social policy, it was their family policy—for their family, not those nameless families that politicians love to whine about." One might think this distinction (family policy versus social policy) would survive when Thomas leaves home and has to make policy with precisely such "nameless families" in mind. In fact, in his various public roles, Thomas arrived at his desk with this mantra intact. "Family Policy, Not Social Policy." Don't leave home without it.[9]

## A Few Humble Feet above the Maddening Crowd

Thomas's confidence in his own familial truth is in turn traceable to his belief that he has the expert's eye for a reality that lies outside the frenzy of politics. In these days of widespread skepticism about claims of simple truth, Thomas has no difficulty urging his Republican allies to embrace natural law (somehow defined) and "begin the search for standards and principles with the self-evident truths of the Declaration of Independence." For Thomas, natural law "both transcends and underlies time and place, race and custom." Moreover,

Our political way of life is by the laws of nature [and] of nature's God, and of course presupposes the existence of God, the moral ruler of the universe, and a rule of right and wrong, and of just and unjust, binding upon man, preceding all institutions of human society and of government.... Without such a notion of natural law, the entire American political tradition, from Washington to Lincoln, from Jefferson to Martin Luther King, would be unintelligible.... All our political institutions presuppose this truth.[10]

*Res ipsa loquitur*. Thomas compounded this exhortation with his much-publicized reference, in the same speech, to an antiabortion pamphlet by Nicholas Lerhman that appeared in the *American Spectator*, the magazine that gave birth, in article form, to David Brock's book *The Real Anita Hill*. Thomas described Lerhman's offering as a "splendid example of applying natural law." For Thomas, "human nature provides the key to how men ought to live their lives." This self-evident truth about "men['s]" lives has some predictable consequences in Thomas's case law on a woman's right to choose. Yet it would be far too simple, and it would understate Thomas's personal moral responsibility for his decisionmaking, if we laid the blame at religion's doorstep. The church has played a central role in much of the

American civil rights movement. It continues to give us our foremost civil rights and intellectual leaders. Apart from mainstream black American churches, there is a strong Franciscan element, within the Catholic Church, that is socioeconomically progressive. Thomas's own early schooling was carried out by white Franciscan nuns from Ireland who ventured to serve in the segregated American South where they were reviled and publicly abused as the "nigger sisters." [11] Moreover, Thomas's own grandfather was propelled into the civil rights struggle by the idea that civil rights came from God, not man, and that the Jim Crow regime, as "legal" as it might seem, was not consistent with divine law. Thomas defenders thus cannot blame the details of his pro-Reagan agenda on any church, nor on any legal theory. It is Thomas's manipulations, seldom intellectually consistent, of various theories in order to reach results consistent with Reaganite ideology that form the basis for criticism. The NAACP Legal Defense Fund, in a thorough review of Thomas's speeches and writings, suggests persuasively that "it is as though Thomas had several right-wing speech writers, one a libertarian, one a natural law advocate, one an executive branch-statist, one a neo-McCarthyite, who took turns framing his views." [12] Thomas's natural-law rhetoric may indeed merely have furnished grandiose underpinnings for his political agenda. But whether or not his resort to various theories was deliberately opportunistic, Thomas's natural-law incantations are consistent with his frequent claims that, as an unfettered persona, he is best placed to find truth. Thomas and his supporters frequently emphasize the supposed unfetteredness of his intellect. One headline proclaims: "Clarence is nothing if not an independent thinker." Assisted by this unfetteredness Thomas can — quite apart from divine intervention — discern what's best for people: "As your front-runner, I have gone ahead and taken a long, hard look. I have seen two roads from my perch a few humble feet above the maddening crowd."

This picture of the wise man, separate from the flux and fortified, therefore, in divining the true "road" to racial salvation, is a role that Thomas treats with monklike seriousness: "I pay little heed to our critics [because] my personality and my style of operating approach is that of a monastic recluse." And Thomas has no doubt that his cloistered wisdom is superior to the folly of others. Of the two roads that Thomas spots from his perch above the maddening crowd, he continues, "On the first [road], a race of people is rushing mindlessly down a highway of sweet, intoxicating destruction, with all its bright lights and grand promises constructed by social scientists and politicians. To the side, there is a seldom used, overgrown road leading through the valley of life."

Thomas is in no doubt that such divinations are superior to what he calls the "ludicrous ... perceptions" of many African Americans. In 1987 he praised fellow Toughs, Sowell and Parker, for standing steadfast and "refusing to give in to the cult mentality and childish obedience that hypnotize black Americans into a mindless political trance. I admire [Sowell and Parker] and only wish I could have a fraction of their courage and strength."

Since joining the Court, Thomas has continued to present himself as a lonely and heroic questioner of "current social and cultural gimmicks." In the midst of the Guinier affair, a Thomas speech criticized mainstream civil rights hostility to those, like himself, who questioned "popular political, social or economic fads." Years earlier, in 1985, Thomas told a series of professional groups in a number of speeches that upon his arrival at the EEOC, "The civil rights community did not hail me as a champion of their cause, but that was good. There was no nonsense to get in the way of doing the hard work that had to be done."

Thomas further opined in this speech that the civil rights community was "wallowing in self-delusion" and ignoring "reality." He assured his audiences that, because of his personal experience of race-based humiliation, he "find[s] it very difficult to criticize publicly anything that minorities perceive to be beneficial or positive." The clear implication is that a monkish discipline has enabled him to overcome the seductions of group adulation and to make hard choices for the authentic benefit of those he cares about. This notion of unflinching expertise pervades Thomas's writings. He has the expert's disdain for emotive debate and the expert's preference for rational argument (as though the two were necessarily in conflict):

People are very passionate about their rights.... This is only natural. But careless, irresponsible and often manipulative rhetoric can and does raise such passions to a feverish level. Fear, anger and hostility dominate people's reactions. They overwhelm and displace rational thought and precise analysis among those who feel the most threatened, and who are the most vulnerable in our society.

Thomas thus carries Julien Benda's disdain for mere passions into his role as head of the EEOC, which he himself described as "one of the most visible and controversial agencies in the United States Government." Upon arrival, Thomas eagerly adopted the role of the rational administrator faced with an undisciplined, chaotic constituency. According to Thomas, the activists' displacement of rationality by passion leads to "further polarization of groups. These fears can register voters, fill ballot boxes or supply audiences for skilled orators who bleed them for cheers, applause, popularity and adulation."

What is most revealing here is the characterization of the political process as an ugly intrusion on his EEOC work. Thomas has mistaken the EEOC's domain as, ideally, an apolitical sphere wherein a neutral expertise can and should prevail. Julien Benda, addressing those prepared to declare that their kingdom is not of this world, lamented that "never were there so many political works among those which ought to be the mirror of disinterested intelligence." Clarence Thomas, in 1985, appointed to head the controversial EEOC, regurgitated, with no self-consciousness whatsoever, this Bendaresque sentiment.

This antipassion sentiment, in turn, underpins Thomas's adherence to an ideal of professionalism. Thomas has disclosed that he was insulted when initially offered the EEOC position because the offer appeared to be based on his presumed interest in racial matters, rather than on his inherent neutral competences. Likewise, he "always found it curious that, even though my background was in energy, taxation and general corporate regulatory matters, I was not seriously sought after to move into one of those areas." Thomas ultimately took the EEOC post, but immediately became absorbed in getting the "monkey" (his word) off his back: he set out to be a corporate managerial superstar, with the EEOC as a foil for his inherent neutral competences. This profound concern to present a picture of managerial competence is clear in many of Thomas's speeches and much of his writing. Former EEOC colleagues remembered fondly that "in the early days of his chairmanship, he would go down to the finance section so often that he had his own chair there." They were not, though, sure that his micromanagement was a good idea. Undaunted, Thomas boasted to an industry group that "we have begun automating our agency with personal computers and an array of electronic wizardry." Thomas repeatedly emphasized, during his time as EEOC chair, how effectively he was tackling an inherited administrative and managerial disaster. His supporters also pick up this theme, noting that Thomas liked to tell the story of when he first arrived at the EEOC and "neither chair, system nor semblance of organization was to be found. Clarence got himself a chair and a Classic Coke, put his grandfather's and his son's picture on his desk . . . and went to work."

Fully half of a speech Thomas delivered to various professional and business organizations in 1985 is given over to a discussion of these managerial issues. He draws the contrast (politics versus managerialism) explicitly: "These are the boring time-consuming factors that make an organization work. These are the aspects of a manager's job that the politicians, interest groups and news media could not care less about."

An initial response is that the politicians, interest groups, and media have got it right. A person appointed to head a large organization had better have the necessary organizational skills—or else know how to tap them. These skills are *essential,* but also merely instrumental. The EEOC, perhaps, was not set up so that it could be efficiently run as an end in itself and as a tribute to its chairperson's fungible managerial skills. Its mission, rather, is the efficient pursuit of certain ends—*those* are properly of general interest. Nevertheless, in his public appearances on behalf of the EEOC, Thomas consistently presented himself as technocrat, not visionary.

Thomas ended this frequently delivered 1985 speech with what is, for present purposes, a fascinating passage. It reflects both his concern for civil rights goals as well as the facile conception of truth that afflicts Thomas's decisionmaking on the Supreme Court:

I would suggest that we have, unfortunately, permitted sociological and demographic realities to be manipulated to the point of surreality by convenient legal theories and procedures such as "adverse impact" and "prima facie cases." We have locked an amorphous, complex, sometimes unexplainable social phenomenon into legal theories that sound good to the public, please lawyers and fit legal precedents, but make no sense. *If I have my way, the legal theories will conform to reality instead of reality being made to conform to legal theories.* (Emphasis added)

One could hardly ask for a clearer statement of a faith in the existence of an objective pretheoretical reality. It is (per Thomas) the job of a legal concept to describe this preexistent reality. Interestingly, Thomas's objective "reality" is something different from that which sounds good to the public, pleases lawyers, and fits legal precedents. Having announced this eccentric yet objective grip on "reality," Thomas continues:

My goal is to take reality into account while enforcing the law. We at the Commission will steadfastly resist political and public pressure to ignore reality and conform our policies to popular notions rather than to demonstrated facts. We have no interest in unfairly attacking employers, but our job is to defend the rights of all individuals in this society.

Thomas has not explained what reality is, but we are left clear on what it is not: it clearly excludes political and public pressure that, he assumes, is always a distraction from demonstrated facts. There is evidence in the speech that Thomas feels politically pressured by the Right as well as the Left. The point is not that Thomas uses the rhetoric of fact as a deliberate expedient to exclude the voices of the Left. Rather, the point is that Thomas thinks his job as EEOC administrator is, properly, one insulated from politics. This attitude is itself a serious failing, for it saddles Thomas with a danger-laden indifference among competing ideological descriptions of reality and jeopardizes, in practice, the progressive values to which he freely admits in theory.

Finally, this allegiance to apolitical rhetoric intensified as Thomas shifted from bureaucrat to judge. At his confirmation hearings, Thomas repeatedly disavowed controversial aspects of his prior truth telling (his hostility to class-action civil rights claims; his hostility to race-conscious remedies; his preference for natural-law theories hostile to a woman's right to choose). Thomas repeatedly denied the relevance of statements made before he became a judge. He said that becoming a judge is "an amazing process. You want to be stripped down like a runner" and to "shed the baggage of ideology." He claimed to have succeeded so well that old friends of Clarence the administrator soon found Clarence the (Court of Appeals) judge a worthless conversationalist. Thomas suggested that judges ought to renounce ideology the better to pursue law as laid down by the language of the Constitution, the Congress, and the Supreme Court's own prior cases.[13] But has he done this?

## Is Thomas Bound by Legal Language?

Are Thomas and the Court, on the evidence of their judicial decisions, bound by the language of the rules laid down by the Constitution, the Congress, and the Supreme Court's prior cases? The earlier discussion established the legal-theoretical arguments against this idea that law binds judges. This section illustrates law's unbindingness by reference to the Supreme Court's actual case law.

The idea that legal language binds judges is often advanced as the best insurance against an unelected Court tyrannizing the country. Yet an ostensible allegiance to language can actually be a useful tool in a judge's hands and can be used in a manner contrary to majority sentiment. The case of *Conroy v. Aniskoff* illustrates this. *Conroy* concerned interpretation of the language of the Soldiers' and Sailors' Civil Relief Act. That legislation ensures that (e.g.) a soldier's house is not sold away from under her should she fail to make mortgage payments while she is away fighting for her country. Conroy failed to pay real estate taxes and the city sold his house. He sued the city and the new owners of the house, relying on the Act's provision that the "period of military service" should be excluded from a time lapse the city had to observe before it could validly take the house. Conroy had not, however, been in a faraway land serving his country. He'd been around and just had not paid his taxes. Could he get the benefit of the Relief Act? Or was that law limited to those who had suffered actual hardship because of military service? Thomas and the Supreme Court concluded that Conroy could get the benefit because the "statutory command" was "unambiguous, unequivocal, and unlimited." Such confident assertions might lead casual observers to believe that the Court has just provided an example of the stable practice of adjudication that the competent lawyer might master through strenuous study. Closer examination suggests otherwise. The trial court earlier dismissed the result the Supreme Court reached, saying it was "absurd and illogical" to give Conroy the benefit of the Relief Act. Maine's highest court, itself bitterly divided, upheld that lower court result—that Conroy was not entitled to the benefit. The Supreme Court was, thus, the *first* court to hold otherwise.

There is a sense in which one might say that the divergent legal results reached by the state courts and the Supreme Court in Conroy were predictable: state courts might be thought to favor their own state taxing authority, whereas the Supreme Court might be thought more impartial. Yet this is itself not a special legal explanation, just a plainly political one. Moreover, the Supreme Court's "impartiality" might easily be redescribed as Reagan-era antitax ideology. The factors in play are thus not peculiarly legal. The "plain-language" analysis in Conroy was thus the site of a political battle, not a means of escape from politics.

Moreover, Scalia's separate concurring opinion demonstrates that a strict judicial allegiance to language can be a useful tool in *resisting* legislative will. Scalia advocated confining the Court's attention to the "law as it is passed." Yet, whatever the basis of Scalia's allegiance to plain language in *Conroy,* it was clearly not a desire to keep the Court in its place and to uphold the will of the elected legislature. Scalia: "The greatest defect of legislative history is its illegitimacy. We are governed by laws, not by the intentions of legislators." This is a useful doctrine for a judge who dislikes the prevailing congressional power balance. Scalia's putsch seems to have alarmed most members of the majority. Stevens wrote that Scalia was apparently willing to assume that the Supreme Court has "a duty to enforce the statute as written even if fully convinced that every member of the enacting Congress, as well as the President who signed the Act, intended a different result. . . . We disagree."

It is thus difficult to argue that confining judges to statutory language is a surefire way to safeguard majoritarian democracy. Justice Thomas joined in all of the Stevens opinion, *except* the above-quoted language in which the majority took issue with Scalia. Moreover, in an opinion he wrote on the court of appeals, before ascending to the Supreme Court, Thomas showed a similar distaste for deference to the legislature, suggesting that such deference might render judicial review "an elaborate farce." Before that, at the EEOC, Thomas emphasized the importance of sticking to one's ideals and being "defiant in the face of [the] petty despots in Congress." He repeatedly praised Oliver North for showing that Congress was "fake" and "out of control." Conversely, during Thomas's tenure at the EEOC, congressional committees repeatedly clashed with Thomas over his neglect of complaints filed under his tenure (thousands of age-discrimination claims simply lapsed), and for a variety of other transgressions. In 1989, no fewer than fourteen chairpersons of House subcommittees cosigned a letter condemning Thomas's "overall disdain for the rule of law." [14] Justice Thomas's allegiance to statutory language as opposed to legislative history and congressional intent is perhaps not democracy's best bet.

## Justice Thomas's Failed Flight from "Policymaking"

Unwilling to defer to the legislature, Thomas and Scalia also—paradoxically—claim to oppose judicial policymaking. (As previously argued, avoidance of policymaking is impossible for a judge.) In *Rowland v. California Men's Colony,* for instance, the question before the Court was whether certain benefits (waivers of court fee and prepayment obligations, etc.) granted to impoverished individual litigants extended to impoverished organizational litigants. The Court's majority concluded that the benefits did not extend to organizational litigants. Thomas, dissenting, argued that the benefits did so extend, and not because the result was a desirable policy outcome (he apparently thought the opposite), but because the result was dictated by plain language of the statute: "Congress has spoken, and we should give effect to its words." The fact that parsing Congress's language had split the Court five to four did not give Thomas pause.

Thomas objected that the majority, in reaching its decision, polluted what should be a pure language-parsing exercise with unnecessary and improper references to legislative history and policy reasoning. He rejected the reasoning that had moved the majority because that reasoning reflected "classic policy considerations—the concerns of a legislature, not a court." In fact, Thomas throughout apparently assumed that the conclusion he was "forced" by plain language to reach was an undesirable policy outcome. He speculated that "while it might make sense as a matter of policy to exclude associations and other artificial entities from the benefits of the in forma pauperis statute, I do not believe that Congress has done so."

Thomas's flight from policy moved Justice Kennedy (who, like Thomas, dissented from the result of the case) to write a separate opinion. Justice Kennedy emphasized that the majority's attempt to "uncover significant practical barriers to including artificial entities within [the benefits in question] is quite appropriate and ought not to be condemned as policymaking." For Kennedy, the problem was that the Court had failed to show that extension of the benefits in question was in fact unworkable.[15] Kennedy's opinion clarifies that what was at stake in the case was not whether to undertake or to avoid policymaking, but rather *which* policy to make.

We are thus left with a paradox that illustrates an important problem. Thomas reached a result consonant with progressive policy, not because he thought it was good policy—he appeared to think it was bad policy—but because he claimed that it was compelled by plain language. The fact that Thomas thought that extending poverty benefits to inmates pressing a civil rights claim was bad policy is itself a paradox, given his espoused concerns. Moreover, while Thomas announced himself forced by language to reach this result notwithstanding his own personal and policy opposition to it, all judges inevitably make policy. No judges don't make policy. And Supreme Court justices make more policy than most.

### A "Lexicon of Death"

Matters as serious as the fate of criminal defendants frequently hinge on word games. In *Smith v. U.S.* the Court faced the question of whether the reference to "use" of a firearm in federal sentencing guidelines required enhancement of a convicted felon's sentence where a gun was offered as payment for drugs. The felon had bought drugs from an undercover officer, tendering the gun in payment. To "use" a gun is, one may think, to menace or to wound rather than to tender as payment. Yet this view was corralled into the dissenting opinion. O'Connor's majority opinion conceded that the natural or plain meaning was to menace or wound, but denied that that meaning "excludes any other use." O'Connor thus implicitly argued that the Court has the discretion to apply any meaning of a word not positively excluded by a statute (how a legislature is to exclude all imaginable meanings is not explained).[16]

Again, in *Arave v. Creech*, a death-penalty case, Justice Blackmun made the point that language games ought not to become an end in themselves but should always be a means towards a right result. He remarked that it was weird to make a person's life hinge on a dictionary: that there was "something absurd in the very project of parsing this lexicon of death." But, he added, "as long as we are in the death business, we shall be in the parsing business."[17] Thomas did not vote with Blackmun against death (the substance of Thomas's death penalty jurisprudence is treated at length below).

While the foregoing discussion ought to fray the false distinction between unfettered subjectivity and disciplined rule application, Thomas and Scalia continue to rely heavily on this distinction. While others apparently impose their ungarnished policy views, Scalia and Thomas claim to enforce the Word. They call a decision with which they disagree "wildly delirious" and beyond the imaginable. With zeal, they insist that their view of the Word is the only truth:

In the end nothing but personal intuition supports the dissent's contention that the statute is [what they say it is]. . . . Like most intuitions, it finds Congress to have intended what the intuitor thinks Congress ought to intend. . . . *Once text is abandoned, one intuition will serve as well as the other. We choose to follow the language of the statute.*[18] (Emphasis added)

This passage is a replay of the Ronald Dworkin's legal theory: the supposed evil of unfettered discretion is, for Thomas and Scalia, solved by the supposed constraints of language. Yet their claim that they follow language does not generate any effectual constraints. Dworkin's theory merely furnishes a language for Thomas's self-righteousness.

## When's an Old Rule New?

A final good example of the unbindingness of legal rules is the harshly criticized decision of *Teague v. Lane*.[19] The *Teague* rule holds that a person applying for habeas corpus relief must do so on the basis of the law at the time of her trial. If the basis for the petition is a "new rule"—one that arose after a petitioner's conviction and sentencing—the petitioner's challenge will fail.

The Court, in *Teague,* has set itself a range of wonderful tasks. First, the Court must decide what the rule at the time of the trial was. Then it must decide whether a claim asserted by a petitioner can be said to be based on the law as it was at the time of the trial, or whether it is instead based on a "new" rule—which is in turn to be distinguished from a mere extension of an old rule. Finally, the Court must determine whether, even if its own view of what the old rule was is different from the version of the old rule enforced by the lower court, that lower court conclusion ought nevertheless to be respected as within the reasonable range of interpretation of the old law.

It should come as no surprise that Thomas and his colleagues have been able to pursue an untrammeled counterprogressive agenda with *Teague's* rhetoric. In *Gilmore v. Taylor* [20] a petitioner who had been convicted of murder sought the benefit of a rule established in a case called *Falconer v. Lane.* [21] That rule required that a jury expressly be told that it could not return a murder conviction if it found that the defendant possessed a mitigating mental state. The jury instruction under which Taylor was convicted clearly did not meet this standard and was therefore, by this standard, unconstitutional. But the *Falconer* case, establishing this standard, was decided after Gilmore's conviction and sentencing (though while his appeal was pending). The question was therefore whether the *Falconer* rule, on which Taylor sought to rely, was "new" or not. If it was new, Taylor's attempted reliance would fail.

The *Falconer* case announced itself as relying on the Supreme Court case of *Cupp v. Naughten,* [22] a case that clearly preceded Gilmore's own and so might seem an old rule, not new. The Court thus had to decide whether *Falconer* was "compelled" by the previous case of *Cupp* or was, rather, a new rule. The district court held that *Falconer* was new, not compelled by *Cupp.* The Court of Appeals reversed, concluding that *Falconer* was actually old, not new. Yet the Court of Appeals did not agree that *Falconer* was compelled by *Cupp,* since *Cupp* was "too general" to have compelled the *Falconer* result. Rather, the Court of Appeals found that *Falconer* was compelled by entirely different old cases: *Boyde v. California* and *Connecticut v. Johnson.* [23]

The Supreme Court then tried its hand. Rehnquist, writing for Thomas, Scalia, and Kennedy, agreed with the Court of Appeals that *Cupp* was an "unlikely progenitor" of the *Falconer* rule. Did Rehnquist and Thomas then agree with the Court of Appeals that the *Boyd* and *Johnson* cases compelled the result? Nope. The Court of Appeals, too, had gone astray. The cases it cited did not compel the *Falconer* rule. *Falconer* was clearly new and compelled by none of the three cases that two courts below held compelled the result.

The dissenters sensibly avoided unbinding wrangling over whether *Falconer* was really a new rule. Instead, they said that even assuming, for the sake of argument, that the rule was new, it was nevertheless within an exception to the *Teague* rule. Under *Teague* the petitioner may have the benefit even of a new rule, if the rule is of a special sort: if it either decriminalizes a class of conduct or is a "watershed rule of criminal procedure implicating the fundamental accuracy and fairness of the criminal proceeding." The dissenters concluded that Taylor's case was within the second exception.

This exception clearly lacks that crisp, binding bite that legal rules are supposed to have. In rejecting this exception Thomas and Rehnquist simply announced that misleading jury instructions were not within the small core of cases that were within the exception. They simply asserted that the exception is a narrow one. Yet, their assertion is not the result of the inner nature of the rule. It follows from nothing other than their ideological preconceptions.

The dissenters, Blackmun and Stevens, read the exception as clearly applicable and laid out cogent reasons why it was so applicable. Yet their opinion ultimately also hinged not on the inherent inner nature of the rule but, rather, on their own ideological conclusion that "the principle that [Taylor] asserts is a fundamental one." The question of what is "fundamental" and what is not is patently a matter of straightforward moral reasoning and ideology. *That* process—not the competent divination of a thing called law—is what is unfolding in this decision, as the following battle confirms. Thomas and Rehnquist lead off with this offering:

Justice BLACKMUN in dissent would elevate the instructional defect contained in the Illinois pattern jury instructions on murder and voluntary manslaughter not merely to the level of a federal constitutional violation, but to one that is so fundamental as to come within *Teague*'s second exception. He reaches this result by combining several different constitutional principles—the prohibition against ex post facto laws, the right to a fair trial, and the right to remain silent—into an unrecognizable constitutional stew.

Thomas and Rehnquist here adopt the posture that their ideological notion of the true nature of the rule is the only possible one. The dissenters join battle with the following offering:

The Court's [comment last-cited] ... added by THE CHIEF JUSTICE after the dissenting opinion circulated, hardly deserves acknowledgment, let alone comment. I had thought that this was a court of justice and that a criminal defendant in this country could expect to receive a genuine analysis of the constitutional issues in his case rather than the conclusory rhetoric with which Kevin Taylor is here treated. I adhere to my derided "constitutional stew."

On the most austere and magisterial judicial tribunal in the country, controversial "legal" decisions are generally little more than overt clashes over questions of value. Blackmun and Stevens lost the *Taylor* case not because they parsed a legal problem incorrectly but simply because they were outnumbered by ideological opponents.

## Thomas Choosing Cases—and Choosing Sides

Every day, everywhere, people in community organizations, or on city councils, boards of directors, and councils of elders set agendas. They discuss the things they think are important or require urgent action; they ignore other stuff. They face up to the scarcity of time and resources. The Supreme Court of the United States does this too, mostly through a device called certiorari. The other way to get a case before the Court is by the "obligatory appeal" jurisdiction whereunder the Court theoretically has no choice but to take the case. But courts generally, and the Supreme Court in particular, never really have no choice and it is entirely uncontroversial that the only meaningful path to Supreme Court review of federal and state court decisions is certiorari. If the Court agrees to hear a case, it grants certiorari; if it refuses, certiorari is denied. The denial of certiorari is not, in theory, an endorsement of the lower court's decision. Yet, law happens. If the Supreme Court declines to review—potentially to disturb—the lower court's determination, that lower judge's word is final and settles what "law" is for the parties in that case and, possibly, for future parties with analogous disputes.

Supreme Court certiorari decisions are thus a very important part of its law-making function. The maneuvering that surrounds the granting or denial of certiorari in the thousands of cases the Court might possibly hear is probably at least as important as the coalition building that occurs in the much smaller number of cases the Court actually reviews every year. If it is, for instance, clear that the presiding members of the Court are likely to overturn or restrictively interpret *Roe v. Wade* if a relevant case comes before the Court, a prochoice justice's best option may be to prevent such a case from reaching the Court's docket. If she can persuade three other members to go along, the danger of overturning *Roe* might be averted. Conversely, when Thomas voted against the Court's dissenting conservatives and instead joined the Court's centrist majority to deny certiorari in the 1992 Guam abortion case, it was apparently to avoid what he saw as a likely reaffirmation of *Roe* (after the majority upheld *Roe* in *Casey*, Thomas knew how the vote on the merits would go).[24]

In this way, battles over certiorari resemble congressional filibusters. Whereas it takes fifty votes to carry the Senate, only forty are needed to maintain a filibuster. Similarly, it takes five votes to carry the Supreme Court but only four to deny certiorari. Moreover, just as a Senate filibuster can alter substantive outcomes by allowing time for political coalitions to shift or for scandals to break, the Court's denial of certiorari can allow time for a shift of Court personnel (Thurgood Marshall out, Clarence Thomas in) that might significantly alter the outcome of a case.

Like other "legal" questions, certiorari is "governed" by a rule—in this case, Supreme Court Rule 10.1 (henceforth, Rule Ten Point One). Once this rule is unveiled, members of community organizations, city councils, boards of directors, councils of elders, comfortable with the straightforward agenda-setting exercise previously described, will be tempted to run for cover. Rule Ten Point One seems beyond the layperson's competence. The truth is, it seems, really to be found in a remote text called the *United States Code, Annotated*. But wait. It turns out that Rule Ten Point One says certiorari is "a matter of judicial discretion, and will be granted only when there are special and important reasons therefore." Then follows a list of three considerations (conflicts among federal courts of appeals; conflicts among states' highest courts; issue of such importance that the Supreme Court ought to speak on it) that, "while neither controlling nor fully measuring the Court's discretion, indicate the character of reasons that will be considered." This is hardly the crisp, clear, binding guidance that intimidated laypersons imagine Rule Ten Point One to provide. It turns out that, by law, discretion is the heart of certiorari. The Court, like the rest of us, just does what seems to need doing.

The certiorari application of *Haitian Refugee Center, Inc. v. James Baker, III*[25] arose because people fleeing tyranny in small boats inconveniently headed for America's shores. The Bush administration argued that the refugees were faking it and decided to send them back. A dazzling legal battle ensued on two fronts—one in Florida, the other in New York. The Supreme Court refused to hear the Florida case; it took the New York case and reached a result deferential to President Clinton (who, abandoning campaign pledges, cloned Bush's policy and legal arguments). Heated dissents and conflicting decisions proliferated. The federal court of appeals in the New York case expressly disagreed with the federal court of appeals in the Florida case and openly hoped that this would make the Supreme Court see fit to grant certiorari in the New York case in contrast to its denial of certiorari in the Florida case.[26]

In denying the *Baker* certiorari application (the Florida case), Justice Thomas announced that "under the standards this court has traditionally employed, cf. S. Ct. Rule 10-1, the petition should be denied." And far from expressing indifference to the plight of the Haitians, Thomas declared that he was "deeply concerned" about the treatment allegedly suffered by the returnees. Thomas's stated reason for denying the Haitians relief was not that he didn't care, but that he was bound by something called law.

Yet of all the rules that might conceivably be said to bind a judge, Rule Ten Point One, expressly preserving the judge's discretion, is an unlikely candidate. Justice Blackmun, dissenting, experienced no such constraint. What went on here became clear as Thomas provided a second, different legal rationale for his denial of certiorari. He wrote that despite his own deep concern for Haitian well-being, "this matter must be addressed by the political branches, for our role is limited to questions of law." This is the "political-question" doctrine, the argument that the Supreme Court, and courts in general, ought to eschew issues that are better decided by the nonjudicial branches and instead confine themselves to questions of law. This doctrine is extremely controversial and widely discussed in the legal community. It has been widely criticized, even ridiculed, for resting on a mythical separation of politics from law. Against a backdrop of such academic and professional controversy, the political-question doctrine is, within the legal community, hardly the type of legal principle that commands unthinking allegiance. If the doctrine is employed in the foreign relations context, it is employed with an awareness of its tendency to exalt executive prerogative above competing values (such as the well-being of Haitian refugees). Thomas's resort to the doctrine is, thus, not driven by impartial legal analysis, by a constraint called law, or by concern for the Haitians. The conflicting value of executive prerogative is the only persuasive explanation of the case. The paradox is now clear: How is Thomas's deference to the executive branch, to George Bush, consistent with his expressed concern for the Haitians?

The very existence of Justice Blackmun's dissent is significant in assessing

Thomas's decision. Even on the unlikely assumption that Thomas's resort to Rule Ten Point One, and his invocation of the political-question doctrine, were the result of his best efforts to find a legal argument that would help the Haitians, why didn't he simply, having failed to find good arguments, sign on to Blackmun's dissent? Blackmun's dissent is hardly outrageous, incompetent, or bizarre. Indeed, the legal community would probably be more surprised by Thomas's failure to see how closely the Haitian refugee case matched the relevant criteria in certiorari cases—the criteria of divergent federal decisions in lower courts. Thus, whatever reasons Thomas has for rebuffing the Haitians, he does not have the excuse that law forced him to do it. The straightforwardness of the issue at stake is very clear in Justice Blackmun's dissent:

A quick glance at this Court's docket reveals not only that we have room to consider these issues, but that they are at least as significant as any we have chosen to review today. If indeed the Haitians are to be returned to an uncertain future in their strife-torn homeland, that ruling should come from this Court, after full and fair consideration of the merits of their claims.

The presence of such dissenting opinions will be a recurring problem for Thomas as this survey of his decisionmaking continues. Wherever there is a dissent that would avoid a result he laments, and he yet fails to vote with that dissent, he will find it difficult to explain his judicial decisionmaking in terms that keep him aboard the progressive project of which he wants to be part.

In the subsequent case of *Chris Sale v. Haitian Centers Council*,[27] the Court granted certiorari because of the sudden "manifest importance of the case" and frontally faced the political-question doctrine. The Court overturned the New York federal court's decision in favor of the Haitians. The "legal" questions at issue were no more binding than such language-parsing exercises ever are. The details of the Court's analysis revolved around various questions of statutory, treaty, and case-law interpretation. There was a tremendous variety of opinion, at every level, among the courts that spoke on these issues (district court reversed in part by circuit court, itself reversed by Supreme Court). To parse those issues would be to replay the earlier discussion of whether legal language binds judges. In this setting, all that separated the Supreme Court's view of "the" law from the contrary view reached by competent lower courts was the Supreme Court's relative indulgence of claims of executive prerogative. Thomas and a majority of the current members of the Supreme Court took sides in a controversial political argument over the scope of executive power. And despite Thomas's claim that he had somehow shed ideological baggage upon becoming a judge, he has long believed that the executive should exercise increased power in foreign affairs and beyond. In 1988, when Thomas was still at the EEOC, his speeches argued that Congress exercised "little deliberation and even less wisdom" in its affairs, and he lamented that "in many areas of public policy, including foreign policy-making, members of Congress can thwart or substitute their will for that of the executive." In 1988, a Thomas article also castigated the Supreme Court for pursuing a "voodoo jurisprudence" that had given the Court inordinate power "over the last 50 or so years." Only *Oliver North,* in Thomas's view, had *stayed within* constitutional bounds. In the aftermath of the 1987 Iran-Contra Senate hearings, Thomas suggested that North's attack on the Senate had furthered the cause of "limited government."[28]

Such dizzying stuff was also at work in *Chris Sales.* President Bush's executive order, a central source of the alleged legal authority to send Haitians home, specifically stated that it was "intended only to improve the internal management of the Executive Branch." Yet the Court went out of its way to confer upon this housekeeping measure the controversial and arguably nonexistent plenary authority that some say the executive has in foreign affairs. Justice Blackmun, dissenter on the certiorari question in *Baker,* was again unsettled: "What is extraordinary in this case is that the executive, in disregard of the law, would take to the seas to intercept fleeing refugees and force them back to their persecutors—and that the Court would strain to sanction that conduct."

Conversely, the majority, including Thomas, found itself "bound" by law and unable to respond to what they conceded was a compelling human crisis. As in Thomas's opinion in the *Baker* certiorari decision, the majority here was both deeply concerned and ostensibly unable to help. Yet their failure to help was, whatever the reason, not dictated by a thing called law. Justice Blackmun pointed out that a legal ban on returning the Haitians was "easily applicable here, the Court's protestations of impotence and regret notwithstanding." And it was, in the words of the majority opinion that Thomas signed, an "uncontested finding of fact" that "since the military coup hundreds of Haitians have been killed, tortured, detained without a warrant, or subjected to violence and the destruction of their property because of their political beliefs. Thousands have been forced into hiding."

Placing Thomas's espoused concern for Haitian well-being alongside his voluntary elevation of executive prerogative, it is easy to argue that he betrayed the Haitians, choosing executive privilege over Haitian welfare. But this tempting accusation of treachery is unnecessary for a devastating moral critique. Even if one declines to question Thomas's good faith, the conclusion can hardly be less scathing. One must then believe that Thomas really mistook the controversial "political-question" doctrine for settled law, binding on him, in a case where the president announced the disputed measure as a housekeeping regulation, *not* one of foreign affairs, and where there was a powerful dissent. Whether under the rubric of betrayal or of incompetence, Thomas is morally culpable.

## Reapportionment

Having rejected the hopelessly political subject of refugee rights, Justice Thomas turned to the wholly apolitical task of invalidating electoral districts. The Supreme Court, in *Baker v. Carr,* long ago rejected arguments that redistricting raises nonjusticiable political questions. The Court reviews these issues under the mandate and the framework established by the Voting Rights Act of 1965 (as amended in 1982). These apportionment cases raise complex issues with no simple answers. Racial politics (whites versus blacks) has interacted with party politics (Republicans versus Democrats), creating unholy alliances and unsettling even the most agile analyses.

On June 28, 1993, Justice O'Connor, writing for Thomas and the majority in the controversial North Carolina apportionment case of *Shaw v. Reno,*[29] concluded that "racial gerrymandering *[sic]*, even for remedial purposes, may balkanize us into competing racial factions." The redistricting plan in *Shaw* had, as noted in the dissent, placed black North Carolinian representatives in Congress for the first time since Reconstruction. In that setting, Thomas's *unprecedented* discovery (following O'Connor) of equal-protection obstacles to the plan was particularly striking. The Court found that five white North Carolina voters who alleged a constitutional right to participate in a color-blind electoral process had stated a cognizable equal-protection claim because the challenged district was "so extremely irregular on its face that it rationally can be viewed only as an effort to segregate the races for the purpose of voting, without regard for traditional districting principles and without sufficiently compelling justification."

The dissenters emphasized the novelty of this equal-protection claim. O'Connor and Thomas were in no credible position to deny that the claim was novel. Less than four months earlier, O'Connor had wondered aloud how an equal-protection claim might be evaluated.[30] Thus, whatever reasons Thomas may offer for following O'Connor in her analysis of the North Carolina case, he cannot claim to have been bound by law. *Shaw v. Reno* was, in crucial respects, a case of first impression, where the Court must wrestle with issues that have not previously received significant treatment. In such cases the judge's ability to do what seems best is acknowledged to be very broad. Moreover, it could be argued (as the dissent did) that the case was not at all one of first impression: that since the Voting Rights Act is intended to advance black political participation, the North Carolina plan, furthering that aim, was valid. Ultimately Thomas's "neutral" equal-protection objection to the plan elevated two cosmetic claims above an actual enhancement of black representation in Congress. Thomas endorsed O'Connor's distaste for odd shapes on electoral maps, as well as her independent distaste for race consciousness in American life.

Earlier cases invalidating boundaries of "uncouth shape" were motivated by a desire to prevent dilution of African American voters by white-dominated legislatures. They were not driven by an abstract aesthetic distaste for oddly shaped districts.[31] For O'Connor, in contrast, odd shape became the legal issue. Justice O'Connor actually cited the *Wall Street Journal*'s complaint that the district resembled a "bug splattered on a windshield." O'Connor (Thomas concurring) stated bluntly that "reapportionment is one area in which appearances do matter." It was now not the disenfranchisement of blacks that mattered, but simply the irregular shape of the district itself.

Thomas faces an uphill battle in showing how the elevation of aesthetics above political representation advances the progressive ends he endorses in theory. Thomas's probable explanation is not hard to imagine. While he was at the EEOC, Thomas lamented in 1988 that "many of the Court's decisions in the area of voting rights have presupposed that blacks, whites, Hispanics and other ethnic groups will inevitably vote in blocs."[32] Consistent with his pre-judicial ideology, and notwithstanding confirmation-hearing assurances that he had shed such baggage, Thomas agreed with O'Connor that the challenged district in *Shaw* would reinforce

the perception that members of the same racial group—regardless of their age, education, economic status, or the community in which they live—think alike, share the same political interests, and will prefer the same candidates at the polls. We have rejected such perceptions elsewhere as impermissible racial stereotypes. [In the political context, by perpetuating such notions], a racial gerrymander [*sic*] may exacerbate the very patterns of racial block voting that majority-minority districting is sometimes said to counteract.

Thomas and O'Connor here assume that sharing political interests and acting on them certainly reflects a stereotype rather than the truth. They apparently assume that choosing among three or four candidates in an election is an exercise in nuanced self-expression rather than in rough-and-tumble self-preservation. "Racial block voting" itself suddenly becomes the enemy. Yet the symmetrical assumption that if white block voting is bad, black block voting is also bad, ignores both America's history and the remedial purpose of the Voting Rights Act. It is what Stanley Fish has called a simplistic "moral algebra." If one consults history rather than geometry, it turns out that American whites have not been a discrete and insular minority facing permanent political irrelevance because of the block-voting patterns of America's black majority. Symmetrical application of the Voting Rights Act, to whites and blacks alike, makes as much sense as inflicting criminal sanctions, symmetrically, on the mugger and the mugged.

### Unhappy Truth

Thomas thinks that the law in general and the Constitution in particular were not intended to solve all of society's ills. This ideology is the basis of Thomas's frequent alliances with Justice Antonin Scalia. In a widely criticized death-penalty case in January 1993, Thomas joined Scalia's view that it is simply an *"unhappy truth that not every problem was meant to be solved by the United States Constitution, nor can be."* [33] In making this observation Scalia and Thomas cited a law review article, sarcastically entitled "Our Perfect Constitution," by a Boston University law professor (henceforth, the Boston Scholar) who belongs to the original-intent school of constitutional interpretation. That article argues that most constitutional scholars unjustifiably stretch the actual "constitutional text" and the "structure it creates" beyond all recognition, preferring to give the true text twisted readings consistent with the commentator's mere "principles of political morality." The Boston Scholar urges his audience to discard its wishful perfectionism and instead face the fact that America just does not after all have a perfect Constitution. In a concluding section entitled "Our 'Imperfect' Constitution" the Boston Scholar asserts that "in its historical setting, the original document was remarkably democratic." This is a problematic assertion given widely known facts. The document, far from dismantling slavery, arranged matters on the assumption of its continued existence. It thus countenanced a perverted, not remarkably democratic, idea of representation. Clarence Thomas himself concedes that the original document "was tainted by a deeply rooted history of prejudice." [34]

It is, then, hardly overexacting or perfectionist to leave the literal text of the document behind (assuming the impossible: that we could agree on a shared interpretation of it). Original-intent lawyers indeed generally concede that the document is, in some degree, an evolving one. Few of today's originalists would, for instance, abolish the female franchise. But the Boston originalist puts a different twist on such concessions. He argues that the warts in the original document support the view that the Constitution is not perfect in the sense of guaranteeing a society consistent with prevailing conceptions of justice *(then or now)*. The Bostonian has thus slid from the truism that the original text countenanced injustice, through the tendentious observation that the text was nevertheless somehow a remarkably democratic document, to the conclusion that the original presence of glaring injustice excuses today's own glaring injustices—or at least makes them the concern of something other than the Constitution. He continues:

The constitution has very few ideas to contribute to the social equality, privacy and autonomy claims now pressed by perfectionist commentators. The ideology contained in the constitution is significantly less embracing in scope than the ideology of the American way of life at the end of the twentieth century. It is, therefore, fundamentally wrong to believe that one can ascertain the meaning of the constitution by asking: "Is this what America stands for?" [35]

This is a lawyer's version of Julien Benda's article of faith: that inequality is an inevitable reality. If inequity is to go away, it is to do so through some other means. Yet this truth about the Constitution is not objective. It is ideological, and the Boston Scholar concedes as much: "To be sure, the Constitution embodies an ideology, but it is a limited one."

The question of whether the Constitution countenances what we agree to be serious injustice cannot be solved by investigation, or by simple assertions that the document somehow "contains" Tough ideology. The question is solved, rather, when we choose values. Thomas's commitments to racial (and other) justice would suggest that, all things being equal, he ought to endorse the ideology that advances those commitments. Yet Thomas's judicial decisionmaking instead reflects the hostile antiprogressive truths of the Boston Scholar.

Thomas is forever objecting to the use of the Constitution to "transform" the courts into boards of supervisors of various sorts. In *Doggett v. United States,* he objected to "turning the courts into boards of law enforcement supervision." In *Georgia v. McCollum,* Thomas objected to the "use of the constitution to regulate peremptory challenges" in criminal cases. In *Riggins v. Nevada,* he wrote that if a criminal defendant was forced to take medication against his will, that was a matter for some civil or other proceeding; it neither raised constitutional issues nor invalidated the defendant's conviction. In *Wright v. West,* Thomas argued for deferential review of state court determinations. In *Hudson v. McMillian,* he protested the "pervasive view" that the Constitution addresses all ills. More of the same in *Helling v. McKinney.*[36] And, despite his claim that, as a judge, he had somehow stripped away the baggage of ideology, Thomas's view in these cases predates his becoming a judge. While at the EEOC Thomas objected, in 1988, that "the Supreme Court has used [the Constitution] to make itself the national school board, parole board, health commission and elections commission, among other titles."[37]

Thomas, on and off the Supreme Court, has lost sight of (or ignored) the possibility that, as a Supreme Court justice or as chief EEOC administrator, he is not merely dispensing parental platitudes. It is his job to pronounce on *whether* it is, as the Boston Scholar urges, fundamentally wrong to ascertain the meaning of the Constitution by asking, Is this what America stands for? Moreover, the Boston Scholar's view is, it turns out, not widely held among legal scholars. The Bostonian openly rails against the legal academic consensus. Original intent is, it turns out, an eccentric constitutional theory nowadays. Yet Thomas and Scalia present it as truth in actual Supreme Court cases, wherein life is often literally at stake.

This is an important point because, although he frequently votes with the Court's conservative wing, Thomas's allegiance to racial justice puts an unusual spin on his adherence to original intent. If the unhappy truth of original intent is not objective truth—indeed, not even conventional wisdom within the legal community—Thomas has a problem. He faces an uphill battle explaining his vigorous allegiance to a beleaguered constitutional theory. Either the unpopular theory of original intent represents objective truth that Thomas just literally cannot avoid, or Thomas has been duped into thinking it does. If Thomas believes original intent represents objective truth, he has dropped the ball by failing to exploit the progressive possibilities opened up by contemporary skepticism about claims of objective truth. If

Thomas has been duped into this belief, he has dropped the ball in an even more obvious sense.

If, conversely, Thomas knows that original intent is not objective truth, and he has not simply been duped, then he must think that the outcomes generated by his chosen theory of original intent are themselves a benefit. However, neither Thomas nor Scalia nor their Boston Scholar even hazard the view that original intent generates *preferable* policy outcomes. They concede exactly the opposite. Original intent and the imperfect Constitution are, in their own words, *unhappy truths.* They'd love to help. Just can't. Hands tied. By "law."

### Muddled Partisanship

Thomas's tied hands are problematic because often he is clearly attempting to pursue some version of racial justice. He goes wrong in ways that are more complex than would flow from a single-minded and consistent hostility to African America. The cases grouped in this section will address Thomas's halting attempts to pursue the aims of racial justice within the ideological binds with which he fetters himself.

Most sensational is the Aryan Brotherhood case, *Dawson v. Delaware.*[38] There the Court, led by Chief Justice Rehnquist, forbade admitting into evidence, at a criminal trial, a stipulation of a defendant's membership in a white racist prison gang. Rehnquist held that the stipulation was not relevant to the defendant's sentencing and should have been excluded from the trial. Rehnquist adopted a First Amendment argument—a novelty in this context—and held that as the stipulation merely disclosed abstract beliefs, it was not relevant to criminal sentencing since sentencing was properly confined to the defendant's conduct. Rehnquist also denied that Aryan Brotherhood membership was "bad character" evidence in its own right. The *Dawson* majority's decision gives new force to the view that the First Amendment has today become the First Refuge of Scoundrels.

Thomas dissented. First, he argued that since jurors don't "leave their knowledge of the real world behind them," they can themselves weigh the importance of Aryan Brotherhood affiliations—at least as easily as they can weigh the more charming affiliations (family ties, etc.) that the defendant had adduced to mitigate his sentence. Second, Thomas challenged the core idea of Rehnquist's novel free-speech argument. Thomas argued that abstract beliefs themselves could be relevant to the character inquiry in sentencing decisions; that racist beliefs themselves were probative of character; that the First Amendment had never previously been read to limit the scope of the character inquiry in penal sentencing; and that it was strange that the First Amendment should suddenly apply where racism was the character evidence in question. (Scalia did not join Thomas's dissent but rather joined Rehnquist's opinion in its entirety.)

Underlying Thomas's disagreement with Rehnquist was the chameleonlike manner in which free-speech analysis responds to the individual judge's view of the values that are set up in opposition to the First Amendment. Rehnquist, Thomas implicitly argued, just didn't think racist beliefs in themselves enough to enhance a criminal's sentence. Thomas, placing a higher value on racial justice, disagreed. Yet when a white youngster burned a cross, Klan style, on a black family's lawn in Minnesota, Thomas's reckoning of the balance between "free speech"[39] and racism changed. In that case, *R.A.V. v. City of St. Paul,*[40] Minnesota's highest court had upheld a hate-speech law as reflecting that state's aversion to messages "based on virulent notions of racial supremacy." And the Supreme Court, Thomas concurring, knocked it down.

Thomas's conclusion in *R.A.V.* does not sit well with his arguments in *Dawson.* In *Dawson,* where Rehnquist required conduct, not mere gang membership, before "free speech" was overridden, Thomas was mystified. In *Dawson,* Thomas thought it absurd not to infer illicit conduct from gang membership. Conversely, in *R.A.V.* there was actual and overt conduct—cross burning—yet the guy who burned the cross escaped enhanced punishment. In *Dawson,* Thomas argued that racist ideology was, worse than valueless, positively evil: it was a reason to enhance a criminal's sentence. One might, then, think that Thomas would agree with Justice Blackmun in *R.A.V.,* who saw "no First Amendment values that are compromised by a law that prohibits hoodlums from driving minorities out of their homes by burning crosses on their lawns, but [who saw] great harm in preventing the people of Saint Paul from specifically punishing the race-based fighting words that so prejudice their community."

Actually, Thomas took the opposite view, that the cross burning was worthy of constitutional protection. Thomas agreed with Scalia's argument that the cases mentioned by the dissenters, in support of the Minnesota statute, didn't mean what they said (were not "literally true").

Conversely, the Scalia opinion was, in the dissenting Justice White's words, "an arid, doctrinaire interpretation [that is] mischievous at best and will surely confuse the lower courts." The Scalia opinion, joined by Thomas, "casts aside long-established First Amendment doctrine without the benefit of briefing and adopts an untried theory," said Justice White. Whatever explanation Thomas may have for his *R.A.V.* concurrence, it cannot be that he was bound by law. And a reason for Thomas's discrepant behavior in *Dawson* as compared with his decision in *R.A.V.* is not difficult to uncover. The campaign against "political correctness," the campaign to protect race baiters, was not a factor in *Dawson*. Thomas's view in *Dawson* would have enhanced a prisoner's sentence and so would have straightforwardly accorded with law-and-order ideology. In *R.A.V.*, there was an additional issue: law-and-order concerns were complicated by concerns over whether to enable communities to address the harms inflicted by race baiters. Thomas thus faces another uphill battle in explaining how joining the anti-p.c. bandwagon in *R.A.V.* advanced racial justice. In contrast, in a subsequent case not involving a hate-speech statute, but rather a statute enhancing a felon's sentence if he or she intentionally selected a victim on the basis of race, Thomas had no problem voting with a unanimous Court that the penalty enhancement was valid. In this case, *Wisconsin v. Mitchell,*[41] Mitchell, the defendant, was black.

In summary, Thomas's racial-justice partisanship in *Dawson,* appearing to suggest that racial animus is a distinct harm, quickly became muddled when subjected to the tensions of the anti-p.c. ideology in *R.A.V.*—then re-emerged, ironically, to the detriment of a black criminal defendant in *Mitchell.*

A further notable instance in which Thomas was responsible for significant, but again disappointing, infusion of racial-justice insight in Supreme Court deliberations was the case of *U.S. v. Fordice.*[42] There a unanimous Court held that merely implementing race-neutral university standards did not necessarily fulfill a state's duty to disestablish its prior segregated system, where the original enactment of those standards was meant to discriminate. Mississippi's intransigence in dismantling segregation was well documented, and was noted by the Court. The unanimous decision of the Court is therefore relatively unsurprising. Even Justice Scalia, finding it impossible to resist the celebratory rhetoric that fuels the case law under *Brown,* entered a (tortured and extremely reluctant) concurring opinion.

Thomas's separate concurring opinion emphasized the race-conscious point that the goal of desegregated education was not the simple elimination of all observed racial imbalance, especially if that would simply mean the destruction of black colleges. Scalia, in contrast, speculated that the elimination of these colleges "may be good social policy." Whereas Thomas embraced such colleges, Scalia merely noted that "the present petitioners ... would not agree" that elimination of these colleges was a good idea. Scalia was merely interested in defending the ideological position that few things under the sun are barred by the "imperfect" Constitution—and black colleges are not among the things barred. The contrast with Thomas's affirmative concern for these colleges illustrates that Thomas is a partisan of racial justice. Yet, even here, Thomas dropped the ball.

The issue that none of the justices faced squarely in *Fordice,* and on which Thomas dropped the ball, was whether there might be a constitutional obligation, given Mississippi's years of intransigence, to provide *restitutionary funds* to Mississippi's historically black institutions. The Court's self-styled centrists might perhaps be expected to recoil at constitutionally mandated funding of what they would see as balkanized higher education. Thomas, part of the antibalkanization crowd in the apportionment cases, momentarily defected in *Fordice.* Thomas invoked W. E. B. Du Bois's clarion call to "repudiate this unbearable assumption of the right to kill institutions unless they conform to one narrow standard." One way to kill institutions is to starve them of cash and strip them of functions. The Court found that Mississippi had done exactly that by manipulating the teaching and research functions (or "mission designations") allotted to the various state institutions:

The institutional mission designations adopted in 1981 have as their antecedents the policies enacted to perpetuate racial separation during the de jure segregated regime. ... *The inequalities among the institutions largely follow the mission designations, and the mission designations to some degree follow the historical racial assignments.* ... The mission designations had the effect of maintaining the more limited program scope at the historically black universities. (Emphasis added)

Yet remedial funding to rectify the deliberate prior deprivation of black public and private colleges was not even seriously on the Court's agenda. The majority framed the issue in such a way as wholly to suppress this important remedial aspect of the petitioner's claim, then icily dismissed it, implying that it was an instance of special pleading: "If we understand private petitioners to press us to order the upgrading of [the historically black colleges] solely so that they may be publicly financed, exclusively black enclaves by private choice, we reject that request."

In sending the case back to the lower court the majority opinion did, however, leave open the question of whether "an increase in funding is necessary to achieve a full dismantlement" of segregation under the standards the Court had outlined. The issue of whether an enhanced funding claim could be pressed under the standard of "full dismantlement" thus remained tantalizingly open for the trial phase of the case. Thomas, far from prying this possibility further open in the separate concurrence he took the trouble to write, completely dropped the ball. He chose to address the issue of whether a state is constitutionally required to maintain its black colleges as such. And Thomas's answer to this question flows inexorably from the familiar unhappy truth about the imperfect Constitution: "A state is not constitutionally required to maintain its historically black institutions as such." Clarence Thomas, Supreme Court justice, included in his opinion a passionate *exhortation* that black colleges not be eviscerated, but could find no way to translate this eloquence into a legal command. Thomas's legal decision is thus little more than an appeal to the empathy of the intransigent Mississippi administrators. And empathy is perhaps not a good legal-political strategy, especially in Mississippi.

Thus Thomas, hero of the black colleges, writing a separate concurring opinion for their ostensible benefit, addressing an issue that the Court's majority left vague and thought should be "carefully explored on remand," succeeded in conjuring a hostile certainty: he made it look as though the lower court, on remand, could *not* find a constitutional obligation to leave the black colleges intact. Justice White, by his more vague and cautious language, may well have been gently steering the reviewing court in the opposite direction. White left open the possibility that the lower court, after careful review on remand, validly could find that closing a historically black college as a "solution" to duplicative facilities would be unconstitutional because of the undue dislocation it would cause its ostensible beneficiaries (black students and faculty). Thomas's would-be helpful concurrence actually clarified Justice White's artful opinion *to the detriment* of the black colleges on whose behalf Thomas was apparently moved to write. Thomas dropped the ball because of the unhappy truth that the Constitution does not solve all the ills of historically black colleges.

## Thomas's Pursuit of Fair Death

There is more Tough Justice in Thomas's death penalty jurisprudence. Civil rights activists have long favored abolition of the death penalty, arguing that it offends humanitarian principles and that the U.S. death penalty regime is not rational, is racially skewed, and is therefore unconstitutional. The late Justice Thurgood Marshall consistently spoke for this view on the Court. In 1976, however, three judges—Justices Stewart, Powell, and Stevens—rejected the view that state-imposed death is inherently unconstitutional, and the Court's cases in this area continue to occasion some of its most bitter dissents and conflicting opinions.

In this setting—intense controversy over whether and in what circumstances the Court will allow death sentences imposed by states to proceed—Clarence Thomas might have continued Thurgood Marshall's argument that death is an unconstitutional penalty in all circumstances. But Thomas's view is different. Like Tough Love lawyer Randall Kennedy, Thomas assumes, without argument, that the death penalty is of benefit to the communities with which he is concerned. Alternatively, Thomas simply assumes that the question, Is death different? is settled law, beyond his power to affect. Finally, Thomas assumes that, even if death is somehow an unduly onerous or unjust punishment, that does not render it unconstitutional since, unhappily, our imperfect Constitution countenances injustice.

Thomas's racially progressive concern is not to abolish death but to make its implementation racially fair. Numerous commentators, academics, judges, bar associations, public-interest groups, civil rights groups, and congressional committees have become convinced that this is a futile course. In early 1994 Justice Blackmun, who was among the Supreme Court's upholders of the death regime in the mid-1970s, concluded that he could no longer in good conscience "tinker with the machinery of death" in the ostensible pursuit of fairness. To Thomas these views are all blind orthodoxy. Thomas goes further even than those who think that a discretionary death penalty is useful in extreme cases. In *Graham v. Collins*,[43] Thomas went out of his way to advocate mandatory death sentences (the issue was, Thomas conceded, not before the Court).[44] Thomas's "fairness" approach to death is, theoretically, an effort to repair the administration of the death penalty so that it helps black and white citizens equally and punishes black and white offenders evenhandedly. That Thomas's view, in practice, happens to coincide with the agenda of America's Dan Quayles and David Dukes is, ostensibly, not a reflection on Thomas's "authentic" commitment to racial (and other) justice. Thomas ultimately asserts that the death penalty is compatible with his allegiances to America's dispossessed.

Thomas, urging that mandatory death sentences advance racial justice, insists that a mandatory regime eliminates the jury's otherwise "boundless discretion," which the jury may exercise on the basis of any number of arbitrary or irrelevant factors, including that of race. Thomas objects to his opponents' insistence that the jury must be able to express a "reasoned moral response." He cautions,

Beware the word "moral" when used in an opinion of this Court. This word is a vessel of nearly infinite capacity—just as it may allow the sentencer to express benevolence, it may allow [her] to cloak latent animus. A judgment that some will consider a "moral response" may secretly be based on caprice or even outright prejudice.[45]

Thomas here argues that discretion is the enemy of the rule of law; that the rule of law, happily, conquers discretion and fends off racism. Thomas does not pause to consider whether the discretion ostensibly exiled from the courtroom is merely cast in another shape or shifted to other, equally arbitrary decisionmakers. Disabling a jury from reaching any sentence but death does not expunge that jury's discretion. Instead, knowing that conviction will inexorably mean death, juries may simply decline to convict those with whom they empathize and disproportionately convict those with whom they don't. Moreover, to the extent that the jury genuinely loses any discretion through Thomas's mandatory statutes, *that* discretion does not itself disappear. It is merely handed to the prosecutors, who may then be as arbitrary as they wish in deciding whom to charge with mandatory death offenses and whom not so to charge. District attorneys, frequently selected in ordinary elections amid rhetoric resembling the Willie Horton campaign, could then easily place Negroes on a statutory conveyor belt to certain death. Moreover, this issue is such a conspicuous feature of lawyerly debate that to say Thomas has made a good-faith error is to displace an unseemly charge of betrayal with an unflattering claim of ineptitude. It may be, as Thomas suggests, that the power to be lenient is also the power to discriminate. But it is a strange solution to this problem to turn that discretion over to a single unaccountable prosecutor, having (supposedly) taken it away from twelve jurors supervised by a judge. The attempt to sanitize death by stamping out discretion is a fool's errand.

## The Unhappy Death of the Innocent

Thomas does not abandon, even in the death-penalty context, the unhappy truth that the American Constitution is imperfect. He laments that "the

Court has put itself in the seemingly permanent business of supervising capital sentencing procedures"[46] and asserts that the Constitution simply doesn't outlaw a fallible death-penalty regime. It was in the death-penalty case of *Herrera v. Collins*[47] that Thomas and Scalia invoked the Boston Scholar in order to advance their criticism of the "reluctance of the present Court to admit publicly that Our Perfect Constitution lets stand any injustice, much less the execution of an innocent man." It was in the sensitive context of state-sanctioned death that Thomas and Scalia cited someone called Professor Monaghan and his article, "which discusses the unhappy truth that not every problem was meant to be solved by the United States Constitution, nor can be." It is important to be clear exactly what, in the context of the *Herrera* case, Thomas's unhappy truth meant.

Petitioner Herrera asked the Court to grant him a new trial or at least to vacate his death sentence. Herrera claimed that new evidence (affidavits showing that someone else committed the killing) demonstrated he was actually innocent—a recognized legal basis for "habeas corpus relief." The Supreme Court denied his petition, insisting that habeas corpus relief is designed merely to ensure that individuals are not imprisoned in violation of the Constitution, not to correct errors of fact. Rehnquist (Thomas concurring) wrote that habeas relief was concerned only with unconstitutional *detention,* not unconstitutional *conviction* of an accused. This distinction is eminently pedantic. The detention (in this case, *execution*) of the petitioner is entirely predicated on the conviction. If new doubts cloud the conviction, it is hard to see how the detention and execution retain their legitimacy. It is here that the specter of unhappy truth arises. Rehnquist (with Thomas) suggests the harsh truth that "due process does not require that every conceivable step be taken, at whatever cost, to eliminate the possibility of convicting an innocent person." The imperfect Constitution alas requires, said Thomas and Rehnquist, a showing of an "independent constitutional violation" in addition to mere innocence.

Justices O'Connor and Kennedy, who furnished two vital votes for Rehnquist's opinion, wrote separately to emphasize a different view: that "the execution of a legally and factually innocent person would be a constitutionally intolerable event." The O'Connor-Kennedy concurrence rested on the "fundamental fact" (persuasively rejected by the dissenters) that Herrera was *actually* "not innocent in any sense of the word," since the new evidence "was bereft of credibility."

Scalia and Thomas, meanwhile, urged the contrary gospel of the imperfect

Constitution. Their separate concurring opinion directly contradicted the O'Connor-Kennedy view that the Constitution precluded execution of the actually innocent. Thomas and Scalia plainly said the Constitution did *not* forbid "the execution of an innocent man who has received, though to no avail, all the process that our society has traditionally deemed adequate." And they explicitly signaled lower courts not to adopt a "strange regime" that assumes that such a constitutional right exists. Invoking their Boston Scholar, they reminded lower courts of the "unhappy truth that not every problem was meant to be solved by the United States Constitution, *nor can be*" (emphasis added).

But what does this "can" mean? In other contexts it refers to the supposedly inherent limitations on what (e.g.) the state bureaucracy can do to raise the morale of black inner-city youth or to eliminate the despair of white Wall Street cocaine addicts. Here, however, the task is simpler. The Supreme Court is merely giving marching orders to lower courts about what to do in habeas corpus cases. The only question here is, What *should* the Supreme Court tell the lower courts to do? The "can" misleadingly suggests a nonexistent limit to the institutional competence of the Court in this area.[48] Scalia and Thomas are no doubt in the habit of voicing such institutional pessimism. But whatever the slim validity of such reasoning in other contexts, it is strikingly out of place where the Supreme Court is simply doling out instructions to lower courts. Scalia and Thomas here presented ideological prescription as fact. They think habeas review *ought* to be narrow. They present this controversial opinion as though it represents neutrally discernable original intent and objective fidelity to the Constitution's "historical moorings." They went beyond the Rehnquist majority opinion, itself criticized by Justice Blackmun, dissenting, as "perilously close to simple murder." Blackmun's harsh comment on the majority opinion is actually *overgenerous* if applied to the Scalia-Thomas opinion. The Thomas-Scalia opinion took the remarkable view that, unhappily, the Constitution does not bar simple murder of the actually innocent, once it is performed by a state after compliance with certain procedures.

How can Thomas explain this suggestion in terms of loyal dissent? If Thomas simply thinks that original intent is the best neutral legal reading of the Constitution, he must explain why so few legal scholars take it seriously. Perhaps he thinks that his version of originalism leads to preferable outcomes in the cases before him, but this argument looks odd alongside his own description of originalism's limits as *unhappy* ones. Once we point out that all interpretations of the Constitution are ideological, and no reading is privileged, we have cut Thomas some slack to pursue his values. He may now, as keeper of this improved and flexible Constitution, do more than he previously felt possible. Suddenly, it's no problem for the Court to be a Board of Supervision of this and that—the only remaining question being whether supervising this or that is itself a good thing. Now Thomas must squarely face the question, Given the current state of affairs, would it be better or worse for the dispossessed in a fallible criminal-justice system if lower courts could rescue people from death upon the production of new evidence of their innocence? Thomas is forced to face that moral question, that *ought*. He can no longer hide behind unhappy truth.

Within this picture of justification, Thomas will have a hard time explaining the death penalty case of *Lockhart v. Fretwell*,[49] where the facts were, in a crucial sense, the exact opposite of *Herrera v. Collins*. In *Herrera*, the majority felt that the petitioner's evidence of actual innocence was flimsy—was unlikely to have affected anything even had it been available at trial (the dissenters disagreed). Conversely, in *Fretwell*, the Court did not doubt that the basis of the petitioner's complaint could easily have changed the result of his trial. The petitioner was sentenced to death for murder committed during a robbery. Under the applicable sentencing statute, the fact that a defendant committed a crime for money was itself a reason (an "aggravating factor") for the jury to impose a death sentence. Since pecuniary gain is, however, already an element of the crime of robbery, its reintroduction as an independent aggravating factor in determining the defendant's sentence was double counting, and violated the applicable law at the time. But the prisoner's lawyer did not raise this crucial issue at his trial, and the prisoner was sentenced to death. After his conviction and sentencing, the prohibition of double counting was overruled. The question before Justice Thomas and the Supreme Court was whether, against this backdrop, the petitioner's death sentence could stand. The Court held that the sentence was valid even while conceding that the petitioner's claim would *actually* have affected the outcome of the case.

Whereas the Court in *Herrera* treated the petitioner's new evidence as a mere formality because it would have had no actual impact on the result, the Court in *Fretwell* argued that although the petitioner would actually have escaped death but for the proven defect, this too was an insufficient basis for invalidation of a death sentence. Rehnquist in *Fretwell* suddenly rejected "an analysis focusing solely on mere outcome determination without attention to whether the result of the proceeding was fundamentally fair."

Placing *Herrera* alongside *Fretwell,* both decided by the Supreme Court on the *same day,* suggests the following: a petitioner who raises a procedural challenge must also show that the alleged failure of procedure actually affected the substance of the result; yet a petitioner who proves that her challenge would actually have changed the result must, additionally, show a procedural deficiency—and one that is not merely technical, but "fundamental." The only apparent principle here is the dismantling of protections afforded individuals accused of crimes. Justices Stevens and Blackmun dissented, emphasizing that the Court's doctrinal zig-zags "cannot be reconciled with [its] duty to administer justice impartially." Justice Thomas, for his part, "join[ed] the Court's opinion in its entirety."

## The Unhappy Truth of Imperfect Trials

The Court's maneuverings continued in *Doggett v. United States,*[50] where Thomas (joined by Scalia and Rehnquist) wrote a dissent from Souter's decision. The Souter majority held that an eight-and-one-half-year delay between a person's indictment and arrest violated the Constitution's speedy-trial clause and that long delay was presumptively prejudicial to the defendant's ability to defend himself.

Thomas, dissenting, stood by the unhappy truth that the courts simply are not "boards of law enforcement supervision." Thomas cited British case law from a nineteenth-century treatise and proclaimed—overlooking 1776— "Time doesn't run against the King." Thomas argued that the Sixth Amendment simply doesn't protect against mere prejudice to a party's defense or mere disruption of a party's now-law-abiding life. While the petitioner had undisputedly become a model citizen, Thomas insisted that "however uplifting this tale of personal redemption, our task is to illuminate the protections of the Speedy Trial Clause, not to take the measure of one man's life." Unhappily, the accused's personal story, and his admitted present rectitude, were irrelevant to matters of crime and punishment.

Yet in the days immediately following his nomination to the Court, amid all the anecdotes about growing up in Pin Point, Georgia, Thomas told another story. He told of arriving to serve in Washington, D.C., and seeing, outside his office window, handcuffed blacks being put in prison vans. His widely broadcast response: "There but for the grace of God go I." Remarks like this furthered the disarray of Thomas's opponents and fanned the hopes of some that, on the bench, Thomas would be unable to renounce his "life experiences." They felt he would inevitably decide cases in accord with the empathy obviously reflected in this anecdote. But now that Thomas has the judge's job, justice is apparently someone else's work.

In *Riggins v. Nevada*,[51] a handcuffed man petitioned for a fair trial—including a fair chance to press his mental-illness defense—in which the jury might observe his natural demeanor. The state insisted on drugging him. When he just said no, they went ahead anyway, claiming the drug was necessary to render him competent for trial. The man argued that since his defense was mental incompetence (insanity), and the state wished to drug him in order, precisely, to render him competent for trial, the state was seeking to disable his defense. The Court's majority agreed and rejected the view that expert testimony was an adequate stand-in for an unexpurgated display of the defendant's drugless demeanor. Justice Kennedy, writing separately, doubted that a state could ever make the "extraordinary showing" necessary to render constitutional forced drugging intended to secure the accused's trial competence. Justice Kennedy suggested that a state's force-feeding of drugs for the "avowed purpose of changing the defendant's behavior" was like tampering with trial evidence.

Justice Thomas, with Scalia, dissented. Thomas, ignoring Kennedy's powerful evidence-tampering analogy, suggested that the forced drugging did not derogate from a "fundamentally fair hearing." It was evidently not Thomas's job to require that trial courts prevent the state from force-feeding drugs to prisoners it is trying to convict. Thomas urged that even if the state improperly force-fed the drug, that was a matter for a separate civil lawsuit. In Thomas's view, the defendant ought, once convicted and comfortably settled in his jail cell, to retain an attorney and initiate a brand-new lawsuit against the state.

## Unhappy Prison Conditions

According to Thomas prisons are, unhappily, uncomfortable places. In *Hudson v. McMillian*,[52] the majority (Thomas dissenting) held that excessive physical force by prison guards is unconstitutional cruel and unusual punishment, even in the absence of serious injury. The absence of serious injury, wrote Justice O'Connor, does not end the constitutional inquiry. Thomas

(Scalia concurring) disagreed. Invoking once again the unhappy truths of original intent and of the imperfect Constitution, Thomas again railed against the pervasive view that the Constitution addresses all of society's ills. The truth is, Thomas assured us, that excessive force occasioning "insignificant harm" is not within the reach of the Constitution. Such force may be immoral, tortious, criminal, or even unconstitutional in some (unspecified) way. It simply isn't a violation of the cruel and unusual punishment clause. Thomas asserted that "punishment," in its original meaning, refers strictly to pain inflicted as "part of the sentence for a crime . . . and not generally to any hardship that might *befall* a prisoner during incarceration" (emphasis added). Excessive force at the hands of a prison guard is, apparently, a random misfortune: like winning the lottery, except less fun. Just one of life's hard knocks. On this view, guards could beat prisoners and blame fate. Justice Blackmun, concurring in the opinion from which Thomas dissented, offered an unsettling list of punishments that might inflict pain without leaving traces of serious injury: leather straps, rubber hoses, naked fists, electric current, asphyxiation short of death, intentional exposure to heat or cold, and injection with psychosis-inducing drugs. And Blackmun cited cases where U.S. courts have found that such abuse has actually occurred in U.S. prisons.

Faced with this litany of pain, Thomas deferred to (his version of) the historical moorings of the Eighth Amendment. He lectured that "historically, the lower courts routinely rejected prisoner grievances by explaining that the courts had no role in regulating prison life." Thus, while "abusive behavior by prison guards is deplorable conduct that properly evokes outrage and contempt, that does not mean that it is invariably unconstitutional. The Eighth Amendment is not, and should not be turned into, a National Code of Prison Regulations."

Thomas continued: the "primary responsibility for preventing and punishing such conduct rests not with the Federal Constitution but with the laws and regulations of the various states." Someone else's job. And if they don't do it, nothing. Yet isn't it the role of courts to make stuff happen when it should happen but, for whatever reason, isn't happening? Thomas pronounces himself unhappily bound to allow prison-guard violence, even as he *dissents from* the outcome he ostensibly wants to reach. Yet few criticized the Court's majority for violating the true Constitution when they voted the happy way in *Hudson*.

Months later, the Court revisited prison conditions in *Helling v. McKin-*

*ney.*[53] There a prisoner said that the state, by confining him to a cell with a smoker, unconstitutionally exposed him to passive smoking and its attendant health risks. A magistrate dismissed the case without a hearing. The Court of Appeals reversed, directing a full hearing on the merits. A majority of the Supreme Court (Thomas and Scalia dissenting) declined to reverse the Court of Appeals and remanded the case for a hearing on the merits. In *Helling,* Thomas conceded that contemporary popular and legal culture both adopt a broader view than his own of the Constitution's scope, yet he stood by his narrower opinion, saying that it was dictated by the dictionary and by history. Indeed, Thomas stood by his narrow reading while conceding that it was *not* dictated by dictionary and history. While conceding that "the evidence is not overwhelming" in favor of his narrow view, Thomas claimed to find sufficient support in the history of the Eighth Amendment so as to "shift the burden of persuasion to those who would apply the Eighth Amendment to prison conditions." Thomas insisted that the burden had not yet been discharged, even while conceding that the view he opposes represents consensus. The idea that law forces a reluctant Thomas to abuse the dispossessed is perhaps wearing thin.

### Civil Rights: The Unhappy Absence of Meaningful Evidence

Thomas has not yet confronted a Supreme Court case in which the validity of an affirmative action or set-aside program was directly in issue, but there is already much in his record on the Court (to say nothing of his extensive extrajudicial pronouncements) to foreclose optimism. During his brief tenure on the Court of Appeals for the District of Columbia Circuit, before he was nominated to the Supreme Court, Thomas wrote the opinion of the Court of Appeals in *Lamprecht v. FCC.*[54] That decision reflects Thomas's indifference to gender discrimination.

In *Lamprecht,* Thomas's task was to apply the landmark Supreme Court case of *Metro Broadcasting, Inc. v. FCC.*[55] In *Metro Broadcasting,* the Supreme Court upheld the FCC's policy of promoting broadcast diversity by awarding "enhancement" for minority status when issuing licenses. The FCC also permitted a certain limited category of existing licenses (those subject to "distress sales") to be sold only to minority-controlled firms. The pre-Thomas Supreme Court, reversing the D.C. Circuit Court where Thomas was then tenured, held in *Metro Broadcasting* that these FCC policies did not violate the Constitution because they had been specifically mandated by

JUSTICE THOMAS'S SINS 161

Congress and served the important governmental purpose of broadcast diversity.

In the subsequent *Lamprecht* case Thomas wrote an opinion enforcing a narrow construction of *Metro Broadcasting*. Thomas upheld a male complainant's claim that an award of extra credit to a female applicant for a license "deprived him of his constitutional right to equal protection of the laws." Voting with Thomas was the D.C. Circuit Court's Judge Buckley, brother of William F. Buckley of *National Review* and talk-show fame. Judge Mikva, the final vote on the three-judge panel, dissented.

Thomas held that there was no "substantial" relation between the goal of broadcast diversity and the FCC's gender-based preferences because the alleged connection was not supported by "meaningful evidence." At a glance Thomas's opinion appears preoccupied with the parsing of statistics. It contains a four-page appendix of numerical tables, and Thomas repeatedly disparages his dissenting colleague, Judge Mikva, for the alleged weakness of the empirical case underlying Mikva's finding of a sufficient link between gender preference and broadcast diversity.

Yet Thomas's empirical edifice comes crashing down in footnote 9 of his opinion. Thomas there addresses Judge Mikva's argument that "judges have no basis, except their own policy preferences," for concluding that there is an insufficient connection between gender diversity and programming diversity. Mikva emphasized that the Constitution does not identify the "mystical point" at which a statistical correlation is sufficient to survive equal-protection challenge. Thomas, far from resisting this direct challenge to the empirical edifice upon which he built his argument, simply agreed. In fact Thomas, sounding momentarily like a member of the Critical Legal Studies movement, affirmed that Mikva "is not the first to criticize the [applicable legal] test for its indeterminacy." Thomas then admitted that the line he chose to draw in invalidating the program was different from the line drawn by the *Metro Broadcasting* Court, was also different from the line drawn in another similar case, and was, too, different from the line drawn by his very own dissenting colleague, Judge Mikva, in the case at hand.

Thomas's response to this realization was simply to assert that "the line that we draw is neither more nor less principled than the line that he draws; *our lines are merely grounded in different exercise of judgment*" (emphasis added). This confession that his own decision is ultimately a straightforward value judgment is seriously at odds with the empirical paraphernalia (the charts and such) and the empiricist rhetoric that clutter the main text of Thomas's opinion. Despite all those numbers, the question was simply one of moral and political values: Which judgment, whose line drawing, was better? This question is not amenable to a "competent" legal answer. In ostensibly focusing on an empirical exercise in the main body of his opinion, Thomas merely glossed over the straightforward value judgment suppressed in footnote 9. This ideological choice—who would you prefer to win the case?—is always central to allocating burdens of proof in law, since when courts make "findings of fact" they are not finding objective fact, but constructing legal truth. It is thus no accident, shifting our attention, that the most controversial aspect of Title VII civil rights litigation is the allocation of the burden of proof as between the defendant-employer and the plaintiff-employee. The Rehnquist Court's case law in this area is responsible for much of its reputation for right-wing activism.

In *Hazen Paper Co. v. Biggins*,[56] Kennedy's concurring opinion (joined by Thomas and Rehnquist) labored the point, extraneous to the facts of the case, that the Court was not extending the "disparate impact" theory of Title VII to the new context of age-discrimination law. Disparate impact analysis allows a plaintiff to rely on statistical imbalances to raise a presumption of discrimination against her employer. Thomas, at the EEOC, criticized such theories as a surreal departure from reality. The question at stake in such cases, however, is not "reality" but, rather, which party *ought* to bear the risk of inevitable difficulties of proof in Title VII cases. That choice is, patently, one of value judgment as much as factual investigation. It presents a straightforward clash between favoring business defendants or favoring plaintiffs who can point to racial imbalances.

Moreover, in the Title VII case of *St. Mary's Honor Center v. Hicks*,[57] issues of broad statistical analysis were absent, and Thomas nevertheless reached an unhappy conclusion. *Hicks* was exactly the kind of case—where a person is "individually discriminated against"—that Benjamin Hooks, NAACP leader at the time of the Thomas hearings, suggested that Thomas would "go to the ends of the earth" to remedy. Thomas didn't.

The Court in *Hicks* faced the question of who must prove what in Title VII cases. Thomas and the majority held that where the employee alleges discrimination, and the employer comes forth with alleged legitimate reasons for the firing, which the employee in turn proves to be a sham, the employee is *still* not entitled to judgment as a matter of law. The employee still faces a further hurdle: the "ultimate burden of persuading the trier of fact that he has been the victim of intentional discrimination." And even though Scalia agreed that the employee had proven "the existence of a crusade to terminate him," he still had further to prove "that the crusade was racially rather than personally motivated." Scalia, Thomas, and the majority gave the employee a rather full plate of proving to do.

Faced with the argument that an employer who proffers fraudulent non-discriminatory rationales for a firing can hardly complain if judgment goes against her, Scalia (Thomas concurring) responded with the simple truth that dealing with dishonesty was not the Court's job under Title VII: "Title VII is not a cause of action for perjury; we have other civil and criminal remedies for that." The majority result in *Hicks* was, as the dissenting Justice Souter pointed out, that even where an employee discredits an employer's nondiscriminatory explanations, a lower court, hostile to civil rights claims, may continue "to roam the record" to find some possible nondiscriminatory reason that may support an assertion that the employee had failed to make an affirmative showing that race was the reason for adverse treatment.

Perhaps Thomas's view in *Hicks* simply reflected the true legal nature of Title VII, but others differed. The dissenters argued persuasively that the Court was abandoning "decades of stable law." Given this existence of controversy (three justices voted against the result), Thomas cannot claim that he was bound to reach a result onerous to the civil rights plaintiffs for whom we'd been assured he'd go to the wall. Thomas is thus thrown back upon nonlegal arguments. He must argue that the result reached was the ethically right result. This is likely to be an uphill battle for him. In the disparate-impact situation, Thomas's ideological position—itself questionable—is that reliance on broad statistics and group claims is a departure from reality. Thomas opposes disparate-impact analysis because, he says, he prefers individual claims over "surreal" statistical games. Yet the employee in *Hicks* did not invoke broad statistical arguments (themselves entirely desirable). He, rather, specifically showed that there was a "campaign" against him. He very specifically showed that the employer's explanations were lies. All this was, unhappily, not enough to support a legal finding of discrimination.

## Civil Rights: The Unhappy Absence of Real Harm

In *Associated General Contractors v. City of Jacksonville, Florida*,[58] Thomas wrote for the majority that a contractors' association had the legal right ("standing") to challenge a minority set-aside program, without any need to show that one of its members would have received a contract absent the program. The standing doctrine ensures that a party seeking to invoke the machinery of the courts has suffered a material harm going beyond that suffered by persons in general. Standing doctrine denies legal recourse to busybodies and to those with trivial injuries.

Yet the rules governing standing are notoriously unpredictable. In *General Contractors,* the association had not shown that the program it sought to challenge deprived it or any of its members of a construction contract. Moreover, the particular regulation the association sought to challenge had been repealed and replaced, making the whole case, in the eyes of two members of the Court, an impermissible academic exercise (O'Connor and Blackmun, dissenting).

There were thus plausible arguments that the "right" the contractors' association sought to enforce in *General Contractors* was, less than trivial, nonexistent. Justice Thomas nevertheless wrote that the relevant "injury in fact" for the standing analysis was present. In stark contrast, Thomas elsewhere wrote that where a civil rights plaintiff wins an actual legal victory, "mere moral satisfaction" would not meet the standard for a recovery of attorney's fees. Mere moral vindication without a money award was simply too trivial a victory to support an award of attorney's fees. In the latter case, *Farrar v. Hobby,*[59] the Court faced the question of whether a civil rights plaintiff who wins a nominal award of money damages is a "prevailing party" in the sense that would entitle her to an award of attorney's fees under the civil rights statute. The prospect of such a fee award is all, frequently, that induces a lawyer to take a poor person's case.

While Thomas held that Farrar's nominal monetary-damages award satisfied the "prevailing party" analysis because it involved an actual money victory (however small), Farrar was ultimately denied a fee award anyway because, Thomas said, the smallness of the damages award affected the "propriety" of an attorney's fee award. This decision was Tough in two senses.

First, the requirement of actual monetary loss (however small) before a legal victory is considered *real* for purposes of a fee award would exclude many of the most striking civil rights cases. Many such cases were fought and won over precisely symbolic issues (where's the money damage in being denied service at a lunch counter in Alabama?). A widespread criticism of orthodox economics and other social sciences is that these disciplines assume that all motives are monetary and so oversimplify the complex reasons why people do the things they do. While arguments favoring legal recognition of symbolic harms are strongly supported by those opposed to hate speech, such arguments are not the sole property of the Left.[60] Justice Thomas, in *Farrar*, entirely dropped the ball on this issue. While he accepted aesthetic and symbolic harms in *Shaw v. Reno* in order to invalidate a black congressional district, he here rejected symbolic victories and enforced instead the old idea that a legal victory means a monetary award.

Second, the plaintiff's showing, in *Farrar*, of an actual (nominal) monetary award was itself of no avail. Thomas went on to hold that while the nominal-damages award satisfied the "prevailing party" requirement of an attorney's-fee award, the smallness of the victory could nevertheless render a fee award improper. O'Connor stated the Court's view bluntly: "If ever there was a plaintiff who deserved no attorney's fee at all, that plaintiff is Joseph Farrar." *Despite* his money award, Farrar got no fee.

To Thomas the plaintiffs in *General Contractors*, who had not proven—not even *alleged*—monetary damages deserved legal standing. Farrar, who had vindicated a legal right that was difficult to quantify in money, did not deserve an attorney's-fee award. The ultimate issue in *Farrar* was, Should the Court encourage or deter lawsuits like his by holding out to plaintiffs and their potential attorneys the carrot of an award of fees? Thus stated, the fees issue in *Farrar* was very similar to the issue of standing in *Associated General Contractors:* Should the Court encourage or deter challenges to municipal set-aside programs by sending a signal that the Court would be willing to entertain challenges by local business groups, even if they could show no monetary loss? Thomas answered nay on the first, yea on the second. This is not a happy juxtaposition.

Finally, in pronouncing Farrar undeserving of a fee, the Court placed enormous emphasis on the difference between the plaintiff's original claim ($17 million) and the actual award ten years later (one dollar). Yet Thomas and the Court's majority are not consistently disturbed when money awards (fees or otherwise) exponentially exceed actual damages. In *TXO Production Corp. v. Alliance Resources Corp.*[61] Thomas concurred in the Court's upholding of a $10-million punitive-damages award in a case where actual damages were merely nineteen thousand dollars. In *TXO*, the beneficiary of the award was a corporation, not a civil rights plaintiff. And the money went to the party, for its own enjoyment, not to a needy litigant trying to pay his lawyers.

## *Impartiality Is Zealotry*

An important goal of the Negro Criticism woven throughout the discussion of Clarence Thomas and the rest of this book is to expose America's hidden ideology of whiteness, of which judicial impartiality is an important hiding place. The white norm is, in America, a powerful idea that often seems beyond question. And this fact has political consequences. Many have argued that black conservatives fall prey to this powerful idea. Stephen Carter, in his habitually self-incriminating fashion, has placed this point beyond dispute. In declining to join the challenges being launched by Negro Crit lawyers, Carter had this to say: "If one wants to move upward in the professions one must accept that most of the rewards one seeks will be distributed by white people according to rules they have worked out." [62]

Carter's habitual settling of controversy with Tough fact ought by now to be familiar. And capture by an unseen ideology also affects his vision of the judicial role, as evidenced anew by his discussion of the federal confirmation process in "The Confirmation Mess." The heart of Carter's thinking on the issue is simple: an ideal of politically insulated judges, and the idea that two wrongs don't make a right. Though Carter admits that presidents Bush and Reagan packed the courts by appointing ideological kinsfolk, Carter argues, in 1994, that it would be wrong for Clinton to follow suit, because when the next Republican comes, Democrats will lack a basis for "principled opposition." *But where was Carter's own principled opposition during the Reagan-Bush eighties?* Carter's confession of Reagan-Bush sins is, conveniently, announced with a Democrat in office. And notwithstanding this confession, Carter never met a Reagan-Bush Supreme Court nominee worth opposing, *not even Robert Bork.* After commenting, first, that the conduct of some of Bork's opponents was "shameful" and, second, that he personally "never did discover [a] compelling case against [Bork's] confirmation," Carter continued:

Third, I have no illusions that a Justice Bork would have voted in all important cases in the way that I believe the Constitution requires. . . . Fourth . . . I have no illusions that a Justice Bork would have voted in all the important cases in the way that I believe morality compels. Fifth, I do not think that Bork's constitutional theory as he explains it can serve as the basis for a judicial philosophy that is consistent with and serves the needs of the Constitution. Sixth, I do not believe that Bork's judicial philosophy was remotely close to any sort of extremism that has no place in legitimate constitutional theoretic debate. Seventh, none of the matters covered [in this quotation] are legitimate matters of inquiry when the president selects a nominee or when the Senate votes on confirmation.

Despite this litany of serious disagreement, Carter ultimately found common ground with Bork on the "method" of original intent as the basis for constitutional interpretation, though "differ[ing] sharply about what the method entails." And while this method of constitutional interpretation remains obviously flexible, the *one* thing that Carter is clear it excludes from constitutional debate is rancorous public campaigning ("it is not clear why public support for [a] right translates into [its] existence"). In the eighties, Carter's commitment to judicial neutrality displayed that "marketable goodness which makes it possible to give comfortable assent to propositions without in the least ordering one's life in accordance with them" (James Joyce). Suddenly, with Clinton in office, Carter's propositions about judicial neutrality ought to influence a president's choice of real-life nominees.

This is important because, as Negro Crits have shown, the ideology of whiteness continues to have disproportionate sway in popular debate over who can pass as an impartial judge or as a nonideological litigator. Nominees and candidates whose perceptions about racial justice mirror America's unspoken whiteness can better present themselves as mainstream, their opponents as special interests. The idea that impartiality has a place in our politics, our law, even our literature, helps those who want stuff to stay like it is. In the words of the truth master himself, those clamoring for change depart from objectivity and dispassion and are "so left they've left America." [63] Reagan's more-of-the-same crowd regularly launches vicious skirmishes over values under the soothing cover of neutrality and truth.

In this setting, the Tough Love Crowd's advocacy of dispassionate ideals is self-maiming. It is widely recognized, for instance, that the rhetoric of impartiality played a central role in the attacks on civil rights nominee Lani Guinier. Less noticed is an important subtext: Guinier's opponents openly championed an ideal of an "impartial" judiciary as the best way to stall what they viewed as formidable pressures for fair courts and disagreeable social change.

Although Guinier emphasized that issues like civil rights enforcement are by their very nature controversial, an ideal of impartiality nevertheless came to dominate the debate. Under the headline "The Last Frontier," the *Wall Street Journal,* launching the paper's *first* editorial attack on Guinier's nomination, warned of a "gathering gerrymander of the judiciary" as the Voting Rights Act was extended to elected judges. To fend off the encroaching NAACP "wagon trains" (the *Journal*'s phrase), the editorial urged an ideal of "judges as impartial arbiters of law" to displace the powerful competing ideal of *fairness* in judicial appointments.

The casual reader might easily assume that the *Journal* thinks impartiality just *is* the true nature of a judge's job. The *Journal*, however, was aware that it was entering a battle over "the way we see the judicial branch of government." Under the suggested "impartial" strategy, the *Journal* reassured its readers in what was ostensibly an attack on the Guinier nomination, "There isn't much case for bringing about a 'fair' mix among the robed." By opposing a "fair mix" the *Journal* was objecting to the commonsense notion, already endorsed by the Supreme Court, that elected judges, like other elected officials, ought to reflect the diversity of the communities over which they sit in judgment. The *Journal* frankly called for a rehabilitation of the old ideal of judicial impartiality, not because that ideal was intrinsically attractive, but exactly because it would provide an apparently reasoned basis for an otherwise indefensible distaste for a *fair* mix among judges.

This impartial view of judging is (Stephen Carter's confessions are legion) not widely accepted within the legal community. It is, moreover, contradicted by the fact that many judges are chosen in the ordinary rough and tumble of popular elections. And it is contradicted by the Supreme Court's view that the 1982 Voting Rights Act (which governs the roly-poly of ordinary politics) applies to such judicial elections. The *Journal* editorialist actually mentioned all of these facts. The *Journal*'s editorializing was not ill informed but was, rather, a straightforward opposition to these well-established policies. Clarence Thomas has described the 1982 amendments as "unacceptable." [64] Guinier opponents successfully recast *existing* law and policy to resemble threatened and cataclysmic innovation—and their principal weapon was the rhetoric of impartiality.

Like the nation in the Guinier affair, the Toughs are duped into (or, worse, pretend) an allegiance to ideals of impartiality. Stephen Carter's preference for politically insulated justices is a functional variant of the *Journal*'s preference for an "apolitical" selection process. Carter has lamented that "the electoral ethos so pervades the selection and the confirmation of justices that one is moved to wonder why we do not dispense with all the cumbersome constitutional rigor of presidential nominations and Senate hearings and proceed directly to an election." [65]

Carter intends that the idea of straightforwardly elected Supreme Court justices should strike the reader as obviously absurd. He assumes that some impartial depoliticized process is obviously desirable. The foregoing discussion suggests the opposite. An acknowledgment that judicial power is *political* power forces the debate onto the preferable terrain of "fairness"—a battleground that terrifies the *Journal.*

Moreover, acknowledging that judicial power is political power does *not* mean abandoning the Court to majoritarianism. As has been well said, "Constitutional review is intended to be antimajoritarian," and so "to argue against it based on majoritarian principles is pointless."[66] To the extent that judicial review, in practice, is overwhelmed by majoritarian principles,[67] judicial review can be said to be malfunctioning.

Finally, one defense of Guinier offered by some, notably Attorney General Janet Reno, was that the *Journal's* fears were misplaced because Guinier would not be free to enforce her admittedly radical ideas. She would be a member of the Clinton administration, and so bound by its policies. If one bought this argument, one might go on to point out an even more impressive constraint on both Guinier *and* the Clinton administration: the rule of law. For neither Guinier nor the Clinton administration would ever have had the last word on anything. They would all be mere parties before a court. So, why worry? Indeed, if Clint Bolick was right that Guinier was, objectively, an exotic civil rights ideologue, why was he hyperventilating? Surely the supposed objective rule of law would rebuff her zealotry? In fact, the *Journal* was canny enough to know that the law means nothing more nor less than the extent to which it is enforced. Bolick feared adverse political results for causes dear to him should Guinier get her hands on what he called "the civil rights arsenal." Now dawns the reason why the *Journal,* in what was ostensibly its opening salvo against Guinier as an individual appointee and litigator, actually spent most of its energy on the NAACP "wagon trains" seeking fairness among judges. What the *Journal* wanted to avoid was a two-pronged danger. The first: an aggressive, articulate, experienced litigator (Guinier) taking civil rights cases before the courts. The second: fair courts that might listen to strong argument. The *Journal* alluded to supposed evils wreaked by some of the state laws requiring that judges reflect the diversity of the communities over which they preside. These laws had, said the *Journal,* "provided an open door for yahoos and stooges of the trial lawyers." Fair judges are the feared "yahoos" and Guinier's civil rights division, the feared trial lawyers.

The *Journal* placed the word "fair" in skeptical question marks, presumably indicating that its opponents' claims for the fairness of the new judge-selection procedures were not objective, and implying that its own call for judges as impartial arbiters was objective. Clint Bolick objected that the Guinier appointment would "blur the lines between advocacy groups and government agencies, as they were in the *pre*-Reagan [!] years, when the executive branch subordinated law enforcement to its ideological agenda" (emphasis added). Bolick's presentation of right-wing zealotry as impartiality is transparent, yet it worked.

All this success (scuppering Guinier, capturing Justice Thomas, capturing Carter, Randall Kennedy, Sowell, Shelby Steele, making Justice O'Connor seem a "centrist," making Clinton's continuity seem like cathartic change) attests to the continuing influence of the abstract ideal of disinterest in American politics. People remain uneasy with the frank and noisy brokering of values. People prefer to pretend that value conflicts don't exist. This uneasiness is *itself* a valuable political tool for the politically comfortable. The ideal of impartiality is itself a partisan weapon in American politics.

V

Tough Love International

# 9

# Sir Vidia Naipaul's Revolutionary Truth

Naipaul seems ... to be a writer beleaguered by his own truths, unable to get past them.

—Elizabeth Hardwick, 1979

Transfixed by country-and-western music's inventiveness, [Naipaul] remains silent about the blues and jazz. White writers get a full billing as artists; black writers are scaled down to representatives of racial frenzy or despair. In encounters with south-ern churchfolk and political leaders, too, Naipaul manages to uncover the noble pathos of a vanishing past amidst white southern communities, but among black communities, he unearths self-violation and back-to-back dereliction. Predictably, Naipaul finds himself drawn to Booker T. Washington while recoiling in irritation from the more radical W. E. B. Du Bois. Naipaul's general disdain toward southern black culture contains dim echoes of his more violent dismissals of the Caribbean, such as his scoffing account of Trinidadian carnival as "a version of the lunacy that kept the slave alive."

—Rob Nixon, *London Calling: V. S. Naipaul, Postcolonial Mandarin*

## *Tough Love Is an International Affair*

Clarence Thomas's unhappy inability to help Haiti's refugees is merely the most obvious example of the international significance of America's Tough Love Crowd. Beyond the direct impact of Clarence Thomas, Stephen Car-ter's version of the original constitutional design would reduce congressional fetters on U.S. presidential war powers. At the height of the Gulf War crisis, Carter wrote in the *Washington Post* that war making is an executive prerogative and that congressional attempts to micromanage (his word) the executive's war-making power are unconstitutional. More generally, Carter appears willing to exoticize foreigners in order to enhance the persuasiveness of his scholarship before an American audience.[1] Carter's advocacy of an expanded role for religion in American civic life is a good example of this. Ignoring the U.S. role in destabilizing Iranian democracy after World War II, Carter attributes the scary Islamic Republic of Iran to religious zeal and goes on to say that his proposed vision of the U.S. Constitution's establishment clause, while more accommodating of religious sentiment, is not akin to that foreign nightmare. Carter elsewhere bolsters his call for more religion in American life with a reference to "that anarchic no-man's land that the maps still insist is a nation called Lebanon." Carter portrays this Lebanese anarchy as the result of a kind of religiosity that is foreign to America—as an emanation of some other place. America's role in the plight of Lebanon entirely disappears in such asides so that Carter can bolster his argument for greater religiosity in American life. Edward Said has long emphasized the role of an invented "other" in every nation's definition of itself. Carter's invented Lebanon, the product of an ostensibly un-American religious zeal, is invoked to assure Americans that their system can surely accommodate a bit more religiosity without reaching what he calls "the bottom of the slippery slope."

Carter's America is unique among nations. For Carter, this presents a "Uniqueness Puzzle," deserving of serious scholarly attention. That puzzle is "why the American experiment in constitutional government has succeeded so well for so long, when so many other efforts at establishing democracy have failed so miserably." Carter's puzzle might resolve itself if he tried to explain how and why a discrete group of Americans has uncannily remained at the bottom of America's well *throughout* America's history. Or where the Native Americans disappeared to. Or why America's neighbors were so churlish as to question U.S. manifest destiny to rule the Western hemisphere. Such concerns are feather-light fetters on Carter's romantic geopolitics.

Again, in his *Reflections,* Carter recants his prior "glowing reference" to the intervention of the U.S. Marines in Guatemala. Yet he recants not because U.S. adventurism is wrong, but because (in a burlesque of imperialist inexactitude) he got the name of the country wrong. Carter, ostensibly correcting himself, lauds the intervention of the Marines in 1965 to enable "free elections" in the Dominican Republic (not Guatemala). Without entering into an historical excursus, suffice it to say that Carter's version of the American role in the 1965 events in the Dominican Republic is acontextual and self-righteous. Every West Indian school child knows that U.S. policy in the Dominican Republic, and throughout the Caribbean, was and is directed by very specific American corporate interests (e.g., the United Fruit Company and its corporate successors). American support for "democracy" was and is sporadic. U.S. intervention had and has an uncanny tendency to accord with the desires of American property in the region. Bush's and Clinton's modest efforts in the cause of Haitian President Aristide (where the U.S. has little at risk), contrasted with their overkill responses to Iraq (where oil prices are at risk), conform to a pattern that is as old as America. In 1987, even after the U.S. laid mines in Nicaragua's harbors, after the U.S. withdrawal from the International Court of Justice (ICJ), where Nicaragua initiated a lawsuit, and after the ICJ's decisions in favor of Nicaragua, Carter remained comfortable discussing whether, *without regard to international law,* it is "morally desirable" for the United States to "try to prod or pressure the government of Nicaragua into a shape that is like that of some other policies that are called democratic." Carter posed this question while serving as a moderator in a panel discussion entitled "Promoting Democracy." It is clear, in context, that Carter is comfortable with American proddings and pressurings. On the panel, Carter repeatedly addressed the anti-interventionist view with a loaded question that made clear his own opinion. He repeatedly asked not whether the U.S. has a unilateral right to intervene in other countries, but rather whether it has a "right to be indifferent" to the "form of government" in Nicaragua, Angola, and elsewhere. When the discussion turned to South Africa, Carter had to *ask* whether the African National Congress (ANC) should be seen as "primarily for some form of democratic change," and he helpfully pointed out that the South African government (circa 1987) "does not see it that way." The reason for Carter's ambivalence is, as the course of the panel discussion confirms, the Communists under the ANC's bed.

Again, Carter lauds as "sensible" the Reagan administration's self-serving distinction between dictatorships that are acceptable and merely "authoritarian," like Pinochet's Chile, and those that are unacceptable and "totalitarian," like the U.S.S.R. Unsurprisingly, despots who were Reagan allies tended to be classed as benign authoritarians, while U.S. opponents were, with uncanny regularity, classed as totalitarian. Yet Carter is ostensibly mystified when he finds that this distinction was deployed by Reagan in such a way as to preserve trade with the unreconstructed South Africa of the 1980s.

Finally, while Carter is always careful to separate the evils done in the name of American meritocracy from the ideal of meritocracy itself, and the evils done in the name of religion from the ideal of American religion itself, he rushes to conflate the failures (alleged as a generality) of Marxists with Marxism itself, and the failures of Eastern-bloc communism with the failures of both communism and Marxism themselves.[2]

Beyond abandonment (Thomas) and apologetics (Carter), Tough Love is international in a more general sense. Thomas Sowell, for instance, does not confine his social-scientific methods to America's shores. His *Preferential Policies* (1990) provides, according to its subtitle, "An International Perspective." An identical subtitle adorns Sowell's earlier book, *The Economics and Politics of Race* (1983), and others. Moreover, as is by now familiar, we are told on the back covers of these books that "by substituting fact for rhetoric, Thomas Sowell has made an invaluable contribution to our seeing the world as it really is" and that "emotional controversies" are "examined in factual terms, with many myths being exploded along the way."

The ineffectiveness of Sowell's claims to capture underlying realities through empirical enquiry was canvassed earlier and will not be repeated here. What remains interesting, turning to V. S. Naipaul, is that Naipaul's publishers make even more exorbitant claims for their man's truth-finding capacity. They nearly claim that Naipaul out-truths economists like Sowell: "With a few swift and beautifully calculated strokes, Mr. Naipaul brings the essence of a social situation so vividly to life that one begins to wonder whether all the sociologists, anthropologists and political scientists have not laboured in vain."[3]

Naipaul himself encourages such reckonings of his ability to detain essential truth—in *both* his fiction and his nonfiction. He has written, for instance, that "the *novel* is a form of social enquiry" (emphasis added). And Rob Nixon has demonstrated, in a brilliantly condensed discussion, the manner in which Naipaul pursues a "convergence of aesthetic and social scientific conceptions of culture." As Nixon suggests, Naipaul skillfully appeals to an autobiographical genre of writing in order to deflate the easy critique to which a straightforward social scientist (Sowell) or ethnographer might be vulnerable. Naipaul's introspective prose appears to cast off narrow scientific pretensions. Yet Naipaul does not abandon the claim that he can capture essential truths about the various cultures he visits. On the contrary, Naipaul claims that his finely tuned sensibility (or "vision") gives him unusual access to *authoritative* cultural knowledge. Naipaul said in 1993,

In the modern period the rendering of reality has always been an issue. Judgments and forms have constantly varied. Hazlitt (who died in 1830) thought that Byron's personality display obscured the world. Scott was the truer writer, he said, because

Scott did not stand between the reader and the world. To render the truth of his own life Hazlitt had only the essay. It wasn't enough. *The novelists who came after used the novel form to get at truths the essay could not get at, truths about society and mental states, for instance. The great novels of the 19th century still have this quality of truth.* (Emphasis added)

While Naipaul's claim to detain truths about diverse societies and collective mental states recalls Shelby Steele's claim to have discovered a universal destructive African American "anti self," Naipaul's claim appears to have had some success among American critics. Alfred Kazin has called Naipaul "the most compelling master of *social truth* that I know of in the contemporary novel" (emphasis added).[4] Kazin's faith in Naipaul's mastery of something called social truth survives the contrary evidence of Naipaul's own utterances:

Hindu civilization stopped growing a long time ago. Nothing has been happening except plunder, war, decimation.

I don't count the African readership and I don't think one should. Africa is a land of bush.

QUESTION: What is the future, in Africa?
NAIPAUL: Africa has no future.

This sort of truth is a pervasive feature of Naipaul's writing, and postcolonial critics have generally emphasized these failures. Yet Naipaul's claims of access to social truth have remained unchastened. This is how Naipaul describes the failings of Indian and West Indian intellectual activity, respectively:

The sweetness and sadness which can be found in Indian writing and Indian films are a turning away from a too overwhelming reality; they reduce the horror to a warm virtuous emotion. Indian sentimentality is the opposite of concern.

The insecure wish to be heroically portrayed. Irony and satire, which might help more, are not acceptable; and no writer wishes to let down his group. . . . If the West Indian writer is to be blamed, it is because, by accepting and promoting the unimpressive race-and-colour values of his group, he has not only failed to diagnose the sickness of his society but has aggravated it.

This, then, is Naipaul's agenda: to tell the bitter truths for the good of those he cares about. Whereas optimistic placebo analyses fail, Naipaul will unflinchingly diagnose the sickness of his society. Naipaul is confident of the accuracy, indeed the *predictive value,* of the knowledge he has spent his life amassing: "You must read *[The Middle Passage]* and tell me that the chapter on Jamaica is not wonderfully prescient, pre-visionary of what has happened lately. If you can tell me that, *then* attack me" (emphasis original).

Naipaul claims, then, that he is telling truth; that if he is heeded future disaster can be avoided; that past failure to heed him has in fact resulted in present disaster. Naipaul's claim to be contributing to real-world solutions recurs in his innumerable dismissals of postcolonial politics as mere drama. The real solution is, for Naipaul, beyond politics. It is in the hands of the small phalanx of genuinely diagnostic intellectuals—those rare, stern, tellers of unpalatable truths such as Naipaul. Naipaul claims that the intellectual's caustic appraisals (and corresponding actions) are the sole authentic means of progress. It is fair to say that this is an incessant theme of Naipaul's work.[5]

Consistent with Naipaul's self-promotion, his admirers detect no oddity in the most clamorous oxymorons, as where William Walsh says that Naipaul has "the novelist's objectivity and insight." Naipaul's novelistic objectivity is as odd as Stephen Carter's empirical hunchmaking, only more audacious. Naipaul's Western admirers consistently describe him as "beyond partisanship" and therefore capable of detaining truth: "His mind is not weighed down by any heavy inherited Indian burden, biased by subjective and arbitrary convictions, nor hagridden by self-pity. His is a very clear and naked intelligence—his only prejudice is to be in favor of reality."

Examples like this can be multiplied among Western critics, but one example in particular is instructive because its slippery use of language takes us near the heart of the problem. Eugene Goodheart acknowledges (indeed treats as obvious) that Naipaul, like the rest of us, is subject to an "incorrigible subjectivity" that reflects itself in "unattractive prejudices" that are "of course unpleasant." But, Goodheart continues,

To flaunt one's prejudices as Naipaul does can be a rare virtue—or vice—in what I've called the ethos of congeniality, which demands that we publicly tolerate one another, a condition that produces either hypocrisy (in which we affect attitudes we privately disavow) or self-deception (in which we no longer recognize our true feelings). In either case perception and truth suffer.

Goodheart's conclusion that perception and truth suffer in one of the two specified ways is entirely unargued. His hypocrisy claim assumes that even Naipaul's concededly prejudiced utterances contribute to a stockpile of something called "truth." But perhaps truth is not a kind of widget? Goodheart's second claim ("self-deception"), with its attendant notion of our no longer recognizing our true feelings, smacks of the infinite regress of "false consciousness." Even if it is, by some unspecified and metaphysical standard, true that we postcolonials don't "know" our true selves, who is to say that Goodheart knows us better?

Next, from the negative assertion (above) that those without prejudice suffer a loss of perception and truth, Goodheart heroically asserts the affirmative—that Naipaul's prejudice advances his truth telling and clear-sightedness: "Prejudiced utterance is authentic expression. Naipaul's power as an observer of the ideological landscapes of developing nations ... owes a great deal to his prejudiced clear-sightedness. ... [His] anti-faith, anti-ideological skepticism is wedded to a kind of radical empiricism, a passion for observation."

This reference to prejudiced clear-sightedness is offered without irony. Goodheart clearly thinks he has built his case for clear-sightedness by pointing out that Naipaul flaunts his prejudice in defiance of the ethos of congeniality, with its attendant hypocrisy and self-deception. Yet there's a failure of logic: *the preparedness to speak up is no guarantee of the truth of what is said.* A zany willingness to flout the ethos of congeniality may be entertaining to those with a taste for Friar's Roasts, but this in itself hardly confers the privilege of truth upon what is said. Goodheart has been tripped up by his own sleight of phrase: "Prejudiced utterance is *authentic* expression." This "authentic" means "honest," not "accurate." There is perhaps a laudable Nietzschean-individualist streak in Goodheart's instincts here. "More important than the particular prejudices," Goodheart says, "is the freedom to be prejudiced and the power to express it, which is associated with the freedom and power of the imagination itself." Yet this principle is hardly a societal blueprint (which is almost what Naipaul's diagnostic "social truth" aims at). Moreover, Goodheart's sleight of phrase, his slippage from *authentic* prejudiced utterance to the superior *truth* of the view expressed, might have been avoided by a closer reading of Nietzsche: "Truth has never yet clung to the arm of an inflexible man."[6]

Naipaul, too, apparently invests little serious thought in the question of what to dignify as truth: "Unless one hears a little squeal of pain after one's done some writing, one has not really done much. That is my gauge of whether I have hit something true."[7]

This is Tough stuff. Or else it is semiserious, and equally irresponsible. Naipaul, while capable of considerable humor, claims to be more than a simple jester. He claims to care. Naipaul's rhetoric of concern for postcolonial peoples is, however, given short shrift even by his most sophisticated adversaries. Rob Nixon's *London Calling: V. S. Naipaul, Postcolonial Mandarin* discusses at length Naipaul's disdain for frivolous and privileged travel writers (Waugh, Norman, Byron, Greene, Dinesen, Hemingway) and Naipaul's insistence that he is, because of his seriousness and his concern, different from them. Nixon distinguishes Naipaul's admitted "political interest" from his lack of "concern," admitting that Naipaul has the interest but doubting that he has the concern. At a very important level Nixon is indeed correct. Naipaul's regurgitation of nineteenth-century British disdain for brown peoples is the precise opposite of concern for those peoples. Nixon correctly points out that Naipaul's protestations of concern deflect attention from his affinities (of sensibility and of privilege) with the frivolous travel writers from whose company he would depart. Yet Nixon's short way around Naipaul's rhetoric of concern forfeits an important ethical resource. If Naipaul were an avowed imperialist, important moral criticisms would be unavailable to his adversaries. Yet those moral criticisms are in fact available. Naipaul is not an avowed opponent, but rather a failed partisan of postcolonial peoples. This is a view that other critics of Naipaul have reached. Selwyn Cudjoe, a consistently unfriendly postcolonial critic of Naipaul, basing himself on psychoanalytical writings, concludes that "Naipaul's hysteria"—and hysteria is a state of mind to which Naipaul frequently confesses—"tends to displace the reality of the postcolonial world." Cudjoe continues that Naipaul "does not deliberately and consciously defame Third World societies, nor does he believe that he is not telling the 'truth' as he perceives it. Rather he accuses these countries of living a gigantic 'lie.'"[8]

Naipaul's concern for postcolonials in exposing such lies is far more than a casual one. He sees moral concern as *central* to his most profoundly held artistic ideals. Any failure of concern is, for Naipaul, a key ingredient of moral and artistic failure. Naipaul's own manifest failures of concern are thus not merely irrelevant political complaining. They represent the collapse of his own moral and aesthetic project: truth as revolution.

## Naipaul's Ideal of Truth as Revolution

It is impossible to overstate Naipaul's commitment to an ethic of art. For him, writing is a vocation in the strictest sense of the word: "I think that if I hadn't succeeded in being a writer I probably would not have been around; I would have done away with myself in some way."

Writing is a vocation that Naipaul sees as given to him by his father, a journalist and short story writer in the (for Naipaul) culturally barren landscape of Trinidad's colonial society. The son cherishes this vocation all the more because such an impulse of high civilization might so easily have been snuffed out in such an adverse environment. This sense that the artist's vocation is at once the ultimate value, even the only one available to him, coupled with a sense of how random was its successful inheritance from his father, how easily (Naipaul thinks) it might have eluded him, sharpens Naipaul's reverence for the writer's art. Naipaul freely admits this unusual intensity: "I became a writer because of this overwhelming sense of its nobility as a calling which was given to me by my father and probably exaggerated by me."[9]

Naipaul's profound appreciation of the life of art, coupled with a visceral conviction that the societies that were to be his subject, being "backward," could not sustain that life, might easily have fueled a turn inward, a sharp move away from any notion of the artist as any kind of legislator. This would have placed the postcolonial artist, retreating in the face of the irreformable barrenness of Third World life, among those who, like Benda, say "my Kingdom is not of this world." *This is not, however, Naipaul's view.* Naipaul, like the other Toughs, admits and approves that no hermetic seal separates art from civic life. As a young Trinidadian reader, Naipaul tells us, he attempted to enter into British literature but failed because *"no writer, however individual his vision, could be separated from his society."* And in his early experience as a writer, Naipaul found this, to his detriment, confirmed:

I've often said that when I was younger and thought of being a writer, I thought I was serving a thing called art, and that art was something divinely judged, and that what was good would be rewarded. I very quickly found out that this wasn't so, that I was always being judged politically. . . . What a labor it has been to ignore this and break out of it.

And Naipaul's labor was not a private, introspective effort. It was a public campaign. Naipaul wrote in the 1950s, in the *Times Literary Supplement,* that "it isn't easy for the exotic writer to get his work accepted as being more than something exotic, something to be judged on its merits. The very originality of the material makes the work suspect." In making such statements, Naipaul became an active and deliberate participant in a *political* project. When Chinua Achebe envisaged the novelist teaching that the palm tree is a fit subject for poetry, he explicitly linked this project with the further one of helping his society regain its belief in itself. Naipaul is quite self-consciously an adherent of the first project, and (implicitly or else despite himself) he also participates in the second—for the former entails the latter, as Naipaul's own words acknowledge:

> If landscapes do not start to be real until they have been interpreted by an artist, so, until they have been written about, societies appear to be without shape and embarrassing. . . . Fiction or any work of imagination, whatever its quality, hallows its subject. To attempt, with a full consciousness of established and authoritative mythologies, to give a quality of myth to what was agreed to be petty and ridiculous—Frederick Street in Port of Spain, Marine Square, the districts of Laventille and Barataria—to attempt to use those names required courage.

Naipaul's manifesto here might suggest an end product resembling Derek Walcott's *Omeros,* which successfully relocated Homeric epic in a West Indian setting. And Naipaul's novel *A House for Mr. Biswas* is exactly such an achievement. *Biswas* spans three generations and renders a particular West Indian milieu with a vividness that is frequently—and justly—compared to the best of Charles Dickens.

If such work flies in the face of received mythologies, writing becomes literally subversive. In 1993, Naipaul rendered his most explicit statement of this creed to date. The project, which he summed up as *"the ideal of truth as revolution . . .* is a *moral one.* It is the striving after truth, the hard look at the world, and its effect is subversive. That may be too strong a word, but many of the great original writers of the nineteenth century and this have helped to undermine and remake their civilization" (emphasis added).

Naipaul's much earlier criticisms of Indian fiction (specifically that of R. K. Narayan, though Naipaul generalizes the point) further underline his commitment to the *moral* ideal that the writer ought to be a subversive truth teller for the benefit of those he or she writes about. Naipaul detects in Indian fiction an (to him) unsatisfactory fusion of the novel form with the (to him) Hindu belief in the vanity of all human action and human life:

> The form of the novel implies a concern with the conditions of men. Narayan's message in all his books is that the condition of men is not important. So there is this oddity—writing about people as though human life matters, and the deeper pessimistic rejection of a concern with men. *I don't think Indians quite understand what the novel is for. They do not quite accept that it has to do with a concern for human existence.* (Emphasis added)

For Naipaul, art minus human concern is morally and aesthetically unsuccessful. Naipaul rejects any view in which the ultimate value is the somehow untethered pursuit of beauty; he denies that the aesthetic is somehow to be elevated above the human. Rather, the alleged *aesthetic* failure of the Indian novelists is for Naipaul the direct result of a failure of human concern. Thus, arguments that Naipaul is a free, untethered soul can be little more than trite references to his expatriation and frequent travel. For Naipaul, *"It is impossible to think of a writer, a novelist, as being anything but attached"*[10] (emphasis added). The bedrock of Naipaul's aesthetic vision is thus very different from his casual remark, in an interview, that he was "willing to believe that the element of pleasure is almost invariably paramount." Naipaul is closer than might first appear to Achebe's view that the notion of art divorced from service to people is deodorized dogshit. Certainly, many questions remain. The question, for instance, of what constitutes adequate service to people is radically controversial. But it is a project into which Naipaul has avowedly entered. Peter Nazareth quotes the following passage from Naipaul's work: "The people of Elvira . . . have their funny ways, but I could say one thing for them; you don't have to bribe them twice." Nazareth comments: "Uniform contempt for life is not an asset to a novelist."[11] It is less interesting to pronounce on where the fine line between irony and contempt is transgressed than to emphasize that *Naipaul agrees with Nazareth's premise.* Naipaul frequently insists that "one can't write out of contempt." Naipaul always insists that he writes out of *concern.* At a reading in New York, he senses that his audience is troubled by a particular story. His unsolicited response: "I assure you, I write from the deepest sympathy for all my characters." Again, faced with the question of whether he had become an "unstitcher of systems" for himself and his readers, he resists the view that his art is a private self-indulgence enacted at the expense of real people:

Put like that it sounds as though I've decided to look after myself and to try to preserve my own calm and happiness—as though I'm shutting out the distress. To some extent, this may be so, but I also think I have an understanding of what is possible in our world: that the oppressed or depressed cultures of the world have really to look after themselves.

Responding to the criticism that his *Turn in the South* had provided an unduly "charmed and gentle account of redneck culture" in the American deep South, Naipaul insisted that while others urged him to express outrage about slavery, he was concerned about slavery "long before [his critics] were." He sarcastically rejected the view that his critics "care much more" than he does. Naipaul is moreover certain that one needs a "conversation with a society" and that "one cannot write in a total vacuum." Naipaul rejects cloistered art and, for instance, wants India to "do something in the world": "A country with 600 to 700 million people which is now offering the world nothing but illegitimate holymen should be ashamed of itself. . . . For a time I hoped my little proddings would start something."

True, this concern is sometimes, as here, expressed in the past tense. In 1977, for instance, Naipaul said that his "concern for India" had been "beaten out of [him]" and that it was now "every man for himself." But even if this rhetoric were regarded as more representative than the overwhelmingly more consistent rhetoric of concern, Naipaul would still be presenting himself as a disillusioned and battle-weary partisan rather than a person who is indifferent or hostile to postcolonial societies. Despite harsh clashes with West Indian critics, Naipaul has always insisted that "I Cannot Disown Trinidad and It Cannot Disown Me." At any rate, the rare and unrepresentative rhetoric of disillusionment never threatens Naipaul's view that a position of concern is essential to *aesthetic* success. While Naipaul has said, "I write out of a sense of duty to myself, to my talents," his exercise of those talents always remains, purportedly, within the project of concern for postcolonial societies: "When people say 'This book is so pessimistic,' my attitude now is 'But it can't be pessimistic, because I have written it.' And by that I mean I am ancestrally of the culture—so the fact that I have written it might be taken as a sign of a mind at work."[12]

Thus, the view that "the expatriate writer, like Naipaul, enjoys a unique position—he is not 'committed,' except to his private sensibility or vision"[13] is simply wrong. Attention to Naipaul's own rhetoric discloses an ethical commitment to the well-being of postcolonial societies.

### Naipaul's Trojan Truth

Naipaul's commitment to postcolonial peoples hangs, however, by a thread. Naipaul's ideal, like that of Julien Benda, is nonideological truth telling. His commitment is, as he tells it, not to political doctrine in an ordinary (he'd say, vulgar) sense. Rather, Naipaul espouses an unexacting humanist ideal: "I am aware that I have probably been rather feeble and uninvolved. Yet I find it very hard to commit myself to any doctrine except my own private values which I think are liberal and humane."

Naipaul, then, is a committed truth teller. He is concerned but remains ostensibly beyond political doctrine. While Clarence Thomas claims to operate like a monastic recluse immune to political pressures, Naipaul claims to have reached the "Buddhist ideal of non-attachment" to politics. For Naipaul, the novelist must thus be attached to and in conversation with society, yet *un*attached to conventionally political causes.

Predictably, this leads to grief. Naipaul believes that "people with a cause inevitably turn themselves off intellectually." Naipaul makes no pretense, however, that his strong ideological independence is the same as disinterest or neutrality. Naipaul urges that art should be more than a passive process of documentation: the artist who seeks only to record commits the "documentary heresy." Rather, the artist should "impose a vision on the world."

The writer, then, must impose an individual vision while yet avoiding the seduction of political causes. That this is a very fine (nonexistent) line to tread Naipaul does not seem to appreciate. Nevertheless, and with gusto, he sets about imposing his ostensibly private and personal vision. He emphasizes that "I can't go to a place just to see and be any longer. I like to go to a place now to look at something, to investigate a particular aspect. I like a mission." And, speaking of his 1977 book on India, he explains, "I was unwilling always to describe simply; I always try to make a description part of an argument."

Naipaul's theory of individualistic description, wedded always to an argument, gives him a way to avoid voices he would rather not contend with. On his Islamic journey he talks to few political leaders because "their views are well known. . . . They have nothing to tell me." *Nothing?* The point that one might prefer to look at the "real people" is well taken, but unsurprisingly, Naipaul is not consistent in enforcing the idea that politicians are irrelevant. He talks, for instance, to the Guyanese politicians Forbes Burnham and the Jagans in his 1962 Caribbean journey, and on a return journey he revisits the Jagans (in government during his first visit; in opposition during the revisit). My point here is not to prescribe either disregard of or concern with politicians as a general rule, but merely to illustrate the inconsistency of Naipaul's dogma over time. Today the politicians (Burnham, the Jagans) contribute to truth, tomorrow the politicians (of the Islamic world) don't contribute to truth.

Naipaul's dogma, while inconsistent, is not random. He deliberately treats certain artistic reverences and canons of evaluation as fixed and beyond anyone's power to control: "The published book, when it starts to live, speaks of the cooperation of a particular kind of society . . . it has the means of judging the new things that are offered. . . . This kind of society did not exist in Trinidad."

Upon Naipaul's receipt of the 1993 inaugural David Cohen British Literature Prize recognizing "a lifetime's achievement by a living British writer," his acceptance speech affirmed that "writing is more than a matter of spirit. A book is a physical, commercial object. It requires a well-organised society. If you are going to make a living as a writer you need publishers, reviewers, bookshops, libraries, a public looking for new work: a book trade."

Such concessions compromise Naipaul's more grandiose assertions of absolute independence ("I have no enemies, no rivals, no masters; I fear no one"), and they confirm the complaints of his critics that while Naipaul claims to present truth about the dispossessed, his work is accountable to the cultural institutions of the dispossessors. This paradox assures a certain kind of failure.

Naipaul assumes that standards of literary value are unchangeable and are foreign to the places with which he is ostensibly concerned. This view of literary value is, in turn, underlain by Naipaul's more general idea that *real* history and value are a peculiar kind of achievement, off limits to some. Naipaul believes that without such achievement, there can be no authentic human activity. What exactly is this achievement that is vital to authentic history? Naipaul explains:

Let's think. Can you write a satisfactory history of England from pre-Roman time up through the Roman occupation, the Roman withdrawal, the time of the little savage Kings, and their being wiped out by the Danes—the consequence of all this being that nothing happened? It wouldn't make sense to write weighty histories about that; whereas if you make all of this a chapter of something larger, the material conceivably can stand that kind of inquiry. Remember what I said long ago, that history was built around achievement and creation.

Naipaul next takes the now-plausible step of asserting that people lacking "real" history likewise lack authentic personality. He joins in the view that West Indian society

has never assumed any particularly noble aspect. There has been splendour and luxurious living, and there have been crimes and horrors, revolts and massacres. There has been romance, but it has been the romance of pirates and outlaws. The natural graces of life do not show themselves under such conditions. There has been no saint in the West Indies since Las Casas, no hero unless philonegro enthusiasm can make one out of Toussaint. There are no people there in the true sense of the word, with a character and purpose of their own.

This passage, which Naipaul adopted from the nineteenth-century British writer James Anthony Froude, hardly represents objective truth. In 1938, C. L. R. James's *Black Jacobins* provided exactly the kind of compelling account of Toussaint L'Overture and the Haitian revolution that Froude would evidently dismiss as "philonegro enthusiasm." James was, moreover, no indiscriminate celebrant of postcolonial society. James's uncompromising ethical commitments led his more pragmatic political and intellectual contemporary, Eric Williams, to conclude that James was lost to "the absurdities of world revolution." Naipaul nevertheless chose to follow Froude rather than James, actually adopting Froude's language as the *epigraph* of his work on the Caribbean. Naipaul chose to peddle Froude's unhappy truth.

This truth defines history as built on achievement, then defines "achievement" as nothing other than imperialism itself. For Naipaul, imperialism bends the destinies of subject peoples into conformity with the ends of empire and makes the subject peoples a mere chapter of something larger. While Naipaul's view underestimates ever-present indigenous resistance to imperialism, there is at least arguably a sense in which subject peoples, under the empire's boot, indeed lacked the power to implement agendas of their own. But with independence this becomes, precisely, inaccurate. The ends of formerly subject peoples are for the first time at their own disposal. *At the center of Naipaul's work is a denial of the "truth" of this shift.* Postcolonial politics is mere drama. In reality it is impotent maneuvering. This is confirmed, for Naipaul, by the "external policing" and eventual suppression of the Grenada revolution by U.S. intervention. It is confirmed by the U.S. prodding and pressuring that Tough Stephen Carter, for example, takes to be America's worldwide prerogative. It is confirmed, too, by America's pro-Naipaul literary establishment. Alfred Kazin is remarkably explicit when he says that Naipaul makes "clear today, as it was not to Dickens, Balzac and all those realists, that you shall know the truth and it shall *not* make you free" (emphasis added).

Naipaul's lucrative truth is, however, premised on an odd definition of authentic human action. The ideal Naipaul presupposes, that of utter self-determination, is *everywhere* (not just in postcolonial societies) absent. If Americans feel constrained to haggle at the UN or within NATO before attacking another country, or if the real value of the British pound is constrained by that of the deutsche mark within the European Monetary System's exchange-rate mechanism, are British and American citizens therefore incrementally less people "in the true sense of the word" than when laissez-faire gunboat diplomacy held free reign? And in the colonial era, were the British less real because the Spanish had a more sprawling empire? Startlingly, it is far from clear that Naipaul would admit the absurdity of such a view. Naipaul has referred to Britain's increasingly "colonial" sense of security—the sense that all the real decisions are being made in Washington, D.C. For Naipaul, Britain's new plight somewhat resembles the invented Trinidad of his *Loss of El Dorado*. In that book, the real decisions were being made elsewhere (Spain, England), rendering local action insignificant. In the late twentieth century, where *are* the "real" decisions being made? By Bill Clinton, or by his political handlers? By politicians, or by Wall Street? If by Wall Street, then really by its well-heeled Asian investors? When Clinton goes soft on China's human-rights abuses because he wants access to its burgeoning consumer market, are the Communists now ruling us all?

Naipaul's vision is paralyzed by such questions, like that of a deer caught in the headlights. The logic and explicit content of Naipaul's vision increasingly suggest the inauthenticity of *all* human action. The escapist romance of Naipaul's recent work—*The Enigma of Arrival, A Turn in the South, India: A Million Mutinies Now*—has been widely noted (in the last instance Naipaul, for the first time, was criticized for undue *optimism* about India). Naipaul's newest truth, like the old, is very far from the radical empiricism that Western critics have long attributed to him. Naipaul uses the alleged technological backwardness of India, the Middle East, Africa to show that they are outside a "Universal Civilization" built on high technology and liberal humanism. Yet the romantic British countryside of Naipaul's *Enigma* easily resembles the antimodernist pantheism of D. H. Lawrence and has led some of Naipaul's most enthusiastic British readers to blush. While Naipaul has for a long time freely admitted to being "feeble and uninvolved" in conventional political agitation, he led a band of lobbyists in writing an August 1993 letter to the London *Times* campaigning against the reckless high-tech upgrading of the road system near Stonehenge. Naipaul's laudable and uncharacteristic concern in this letter for "larks, lapwings, stone curlews and English partridges" had less to do with a conversion to Greenpeace politics than with the perceived vulgarization of that revered English tableau: "the countryside." Naipaul's latest truth, no less than the earlier variety, reflects his personal preoccupations. While his earlier work screeches venom, his newer offerings remain quietly oppressive.

## Naipaul's Tough Stuff

Naipaul's Tough diagnosis foredooms his suggested solutions. He divines that the problem is history, which is inherently beyond the reach of current mortals. What, then, is to be done about postcolonial societies? "Nothing! There's nothing to be done. Except we mustn't romanticize them. People must do things for themselves." Naipaul believes not only that history is built on (imperial) achievement but also that the dead hand of history's grip is wholly unshakable. In the following interview, this view is emphatic:

QUESTION: [Trinidad] has always had England as a reference and things English as reverences. Do you think it is possible with independence to build or create new reverences?

NAIPAUL: No, no, no, No, no, No. Because you know, whether you like it or not the reverences have already existed. Within a kind of political system one knew that there was a good way of behaving: there was a way of being upright and a way of being good and a way of not being good.[14]

This reinforces Edward Said's view that "Naipaul carries with him a kind of half-stated but finally unexamined reverence for the colonial order."[15] What greater reverence is possible than to make imperial achievement the litmus test of *real* history? Naipaul's bedrock belief that the political and cultural reverences are fixed makes an attitude of despair the appropriate tonal posture for his fiction. In *The Mimic Men* the lead character says, "The empires of our time were short lived; but they have altered the world forever; their passing away is their least significant feature." Yet this felt fixedness emerges from Naipaul's consciousness rather than from simple fact. This realization allows us to criticize Naipaul's account of postcolonial truth. Naipaul's concern reflects what Rob Nixon has called return-ticket progressivism. *The values that underlie Naipaul's descriptive effort betray the values that underpin his concern.* His espoused concern is for those who inhabit postcolonial places and must make something of the pressure to act; his prescriptions make sense only to his Western camp followers. This is an *ethical* failing. It amounts to secular sin. It is entirely plausible that in the still-colonial world in which Naipaul matured through his formative years, British domination might have carried with it cultural baggage that enthroned English reverences. But that is no longer the case. And this last assertion is not just postcolonial bravado. Anthony Burgess, English novelist and virtuoso of a self-conscious style of fiction that some might associate with the most refined culture as judged by traditional reverences, makes a similar suggestion. In a 1991 article entitled "Joseph Kell, V. S. Naipaul, and Me" (Kell is a Burgess nom de plume), Burgess wrote about his own exile from England. As Burgess explained the problems of the modern British writer, the parallel between his situation and Naipaul's own complaint in his 1958 article on the

"Regional Barrier" is striking. Burgess, in this article, which is a 1991 excerpt from his memoirs suggestively entitled *You've Had Your Time,* is doubtless parodying Naipaul, even while he marks the collapse of old reverences:

The problem of the contemporary British novelist—my problem—is knowing who to write for. To write for the British is not enough: it means choosing for subject matter the emancipated women living in Hampstead or holidaying in small hotels by Swiss lakes. . . . To write for America, where the large advances are, is a temptation, but American publishing houses want the British less and less.

This recalls Naipaul in 1958: "The Americans do not want me because I am too British. The public here [Britain] do not want me because I am too foreign. . . . It isn't easy for the exotic writer to get his work accepted as being more than something exotic." [16]

In the contemporary erosion of Britannic reverences—an erosion effected by others' efforts—Naipaul seems eventually to have been swept up. His 1990 book *India: A Million Mutinies Now* treats with a new respect what was once violently dismissed. Whereas the latest work celebrates the suddenly fertile million mutinies that is India, an interview contemporaneous with one of Naipaul's earlier India books records differently Naipaul's response to analogous energies: "Now that the British presence is no longer there, what you are seeing now in India . . . is an awakening of a very old, very village, very petty India, that really has lost its way." This idea of lost European authenticity is present also in Naipaul's 1967 novel, *The Mimic Men,* in which a mediocre Belgian school teacher in the Caribbean island of Isabella is yet able to conjure the magic of the real place across the seas:

There, in Liege in a traffic jam, on the snow slopes of the Laurentians, was a true, pure world. We, here on our island, handling books printed in this world, and using its goods, had been abandoned and forgotten. We pretend to be real, to be learning, to be preparing ourselves for life, we mimic men of the New World, one unknown corner of it, with all its reminders of the corruption that came so quickly to the new.

Conversely, in 1990, Naipaul detects new reverences on the rise in India: "The increased wealth showed; the new confidence of people once poor showed. One aspect of that confidence was the freeing of new particularities, new identities." [17]

That this is framed as a change in India itself does not obscure the likelihood that, as Naipaul says in his harsh 1964 India book, "It was my eye that had changed." (Naipaul made this latter remark upon revisiting Bombay, months after his initial 1964 visit.) The dust jacket of the U.S. edition of

Naipaul's 1990 India book is studded with "Praise for V. S. Naipaul." Heading the list is Joseph Lelyveld's remark, cited from the *New York Times Book Review,* describing Naipaul as "the most notable commitment of intelligence that Post-colonial India has evoked" and opining that Naipaul is "indispensable for anyone who wants seriously to come to grips with the experience of India." Lelyveld's remark is based on Naipaul's track record prior to his latest, revisionist book.[18] On the basis of those early vituperative and anxiety-ridden books, one wonders whether Naipaul had himself as yet come to grips with the experience of India. Naipaul is, doubtless, a notable intelligence. Yet one is reminded of a story the anthropologists tell: a clever boy in a traditional society, told by his mother to "go and find a quiet girl to marry," returned with a corpse.

## *What Naipaul's Tough Stuff Does*

The risks in Naipaul's rudderless truth telling are not difficult to detect. Notice how the impressionable Paul Theroux was influenced by Naipaul when the two were acquainted over a period of time at an African university: "It was Naipaul who showed me that Africa was more comedy than tragedy, and that perhaps I should spend more time writing and less time organizing extra-mural classes [for the locals]."[19]

"Truth" that has this effect is not self-evidently of value. Again, on November 5, 1990, as the war drums rose against Iraq, Naipaul wrote a *New York Times* op-ed piece under the headline "Our Universal Civilization." According to Naipaul's byline, the article was "adapted from the Walter B. Wriston lecture at the Manhattan Institute, a public policy organization." Naipaul, lecturing the policymakers, portrayed a fanatical Islam "where the faith was the complete way, filled everything, left no spare corner of the mind or will or soul." And he contrasted this with the West, "where it was necessary to be an individual and responsible." This Western world was governed, according to Naipaul, by a "pursuit of happiness" that simply "cannot generate fanaticism." Having just denied the possibility of Western fanaticism, Naipaul concludes in language that, ironically, exactly recalls Ronald Reagan's more zealous moments. Where Reagan earlier threatened that America's ideological opponents would end on the "trash heap of history," Naipaul now concurs that "other more rigid systems in the end blow away." On the same day and on the same page—literally alongside

Naipaul's article—William Safire, baying for war, contrasted the world's "civilized capitals" to Iraq, which was a different kind of place. Where Naipaul said that our "universal civilization has been a long time in the making," Safire chorused that immediate attack on Iraq was vital because "we are dealing here with our own survival." Days later, then-President Bush made a unilateral and fateful decision vastly to increase U.S. troop commitments in the region.

Next observe Sir Vidia Naipaul's rendering of the Third World: "To be born on an island like Isabella, an obscure New World transplantation, second-hand and barbarous, was to be born to disorder." Hear now Sir Peter de la Billiere, British commander in the Gulf War, on Saddam Hussein: "It's the sort of behavior you'd expect from the rather low-grade, second-hand sort of person that he is."[20] Taken with U.S. general Norman Schwarzkopf's view that Iraqi soldiers were not part of the same human race, and with the disparate sensitivity of American public opinion to the loss of a few Americans (versus many Iraqis), Edward Said's 1981 remark on Naipaul's book on Islam, *Among the Believers,* is prescient: Said points out that for Naipaul, the "other" people "are to be castigated for not being Europeans, and this is a political pastime useless to them, eminently useful for anyone plotting to use Rapid Deployment Forces against Islam. But then Naipaul isn't a Politician: he's just a Writer."

Naipaul hardly *caused* George Bush's resort to force rather than negotiations with Iraq. Bush's approval rating soared above 90 percent in the war's aftermath, and Bush had long independently held the view that every worthy president ought to be "tested by fire." However, Naipaul's expert and timely op-ed article, contrasting inherent Western reasonableness with inherent Islamic fanaticism, unquestionably *facilitated* Bush's deployments and sanitized the scorched-earth military strategy that followed.

The foregoing provides a context for remarks like the following: "Naipaul has not demonstrated that he has that sense of genuine commitment to the endurance of the human spirit and the upliftment of the human person and the triumph of the human ... [necessary] to give a meaningful criticism of [the then-contemporary "Black Power" movement] taking place in the Caribbean today."[21]

This passage is not simply a wistful cry for new empathy from Naipaul. It is, rather, a straightforward and credible *assertion* that failures of vision derail Naipaul's ability to engage postcolonial societies in *meaningful* criticism. "Criticism" that asserts futility is literally meaningless, since life continues. Naipaul has long denied that humans in postcolonial societies can generate value. This ability has, says Naipaul, been taken away from us by our history. Naipaul, who begins with an ideal of "truth as revolution," ends with the news that reality is fixed. Naipaul commits the very sin of which he misaccuses the Indian novelists: the form of his work entails the worth of human life, while the infused vision denies it.

# Conclusion: What's So Scary about Partisanship?

*Partisanship Is Not Censorship*

Surely more truth is always better and partisanship is bad. Doesn't partisanship smack of self-censorship, and won't it stultify debate? Perhaps not. *First,* the class of absolutely uncontestable truths is very small or nonexistent. The choice, where people disagree, is not between truth and its opposite, but between *enduring* truths and trivial ones. If "censorship" is a problem, it is a problem for everyone. Those who pursue Julien Benda's "disinterest" also need to choose and discard among the many things they can say. Everybody is always already inevitably partisan. We can only try to ensure that we are partisans for the right crowd. Either we set our priorities after careful reflection, remaining skeptical of conventional wisdom; or, unthinking, we adopt conventional wisdom in deciding what to emphasize or ignore.

Furthermore, people who say that partisanship is censorship are wrong if they mean that partisanship implies a net loss to the debate as a whole. In areas like politics, law, and literature we all know that most issues are "eternal" or "recurring." Particular refinements no doubt abound, but genuine ideological novelty is rare. Indeed, some say that "ideological novelty" is incomprehensible since "ideology" comprises the instinctual fabric of our awareness. They say we are, by definition, unable to tame this fabric through conscious reflection. Ideology, in this picture, is the very currency of thought. Every time we think about our ideology, whatever we come up with is itself a product of that ideology. Our thought therefore cannot capture the ideology that shapes it. We can't climb outside our way of seeing. So the idea that partisanship is somehow *more* ideological than Benda's ideal of disinterest simply makes no sense. Champions of disinterest too often assume that "ideology, like halitosis, is ... what the other person has."[1] Nothing is *lost* by replacing disinterest with partisanship.

And where censorship implies a loss of freedom, partisanship loosens things up. Partisan skepticism threatens conventional wisdom. What others take for granted, partisans raise as *questions.* The Toughs exactly mistake conventional wisdom for truth, and therefore add little to what we already know. Partisans, conversely, stir debate. They release suppressed objections and unsettle prevailing thought. Disinterest is self-censorship, and partisanship is its exact opposite.

### Coping with Lies

What of the self-righteous zealot who deliberately distorts things under cover of spurious arguments that "the end justifies the means"? This problem is fatal where the zealot holds a large degree of centralized state power (Ronald Reagan, Oliver North) or centralized private power (Ted Turner, Rupert Murdoch, the *Wall Street Journal*). This is already a big problem in America, says Ishmael Reed: "We live in a country where General Electric, which sponsors one of the chief outlets for anti-black propaganda, 'NBC News,' has been in trouble with the law more times than your average mugger."[2]

How can a mumbling disinterest move us out of this predicament? Effective partisan argument already faces big obstacles in unsettling the contented crowd. The dispossessed already get left out: Bill Clinton forbade Lani Guinier to respond to her critics, then sent her home without the Senate hearing Clarence Thomas got. Since so much stuff muffles the dispossessed's talk, the *last* voice we need is Tough counterfeit calm.

# Notes

*Notes to Chapter 1*

1. Shelby Steele, *The Content of Our Character* (New York: HarperCollins, 1991), 53.
2. Clarence Thomas, quoted by Juan Williams in "A Question of Fairness," *Atlantic Monthly,* February 1987, 80; C. Thomas, speech at Georgetown Law Center, February 20, 1986, 17, quoted in *Clarence Thomas Sourcebook* (Washington, D.C.: NAACP Legal Defense Fund, 1991), 23 (unpublished draft); C. Thomas, "Reason Interview: Clarence Thomas," *Reason,* November 1987, 31–32.
3. Stephen Carter, *Why the Confirmation Process Can't Be Fixed,* U. Ill. L. Rev. 1, 19 (1993); S. Carter, *The Independent Counsel Mess,* 102 Harv. L. Rev. 105, 123, 123, n. 67 (1988); S. Carter, *The Political Aspects of Judicial Power: Some Notes on the Presidential Immunity Decision,* 131 U. Pa. L. Rev. 1341, 1360, 1399 (1983); S. Carter, *The Confirmation Mess,* 101 Harv. L. Rev. 1185, 1195 (1988) (lamenting that Senate staff lack the capacity to address "the ends of government" with the tools of scholarship).
4. *Clarence Thomas Sourcebook,* 2, 5.
5. S. Carter, "Racial Preferences? So What?," *Wall Street Journal,* September 13, 1989, A20; S. Carter, *Reflections of an Affirmative Action Baby* (New York: Harper Collins, 1991), 63–65, 68–69, 115, 116.
6. Henry Louis Gates, Jr., "Black Intellectuals, Jewish Tensions," *New York Times,* April 14, 1993, A21.
7. C. Thomas, speech to Capitol Press Club, September 19, 1983, quoted in *Clarence Thomas Sourcebook,* 98.
8. Tray Ellis, "The New Black Aesthetic," *Before Columbus Review,* May 14, 1989. Ellis dates the movement to the midseventies (specifically, the 1978 appearance of Toni Morrison's *Song of Solomon*).
9. H. L. Gates, Jr., *Loose Canons: Notes on the Culture Wars* (New York: Oxford University Press, 1992), 38 (emphasis original).
10. Daniel Farber and Suzanna Sherry, *Telling Stories out of School,* 45 Stan. L. Rev. 807, 808, 835–36 (1993).

11. C. Thomas, address to the Pacific Research Institute, August 10, 1987, 2.
12. Drucilla Cornell, *The Philosophy of the Limit* (New York: Routledge, 1992), 2, 100; Edward W. Said, *Beginnings: Intention and Method* (New York: Columbia University Press, 1975), 230.
13. S. Carter, *The Dissent of the Governors,* 63 Tul. L. Rev. 1325, 1328 (1989).
14. S. Carter, *Academic Tenure and "White Male" Standards: Some Lessons from the Patent Law,* 100 Yale L. J. 2065, 2072 (1991); S. Carter, "The Black Table, the Empty Seat, and the Tie," in Gerald Early, ed., *Lure and Loathing* (New York: Penguin, 1994), 73, 75.
15. C. Thomas, "Are the Problems of Blacks Too Big for Government to Solve?" *Washington Post,* July 17, 1983, C3. Thomas ultimately accepted the job and it proved a stepping stone to the D.C. Circuit Court and ultimately the Supreme Court.
16. R. Kennedy, *Lani Guinier's Constitution,* 15 American Prospect 36, 47 (Fall 1993); Lani Guinier, *Groups, Representation, and Race Conscious Districting: A Case of the Emperor's Clothes,* 71 Tex. L. Rev. 1589, 1589, acknowledgments (1994); Paul Gigot, "Potomac Watch," *Wall Street Journal,* May 7, 1993.
17. Paul A. Bove, *In the Wake of Theory* (Middletown, Conn.: Wesleyan University Press, 1992), 131.
18. Randall Kennedy, *Reconstruction and the Politics of Scholarship,* 98 Yale L. J. 521, 522 (1989) (the article is arguably agnostic, but suggests considerable comfort with originalism).
19. Thomas Kuhn, *The Structure of Scientific Revolutions* (Chicago: International Encyclopedia of Unified Science, 1962); Paul Feyerabend, *Against Method* (New York: New Left Books, 1975, 1993). These argue that *even* the physical sciences are not value free. Their conclusion applies with double force in the "social" sciences.
20. S. Steele, *Content,* 30.
21. R. Kennedy, 15 American Prospect 39, 44, 45, 46 (Fall 1993); Clint Bolick, "Rule of Law," *Wall Street Journal,* June 2, 1993, A15; Laurel Leff, *From Legal Scholar to Quota Queen: What Happens When Politics Pulls the Press into the Groves of Academe,* 32 Colum. J. Rev. 36 (September/October 1993) (quoting University of Texas law professor Samuel Issacharoff).
22. Kennedy pleads that "acknowledging" the accuracy of Guinier's opponents' perceptions that she was outside the mainstream "does not mean siding with her opponents." Kennedy, 15 American Prospect 40. Even Anthony Lewis, in a laudatory reference to this Kennedy article, was puzzled by Kennedy's attribution of inaccurate Guinier commentary to "low intellectual standards" rather than what Lewis calls "ideological zealotry that had no concern for truth." A. Lewis, "Depriving the Nation," *New York Times,* September 27, 1993, A17. Lewis's bemusement might have dissipated had he read Kennedy's article closely. Having criticized Guinier for overplaying some "racial card," Kennedy could hardly attack her opponents for distorting "truth."
23. *Washington Times,* June 2, 1993. On the very day Guinier's nomination was announced, Clint Bolick was quoted as saying that Ms. Guinier was "breathtakingly radical." C. Bolick, quoted in *Washington Times,* April 30, 1993.

24. R. Kennedy, 15 American Prospect 46.

25. S. Carter, *The Culture of Disbelief* (New York: HarperCollins, 1993) 74, 81, 177; S. Carter, *Dissent*, 63 Tul. L. Rev. 1325, 1332, 1335 n. 29; S. Carter, *Separatism and Skepticism* 92 Yale L. J. 1334, 1338 (1983); S. Carter, *Bork Redux; or, How the Tempting of America Led the People to Rise and Battle for Justice*, 69 Tex. L. Rev. 759, 774, 776 (1991); S. Carter, *Abortion, Absolutism, and Compromise*, 100 Yale L. J. 2747 (1991)

26. R. Kennedy, *Racial Critiques of Legal Academia* 102 Harv. L. Rev. 1763, 1806–7 (1989); S. Carter, *Reflections*, 63–65, 68–69.

27. S. Carter, *Reflections*, 90; *see, further,* S. Carter, "Black Table," in *Lure*, 55, 57 ("the truth is that there is no time to worry, no time and no space, not for the professional.")

28. S. Carter, "Black Table," in *Lure*, 58, 77 (despite admitted political and academic controversy "the profession remains what it is"). *See, further,* Stanley Fish, *Doing What Comes Naturally* (Durham, N.C.: Duke University Press, 1989) 163–246 (esp. 242–46); Drucilla Cornell, *Transformations* (New York: Routledge, 1993), 16–18.

29. *See, e.g.,* Alasdair MacIntyre, *Whose Justice? Which Rationality?* (Notre Dame, Ind.: University of Notre Dame Press, 1988); "Whose Family? Which Values?" *New Republic,* cover story, August 16, 1993.

30. Michel Foucault, "Truth and Power," in Paul Rabinow, ed., *The Foucault Reader* (New York: Pantheon, 1984), 73.

31. Thomas Sowell, "The Real Anita Hill," in *Is Reality Optional?* (Stanford, Calif.: Hoover Institution Press, 1993), 26.

32. *See* Mayer and Abramson, "The Surreal Anita Hill," *New Yorker,* May 17, 1993; Kathleen Sullivan, "The Hill-Thomas Mystery," *New York Review of Books,* August 12, 1993; Deirdre English, "Story of a Smear," *Nation,* June 28, 1993.

33. The *New York Times* reported that on September 30, 1993, the nomination of Janet Napolitano to be United States attorney for Arizona was delayed because of unconfirmed allegations that she "interfere[d]" with the Senate confirmation process in the Hill-Thomas affair by allegedly coaching a Hill witness, Judge Susan Hoerchner, about the dates of Hoerchner's phone conversation with Professor Hill, in the early eighties, in which phone calls Hill disclosed Thomas's harassment to Hoerchner. References to Brock's book comprise fully two paragraphs of the *Times*'s eleven-paragraph account.

34. *New York Times,* October 1, 1993, A19. Controversy centered on whether the 25 percent figure should be measured in dollars (better for the Republicans) or personnel (better for Clinton)—and, if measured in terms of personnel, on which of the departed staffers were really White House staff as opposed to merely being on loan from other federal entities.

35. *See* Martin Kilson, *Anatomy of Black Conservatism,* 59 Transition 4, 12 (Fall 1993) (the new black conservatism rests on "ideological fetish").

## Notes to Chapter 2

1. Roland Barthes, *Criticism and Truth* (1967), trans. and ed. Katrine Pilcher (Minneapolis: University of Minnesota Press, 1987), 44, 46, n. 38. *See, further, The Political Responsibility of Intellectuals,* ed. Maclean, Montefiore, and Winch (Cambridge: Cambridge University Press, 1990), passim; Andrew Ross, *No Respect: Intellectuals and Popular Culture* (New York: Routledge, 1989), 215 et seq. Julien Benda's book has been translated as *The Treason of the Intellectuals* (Boston: Beacon, 1955).

2. Stephen Carter, *Reflections of an Affirmative Action Baby* (New York: HarperCollins, 1991), 253.

3. R. Kennedy, *Racial Critiques of Legal Academia,* 102 Harv. L. Rev. 1745, 1773 n. 116 (1989) (internal quotation marks omitted); C. Thomas, "The New Intolerance," *Wall Street Journal,* May 12, 1993.

4. *Step One: Society is inveterately race conscious.* "The Constitution, by protecting the rights of individuals, is color blind. But a society cannot be color blind, any more than men and women can escape their bodies."

   *Step Two: The policymaker ought to resist race-conscious taint as the best way to restrain these inevitable, unfortunate passions.* "When Founding Father James Madison spoke of the need for 'the reason alone, of the public ... to control and regulate government,' and for government to control and regulate the passions, he wanted exactly what Justice Harlan was pointing to when he endorsed a color-blind Constitution."

   *Step Three: The question of remedying the underlying grievances never arises because those grievances are not "rational," merely passionate.* "Obscuring the difference between public and private would allow private passions (including racial ones) to be given full vent in public life and overwhelm reason."

   C. Thomas, *Wall Street Journal,* October 12, 1987.

5. S. Carter, *Constitutional Adjudication and the Indeterminate Text: A Preliminary Defense of an Imperfect Muddle,* 94 Yale L. J. 821, 823 (1985); S. Carter, *Abortion, Absolutism, and Compromise,* 100 Yale L. J. 2747, 2747 (1991).

6. C. Thomas, "A Second Emancipation Proclamation," *Heritage Foundation Policy Review,* Summer 1988, 84 (emphasis added); C. Thomas, "Rage and Reality," *Wall Street Journal,* October 12, 1987.

7. K. Sullivan, *New York Review of Books,* August 12, 1993.

8. N. Chomsky, "Objectivity and Liberal Scholarship," in *American Power and the New Mandarins* (1968); N. Chomsky, "Universal Principles of Language Structure" (interview, 1972), in Otero, ed., *Language and Politics* (New York: Black Rose Books, 1988); N. Chomsky, *The Prosperous Few and the Restless Many* (Berkeley, Calif.: Odonian, 1993), 70.

9. *See, e.g.,* E. Said, *The World, the Text, and the Critic* (Cambridge: Harvard University Press, 1983), 15, 80; E. Said, *Culture and Imperialism* (New York: Knopf, 1993), 303.

10. This description is prompted by the critical legal scholars' faith in their ability to provide knowledge for politics; their consequent and fruitless pursuit of a some-

how impeccable legal-scholarly "methodology"; and their sometimes collapse into something resembling a parlor game.

11. *See, e.g.,* Roberto Unger, *The Critical Legal Studies Movement,* 96 Harv. L. Rev. 561, 610 (1983) (strategies that isolate racial or gender injustice rest on the "dogmatic and arbitrary assertion of implausible distinctions"); *compare,* Kimberle Crenshaw, *Race Reform and Retrenchment,* 101 Harv. L. Rev. 1331 (1988); Patricia J. Williams, *The Alchemy of Race and Rights,* preface (Cambridge: Harvard University Press, 1991); Richard Delgado, *The Ethereal Scholar: Does Critical Legal Studies Have What Minorities Want?,* 22 Harv. C.R.-C.L. Rev. 301 (1987).

12. *See* Duncan Kennedy, *The Structure Of Blackstone's Commentaries,* 28 Buff. L. Rev. 205 (1979); D. Kennedy, *Form and Substance in Private Law Adjudication,* 89 Harv. L. Rev. 1685 (1976); Peter Gabel and D. Kennedy, *Roll Over Beethhoven,* 36 Stan. L. Rev. 1, 6 (1984); R. Unger, *The Critical Legal Studies Movement,* 96 Harv. L. Rev. 583 (1983).

13. *See* Stanley Fish, "Unger and Milton," in *Doing What Comes Naturally* (Durham, N.C.: Duke University Press, 1989), 399, 422, 427 ("context-breaking power is entirely contextual").

14. A. Ross, *No Respect,* 212–13.

15. Thomas Sowell, *Civil Rights: Rhetoric or Reality* (New York: Morrow, 1984), dedication; S. Carter, *Reflections,* 6, 114, 117, 118, 141, 236 et seq.; S. Carter, "The Black Table, the Empty Seat, and the Tie," in Gerald Early, ed., *Lure and Loathing* (New York: Penguin, 1994), 64 (opting for a black milieu); R. Kennedy, *Racial Critiques,* 102 Harv. L. Rev. 1810, 1773, 1787, 1812, 1815 (1989); R. Kennedy, *Reconstruction and the Politics of Scholarship,* 98 Harv. L. Rev. 521, 537 (1989); V. S. Naipaul, quoted by Charles Michener, "Dark Visions of V. S. Naipaul," *Newsweek,* November 16, 1981, 110; V. S. Naipaul, quoted in Paul Theroux, *Sunrise with Seamonsters* (New York: Penguin, 1986), 110; V. S. Naipaul, quoted by Charles Wheeler, " 'It's Every Man for Himself'—V. S. Naipaul on India," *Listener,* October 27, 1977, 537; V. S. Naipaul, collected in Hamner, ed., *Critical Perspectives on V. S. Naipaul* (Washington, D.C.: Three Continents Press, 1977), 32; S. Steele, quoted in *Washington Post,* October 10, 1990, D1.

16. S. Carter, *Reflections,* 138, citing Crouch as quoted by G. Seymour, "The Great Debate," *Newsday,* October 10, 1990; Stanley Crouch, *Notes of a Hanging Judge* (New York: Oxford University Press, 1990) 3, 7, 10, 15, 18, 174, 175; S. Crouch, "Who Are We? Where Did We Come From? Where are We Going?" in Early, ed., *Lure,* 80–81, 90.

17. Stephen Dedalus in James Joyce, *A Portrait of the Artist as a Young Man,* in *James Joyce* (New York: Gramercy Books, 1992), 385; A. Ross, *No Respect,* 210.

*Notes to Chapter 3*

1. S. Steele, *The Content of Our Character* (New York: HarperCollins, 1990), 29, 30, 159; Toni Morrison, quoted in the *New York Times,* October 8, 1993, A34 (editorial column). Steele elsewhere suggests that race enhances individuality, but

"only when individuality is nurtured and developed apart from race." S. Steele, *Content,* 29. What that means is anyone's guess.

2. J. Joyce, *A Portrait of the Artist as a Young Man,* in *James Joyce* (New York: Gramercy Books, 1992), 390.

3. Steele, *Content,* 13, 91.

4. S. Carter, *Reflections of an Affirmative Action Baby* (New York: HarperCollins, 1991), 239, 241, 252.

5. S. Steele, *Content,* 165; R. Kennedy, *Poverty: A Collective Difficulty, a Collective Challenge,* 77 Cornell L. Rev. 967, 967 (1992).

6. J. Joyce, *Stephen Hero* (Stephen Dedalus speaking) (New York: New Directions, 1944, 1963), 184; S. Steele, *Content,* x, xi–xii, 21, 40–41, 64, 89, 156–57; J. Joyce, *Portrait,* 381 (Cranley speaking).

*Notes to Chapter 4*

1. C. Thomas, speech at Georgetown Law Center, February 20, 1986, 21–22, quoted in *Clarence Thomas Sourcebook* (Washington, D.C.: NAACP Legal Defense Fund, 1991), 85.

2. C. Thomas, Speech to Connecticut Business and Industry Association, December 12, 1985, 13–14, quoted in *Clarence Thomas Sourcebook,* 34; C. Thomas, speech to the American Society of Personnel Administrators, March 17, 1983, quoted in *Clarence Thomas Sourcebook,* 30.

*Notes to Chapter 5*

1. Stephen Carter, *Reflections of an Affirmative Action Baby* (New York: Harper-Collins, 1991), 240; Randall Kennedy, *Racial Critiques of Legal Academia,* 102 Harv. L. Rev. 1745, 1773 (1989); Andrew Ross, *No Respect: Intellectuals and Popular Culture* (New York: Routledge, 1989), 216.

2. S. Carter, "The Right Questions in the Creation of Constitutional Meaning," Boston U. L. Rev. 66, no. 1 (1986). R. Kennedy, *Racial Critiques of Legal Academia,* 102 Harv. L. Rev. 1745, 1815 (1989); Richard Delgado, *Brewer's Plea: Critical Thought on Common Cause,* 44 Vand. L. Rev. 1, 14 (1991); E. Said, *Orientalism* (New York: Pantheon, 1978), 326; S. Carter, *Reflections,* 253; R. Kennedy, quoted in "Political Correctness versus Open Expression on Campus," *New York Times,* June 6, 1991, C18; Scott Brewer, *Introduction to Colloquy,* 103 Harv. L. Rev. 1846 (1990); S. Carter, *Reflections,* 230, directly citing Kenneth Clark, *The Pathos of Power.*

3. R. Kennedy, *McClesky v. Kemp: Race, Capital Punishment, and the Supreme Court,* 101 Harv. L. Rev. 1389, 1394 (1988); *McClesky v. Kemp,* 107 S. Ct. 1756 (1987).

4. H. Bedau and M. Radelet, *Miscarriages of Justice in Potentially Capital Cases,* 40 Stan. L. Rev. 21, 36, 173–79 (1987); and M. Radelet, H. Bedau, and C. Putnam, *In Spite of Innocence* (Boston: Northeastern University Press, 1992), 282–356 (1992), both cited in *Herrera v. Collins,* 113 S. Ct. 853, 876 n. 1 (1993) (Justice Blackmun, dissenting).

5. R. Kennedy, *McClesky,* 1421, n. 157. The assertion that "individual rights" are "more familiar" is itself tendentious.

6. R. Kennedy, *McClesky,* 1394, n. 20.

7. R. Kennedy, *McClesky,* 1420, n. 152.

8. H. L. Gates, Jr., *Loose Canons: Notes on the Culture Wars* (New York: Oxford University Press, 1992), 147.

9. P. J. Williams, quoted in J. Wiener, "Law Profs Fight the Power," *Nation,* September 4, 1989.

10. S. Carter, *Reflections,* 118, 129, 136, 138, 139; S. Carter, *The Confirmation Mess,* 101 Harv. L. Rev. 1185, 1192, 1199 (1988); S. Carter, *Bork Redux,* 69 Tex. L. Rev. 759, 762, 771, 774, 777 (1991).

11. Carter, *Reflections,* 133. *See, further,* Carter, "The Black Table, the Empty Seat, and the Tie," in G. Early, ed., *Lure and Loathing* (New York: Penguin, 1994), 75 (black political divisions create "tremendous risk of losing sharp minds to those some would call the enemy").

12. R. Kennedy, *Racial Critiques of Legal Academia,* 102 Harv. L. Rev. 1745, 1773 (1989), citing R. Merton, *Social Theory and Social Structures* (London: Collier-Macmillan, 1957) (emphasis in Merton's original).

13. Merton, *Social Theory,* 36.

14. Merton, *Social Theory,* 531.

15. Merton, *Social Theory,* 553.

16. Thomas Kuhn, *The Structure of Scientific Revolutions* (Chicago: International Encyclopedia of Unified Science, 1962), 19.

17. Mary I. Coombs, *Outsider Scholarship: The Law Review Stories,* 63 U. Col. Rev. 683, 713 (1992) (good legal scholarship serves "the interests of the outsider community").

18. Paul Bove, *In the Wake of Theory* (Middletown, Conn.: Wesleyan University Press, 1992), 67, 70.

19. R. Kennedy, *Reconstruction and the Politics of Scholarship,* 98 Yale L. J. 521, 530, 537, 538 (1989).

20. Karl Mannheim, *Ideology and Utopia* (New York: Harcourt Brace, 1954), 163.

21. Audre Lorde, "Sexism: An American Disease in Blackface," in *Sister Outsider* (Trumansburg, N.Y.: Crossing Press, 1984), 60, 64 (citing Mary McAnally; footnotes and internal quotation marks omitted; capitalization original).

22. R. Kennedy, *Celebration,* 86 Colum. L. Rev. 1622, 1629, 1641, 1660, 1661 (1986).

23. Kennedy, *Celebration,* 1659–60.

24. Kennedy, *Distrust,* 99 Harv. L. Rev. 1327, 1340 (1986).

25. R. Kennedy, *Racial Critiques,* 1760, 1809, 1811.

26. Kennedy, quoted in *Nation,* September 4, 1989. The misrepresentation centers on the unsaid: Negro Crits allegedly practicing some deviant "politics," everyone else evidently doing nonethnic, nonpolitical truth seeking.

27. R. Kennedy, quoted in *Nation,* September 4, 1989.

28. R. Kennedy, *Racial Critiques,* 1815.

29. R. Kennedy, 98 Yale L. J. 999, 1005 (1989).

30. Roland Barthes, *Criticism and Truth* (1967), trans. and ed. Katrine Pilcher (Minneapolis: University of Minnesota Press, 1987), 33.

31. Charles Rothfeld, "Minority Critic Stirs Debate on Minority Writing," *New York*

*Times,* January 5, 1993, B6; Derrick Bell, "Shed Light in All Corners of Academic Tenure," letter, *New York Times,* January 26, 1990.

32. R. Kennedy, quoted by David Margolick, *New York Times,* September 13, 1992.

33. Peter Berger, "Who's Afraid of Religious Values?" *New York Times Book Review,* September 19, 1993.

34. S. Carter, *Chicago Daily Law Bulletin,* July 17, 1992.

35. S. Carter, *Reflections,* 100. But evidently not when students *agree* with him. Carter for instance has taken the unusual step of citing a then-unpublished student paper in one of his law review articles. S. Carter, *The Political Aspects of Judicial Power,* 131 U. Pa. L. Rev. 1341, 1383, n. 170 (1983).

36. Liza Featherstone, "The Joy of Sex," *Nation,* October 4, 1993. The role of "infantilization" in sustaining arbitrary power balances, and illegitimate disciplinary mechanisms, is a familiar one. *See,* Foucault, *Language, Counter-Memory, Practice* (Ithaca, N.Y.: Cornell University Press, 1980), 210.

37. S. Carter, *Reflections,* 190; S. Carter, *From Sick Chicken to Synar,* B.Y.U. L. Rev. 719, 792 (1987). *See, further,* S. Carter, *The Independent Counsel Mess,* 102 Harv. L. Rev. 105, 126, n. 75 (1988) (referring to his previous "defen[se]" and discussion of "ancestor worship").

38. S. Carter, *Constitutional Improprieties,* 57 U. Chi. L. Rev. 368 n. 39, 375, 382, 395 (1990).

39. Yet Carter elsewhere concedes that the difficulties of elaborating the "rules of recognition" that might guide us as to what constitutes sufficient national dialogue as to constitute a Founding Event "may be insuperable." S. Carter, *The Right Questions in the Creation of Constitutional Meaning,* 66 B.U. L. Rev. 71, 89 (1986).

40. R. Kennedy, *Reconstruction and the Politics of Scholarship,* 98 Yale L. J. 521, 523, 529, 533 (1989).

41. S. Carter, *Independent Counsel Mess,* 105, 122.

42. S. Carter, *Constitutional Adjudication and the Indeterminate Text: A Preliminary Defense of an Imperfect Muddle,* 94 Yale L. J. 821, 823 (1985). The substance of the "deligitimation" critique is defended below in the discussion of whether and how law binds judges.

43. S. Carter, *Michael J. Perry's Morality, Politics, and Law: The Dissent of the Governors,* 63 Tul. L. Rev. 1325, 1332 (1989).

44. S. Carter, *Constitutional Improprieties,* 57 U. Chi. L. Rev. 357, 392 (emphasis added) (1990).

45. Carter, *Indeterminate Text,* 845, n. 90.

46. S. Carter, *Dissent of the Governors,* 1325, 1334, 1337 (1989); S. Carter, *Do Courts Matter?* 90 Mich. L. Rev. 1216, 1223 (1992).

47. S. Carter, "An Old Soldier of Liberalism Musters Out," *Wall Street Journal,* July 1, 1991.

48. S. Carter, *Independent Counsel Mess,* 105, 124; S. Carter, *Indeterminate Text,* 869.

49. S. Carter, *Constitutional Improprieties,* 357, 392; S. Carter, *The Constitution, the Uniqueness Puzzle, and the Economic Conditions of Democracy,* 56 Geo. Wash. L. Rev. 136 (1987).

50. Carter's vision of the state as the principal conduit for legitimate dialogue is, importantly, the exact opposite of what Robert Cover has in mind in his well-known essay. *See,* R. Cover, *The Supreme Court 1982 Term—Foreword: Nomos and Narrative,* 97 Harv. L. Rev. 4, 44 et seq. (1983).

51. S. Carter, *Do Courts Matter?* 1223; S. Carter, *The Right Questions,* 71, 88, n. 71, 89; S. Carter, *Reflections,* 164, 191 (1991); S. Carter, *Dissent of the Governors,* 1325, 1339; R. Kennedy, *Martin Luther King's Constitution,* 98 Yale L. J. 999, 1000 (1989); Elaine Brown, "Attack Racism, Not Black Men," *New York Times,* May 5, 1993, A23; S. Carter, *Independent Counsel Mess,* 105, 136, 137; Stanley Cavell, *The Claim of Reason: Wittgenstein, Skepticism, Morality, and Tragedy* (Oxford: Oxford University Press, 1979), 95; R. Kennedy, quoted by D. Von Drehle, *Washington Post,* June 4, 1993.

## Notes to Chapter 6

1. Whoopi Goldberg, reported in the *New York Post,* October 11, 1993, 5. Goldberg, an African American, defended her white lover, Ted Danson, after he appeared in blackface and performed a comedy routine that New York mayor David Dinkins, present at the event, described as "way, way over the line."

2. Derek Bok, *Beyond the Ivory Tower* (Cambridge: Harvard University Press, 1982), 11.

3. S. Carter, *The Culture of Disbelief* (New York: HarperCollins, 1993), 253 (rejecting the view that definitions of life based on religious sentiment are "out of bounds"); S. Carter, *Abortion, Absolutism, and Compromise,* 100 Yale L. J. 2747 (1991).

4. H. Wechsler, *Neutral Principles,* 73 Harv. L. Rev. 1 (1959); S. Carter, *The Right Questions in the Creation of Constitutional Meaning,* 66 B.U. L. Rev. 71, 87 (1986); Mark Tushnet, *The Degradation of Constitutional Discourse,* 81 Geo. L. J. 251, 251 n. 3 (1992); Steven D. Smith, *Idolatry in Constitutional Interpretation,* 79 Va. L. Rev. 583, 587, 631 (1993).

5. Stanley Cavell, *The Claim of Reason* (Oxford: Oxford University Press, 1979), 12–13 (emphasis added).

6. M. Tushnet, *Degradation,* 251, 277; Lloyd Cohen, *A Different Black Voice in Legal Scholarship,* 37 N.Y.U. L. Rev. 301, 309, 310 (1992).

7. *The Stories of the Law,* Book Note, 105 Harv. L. Rev. 779, 782 (1992); P. J. Williams, *The Alchemy of Race and Rights* (Cambridge: Harvard University Press, 1991), 73, 175–76.

8. Edward Rubin, *On Beyond Truth,* 80 Cal. L. Rev. 889, 904, 923–24, 932, 963 (1992).

9. D. Farber and S. Sherry, *Telling Stories out of School,* 45 Stan. L. Rev. 807, 809, 824, 832–33, 835–36.

10. E. Gellner, "La trahison de la traishon des clercs," in *The Political Responsibility of Intellectuals,* ed. Maclean, Montefiore and Winch (Cambridge: Cambridge University Press, 1990), 26 (attacking the prevalence of Benda's work).

11. *See,* E. Said, *The World, the Text, and the Critic* (Cambridge: Harvard University Press, 1983), 54–89.

12. Martha Minow, *The Supreme Court 1986 Term—Foreword: Justice Engendered,* 101 Harv. L. Rev. 10, 77 (1987), citing C. Larmore, *Patterns of Moral Complexity,* 59–66 (1987).
13. P. J. Williams, *Alchemy,* 151–52.
14. "The Week in Review," *New York Times,* January 31, 1993, 4.

*Notes to Chapter 7*

1. *See,* Pierre Schlag, *Normativity and the Politics of Form,* 139 U. Pa. L. Rev. 801, 802–4 (1991) (suggesting that idealistic normative questions "reprieve legal thinkers from recognizing the extent to which the cherished 'ideals' of legal academic thought are implicated in the reproduction and maintenance of precisely those ugly 'realities' of legal practice the academy so routinely condemns").
2. Anonymous Thomas defender, quoted in "Leon Higginbotham's Farewell to Gavels," *Pennsylvania Gazette,* February 1993, 36.
3. *Conroy v. Askinoff,* 113 S. Ct. 1562 (1992); *Concrete Pipe & Prod. v. Construction Laborers Pension Trust,* 113 S. Ct. 2264, 2270 (1992); *Sassower v. Reno,* 114 S. Ct. 2 (1993).
4. *See, e.g.,* John Stick, *Can Nihilism Be Pragmatic?* 100 Harv. L. Rev. 332, 353, 354 (1986); Brian Leiter, *Objectivity and the Problems of Jurisprudence,* 72 Tex. L. Rev. 187, 208 (1993).
5. Joseph W. Singer, *The Player and the Cards: Nihilism and Legal Theory,* 94 Yale L. J. 1, 58 (1984).
6. Joan Williams, *Critical Legal Studies: The Death of Transcendence and the Rise of the New Langdells,* 62 N.Y.U. L. Rev. 429, 442, n. 95 (1987). Stanley Fish regurgitates a similar account of Cohen's work. S. Fish, *There's No Such Thing as Free Speech . . . and It's a Good Thing Too* (New York: Oxford University Press, 1994), 210. *Compare,* F. Cohen, *Transcendental Nonsense,* 35 Colum. L. Rev. 848 (1935) (postponement of the problem of values for the purpose of somehow value-free inquiry is futile and undesirable).
7. J. Williams, *New Langdells,* 429.
8. Wittgenstein's work is notoriously controversial. The question is not what did "he" say, but which reading of Wittgenstein to prefer. Joan Williams cites and prefers Stanley Cavell's (and Hanna Pitkin's, which avowedly follows Cavell's). So do I. She misreads Cavell. That is the subject of this section. *See,* A. C. Grayling, *Wittgenstein* (Oxford: Oxford University Press, 1988), vi ("The wide latitude for competing interpretations of Wittgenstein's work . . . creates problems. Every commentator tries to give as accurate an account as he can, only to find himself charged with distorting Wittgenstein's views by those who have a different response to them. . . . The views [one] attribute[s] to him are what [one] interpret[s] those views to be.") Joan Williams champions a reading of Wittgenstein that is not supported by Stanley Cavell, whom she invokes, and that is unattractive (and wholly unargued) on its own merits.
9. Note Williams's failure to distinguish two senses of "can." The first (which she intends) translates "with likelihood of swaying the court." The second, which

preserves for the judge, if not the advocate, a radical freedom as to the outcome of the case, connotes "without declining into conceptual gibberish."

10. J. Williams, *New Langdells,* 495, n. 463.

11. Roberto Unger is surely the last theorist one wants to cite in support of the idea that legal concepts legitimately derive determinacy from prevailing "forms of life." Unger advocates a "deviationist" concept of legal doctrine that would integrate political controversy into standard doctrinal argument. He further advocates "expanded doctrine" in which "the class of legitimate doctrinal categories must be sharply enlarged." R. Unger, *The Critical Legal Studies Movement,* 96 Harv. L. Rev. 561, 577 (1983). Unger's concern is to "expose how power-ridden and manipulable materials gain a semblance of authority, necessity and determinacy" (579). Finally, Unger's rejection of a judicial role in which prevailing "forms of life" bind judges is explicit:

> [Judges] are neither servants of the state (not at least in the conventional sense) nor their technical assistants. We have no stake in finding a preestablished harmony between moral compulsions and institutional constraints. We know, moreover, that the received views of institutional propriety count for little except as arguments to use against those who depart too far from professional consensus. (581)

12. In a subsequent piece, *Culture and Certainty: Legal History and the Reconstructive Project,* 76 Va. L. Rev. 713, 743–44 (1990), attempting to show that she recognizes the contestability of culture, Joan Williams nevertheless ends by reasserting that "legal culture 'makes thinkable' a narrower band of political possibility than does political culture in general."

13. S. Cavell, *The Claim of Reason,* 12–13 (Oxford: Oxford University Press, 1979). Cavell distinguishes the judge's role in law as compared both to situations where there are "objective" external criteria *and* to cases where, through there aren't "objective" criteria, Wittgensteinian criteria provide sufficient certainty. Law is, for Cavell, a special *third* class of case.

14. Cavell, *Claim of Reason,* 15, 36, 94, 247.

15. S. Cavell, *Conditions Handsome and Unhandsome* (Chicago: University of Chicago Press, 1990), 64 (emphasis added).

16. S. Cavell, *Claim of Reason,* 118.

17. Margaret J. Radin and Frank Michelman, *Pragmatist and Poststructuralist Critical Legal Practice,* 139 U. Pa. L. Rev. 1019, 1042, n. 112 (1991). Winter accepts that he has common ground with the dialogists. Steven L. Winter, *Indeterminacy and Incommensurability in Constitutional Law,* 78 Cal. L. Rev. 1442, 1505 n. 330 (1990).

18. S. Winter, *Indeterminacy,* 1442, 1505.

19. S. Winter, *Bull Durham and the Uses of Theory,* 42 Stan. L. Rev. 639, 656, 656 n. 93, 657, 678 (1990).

20. S. Winter, *Indeterminacy,* 1453, n. 39.

21. Joseph W. Singer, *The Reliance Interest in Property,* 40 Stan. L. Rev. 611, 625, n. 40 (1988).

22. S. Winter, *Indeterminacy,* 1490.

23. S. Winter, *Indeterminacy,* 1506, 1520.

24. S. Winter, *Transcendental Nonsense, Metaphoric Reasoning, and the Cognitive Stakes for Law*, 137 U. Pa. L. Rev. 1105, 1113, 1115, 1130, 1133, 1152, 1182–83, n. 252 (1989).

25. S. Winter, *Indeterminacy*, 1453.

26. Noam Chomsky, *Language and Politics*, ed. Otero (Black Rose Books, 1988), 534.

27. S. Winter, *Cognitive Stakes*, 137 U. Pa. L. Rev. 1106–7, 1109, 1112–13, 1114, 1153 n. 145 (1989); S. Winter, *Bull Durham*, 670, n. 162; Thomas Kuhn, *The Structure of Scientific Revolutions* (Chicago: International Encyclopedia of Unified Science, 1962, 1973), 19, 206 (1969 postscript).

28. Herbert Dreyfus and Paul Rabinow, *Michel Foucault: Beyond Structuralism and Hermeneutics* (Chicago: University of Chicago Press, 1982), 32.

29. Michel Foucault, *The Order of Things* (New York: Vintage, 1973), 321, 336.

30. Duncan Kennedy and Peter Gabel, *Roll Over Beethoven*, 36 Stan. L. Rev. 1, 3, 6, 25, 33, 48, 52, 53 (1984).

31. Kennedy, *Freedom and Constraint in Adjudication: A Critical Phenomenology*, 36 J. Leg. Educ. 518, 521, 522, 549, 550 (1986).

32. Stanley Fish, "Working on the Chain Gang," in *Doing What Comes Naturally* (Durham, N.C.: Duke University Press, 1989), 93 (emphasis original); S. Fish, "Fish v. Fiss," in *Doing What Comes Naturally*, 131; S. Fish, *There's No Such Thing as Free Speech*, 158–59.

33. S. Fish, "Change," in *Doing What Comes Naturally*, 157.

34. S. Fish, "Fish v. Fiss," 136–37.

35. S. Fish, "Posner on Law and Literature," in *Doing What Comes Naturally*.

36. James A. Gardner, *The Ambiguity of Legal Dreams: A Communitarian Defense of Judicial Restraint*, 71 N.C. L. Rev. 806 (1994). Gardner's counsel of judicial abdication is, of course, unattractive on its merits.

*Notes to Chapter 8*

1. C. Thomas, speech to Bureau of the Census, May 2, 1983, 12, in *Clarence Thomas Sourcebook* (Washington, D.C.: NAACP Legal Defense Fund, 1991), 23.

2. C. Thomas, commencement speech, Savannah State College, June 9, 1985. Rpt. as "Climb the Jagged Mountain," *New York Times*, July 17, 1991, A21, col. 2; C. Thomas, quoted by United Press International, September 11, 1991 (asserting that civil rights predecessors paved his way to the Court).

3. Timothy M. Phelps and Helen Winternitz, *Capitol Games* (New York: Hyperion, 1992), 83–84 (the Thomas-Parker memo was not released during the hearings); C. Thomas, speech to ABA Business Law Section, August 11, 1987, in *Clarence Thomas Sourcebook*, 93.

4. 958 F. 2d 382 (D.C. Cir. 1992).

5. 112 S. Ct. 2791, 2874, 2884–85 (1992).

6. Thomas said his sister "gets mad when the mailman is late with the welfare check, that is how dependent she is." Thomas, quoted in Phelps and Winternitz, *Capitol Games*, 85.

7. Phelps and Winternitz, *Capitol Games*, 59.

8. *Firefighters v. Stotts,* 467 U.S. 561 (1981). *See* Phelps and Winternitz, *Capitol Games,* 103 (suggesting that the expansive reading of *Stotts,* championed by the Thomas EEOC, was the initiative of William Bradford Reynolds, a Reagan official with a tenacious anti–civil rights agenda).

9. C. Thomas, speech at the University of Virginia, October 19, 1983, 32, in *Clarence Thomas Sourcebook,* 28; speech at the University of California, July 28, 1983, 8, in *Clarence Thomas Sourcebook,* 28; *Talking Points,* November 4, 1983, 2; C. Thomas, "Why Black Americans Should Look to Conservative Policies," *Heritage Foundation Reports,* June 18, 1987; C. Thomas, "Are the Problems of Blacks Too Big for Government to Solve?" *Washington Post,* July 17, 1983; C. Thomas, "Reason Interview: Clarence Thomas," *Reason,* November 1987, 31, quoted in *Clarence Thomas Sourcebook,* 90; C. Thomas, "Right Thinking," *Forbes,* October 14, 1991, 30 (emphasis added); C. Thomas, "Judge Thomas Speaks on Blacks and Conservatism," *San Francisco Chronicle,* July 10, 1991, A19; C. Thomas, "Job Discrimination Is Still Very, Very, Serious" (interview), *U.S. News and World Report,* March 14, 1983; Phelps and Winternitz, *Capitol Games,* 99; C. Thomas, "Climb the Jagged Mountain"; C. Thomas, *U.S News and World Report,* March 14, 1983.

10. C. Thomas, "Why Black Americans Should Look to Conservative Policies."

11. Phelps and Winternitz, *Capitol Games,* 37, 38, 109–10.

12. *Clarence Thomas Sourcebook,* 4. *See, further,* Stanley Fish, "Play of Surfaces: Theory and the Law," in *There's No Such Thing as Free Speech . . . and It's a Good Thing Too* (New York: Oxford University Press, 1994), 181–82 (arguing that legal theories do not determine outcomes).

13. R. Gaull Silberman, "He Is Nothing If Not an Independent Thinker," *Los Angeles Times,* July 7, 1991, M1; C. Thomas, "Climb the Jagged Mountain"; C. Thomas, *The Equal Employment Opportunity Commission: Reflections on a New Philosophy,* 15 Stetson L. Rev. 29, 35 (1985); C. Thomas, *Symposium: Black America under the Reagan Administration,* 34 Policy Rev. 32 (1985); C. Thomas, "Why Black Americans Should Look to Conservative Policies"; C. Thomas, "The New Intolerance," *Wall Street Journal,* May 12, 1993, A15; C. Thomas, "Why Black Americans Should Look to Conservative Policies"; C. Thomas, "Address to the Employers Resource Council" (formerly Associated Industries of Cleveland), rpt. in *Industry Week,* August 4, 1986; Linda Greenhouse, "In Trying to Clarify What He Is Not, Thomas Opens Questions of What He Is," *New York Times,* September 13, 1991, A19 (quoting Thomas's testimony).

14. *Conroy v. Aniskoff,* 113 S. Ct. 1562, 1564, 1567 (1993) (emphasis added), 1567, n. 12; *Lamprecht v. FCC,* 958 F. 2d 382 (D.C. Cir. 1992); C. Thomas, speech at Harvard University Federalist Society, April 7, 1988, 13; speech at Tocqueville Forum, April 18, 1988, 21; speech at University of Virginia Federalist Society, March 5, 1988, in *Clarence Thomas Sourcebook,* 45–46.

15. *Rowland v. California Mens Colony,* 113 S. Ct. 716, 731, 732 (1993).

16. *Smith v. U.S.,* 113 S. Ct. 2050, 2055 (1993).

17. *Arave v. Creech,* 113 S. Ct. 1534, 1550 (1993).

18. *Deal v. United States,* 113 S. Ct. 1993, 1998 n. 3, 1998 (1993) (Justice Scalia, Justice Thomas joining); *Dobbs v. Zant,* 113 S. Ct. 835 (1993) (Scalia, Thomas joining).

19. *Teague v. Lane,* 489 U.S. 288 (1989). For lay criticism, *see, e.g., New York Times,* Editorial, August 14, 1993.
20. *Gilmore v. Taylor,* 113 S. Ct. 2112, 2119, 2119 n. 4, 2123, 2129–30 n. 5 (1993).
21. *Falconer v. Lane,* 905 F. 2d 1129 (1990).
22. *Cupp v. Naughten,* 414 U.S. 141.
23. *Boyde v. California,* 110 S. Ct. 1190 (1990); *Connecticut v. Johnson,* 103 S. Ct. 969 (1983).
24. *See,* Sanford Levinson, *Strategy, Jurisprudence, and Certiorari,* 79 Va. L. Rev. 717, 728 (1993).
25. *Haitian Refugee Center, Inc. v. James Baker, III,* 112 S. Ct. 1245, 1246 (1992).
26. *Haitian Centers Council, Inc. v. McNary,* 969 F. 2d 1350, 1367 (2d Cir. 1992).
27. *Chris Sale v. Haitian Centers Council,* 61 LW 4684, 4686 (internal quotation marks omitted), 4688, 4693, 4698 (emphasis added), June 21, 1993.
28. *See, e.g.,* C. Thomas, speech at Brandeis University, April 8, 1988, 4–12, in *Clarence Thomas Sourcebook,* 47, 51. This point recurred in other 1988 speeches; C. Thomas, "Civil Rights as a Principle versus Civil Rights as an Interest," in D. Boaz, ed., *Assessing the Reagan Years* (Washington, D.C.: Cato Institute, 1988), 391; C. Thomas, address to the ABA Business Law Section, August 11, 1987, 13, in *Clarence Thomas Sourcebook,* 56; C. Thomas, speech before the Cato Institute, October 2, 1987, 13, in *Clarence Thomas Sourcebook,* 47.
29. *Shaw v. Reno,* 1993 WL 224459 *3, *7, *10, 113 S. Ct. 2816 (1993).
30. *Voinovitch v. Quilter,* 113 S. Ct. 1149, 1157 (1993).
31. *Gomillion v. Lightfoot,* 364 U.S. 339 (1960).
32. C. Thomas, speech at the Tocqueville Forum, April 18, 1988, 17, *Clarence Thomas Sourcebook,* 57.
33. *Herrera v. Collins,* 113 S. Ct. 853, 875, n. 1 (1993).
34. C. Thomas, speech to Missouri Human Rights Conference, May 20, 1983, 2–3.
35. Monaghan, *Our Perfect Constitution,* 56 N.Y.U. L. Rev. 353, 356, 395, 396 (1981) (internal quotation marks and citations omitted; emphasis added).
36. *Doggett v. United States,* 112 S. Ct. 2686, 2700 (1992); *Georgia v. McCollum,* 112 S. Ct. 2348, 2359 (1992); *Riggins v. Nevada,* 112 S. Ct. 1810, 1821 (1992); *Wright v. West,* 112 S. Ct. 2482 (1992); *Hudson v. McMillian,* 112 S. Ct. 995, 1010 (1992); *Helling v. McKinney,* 113 S. Ct. 2475 (1993).
37. C. Thomas, speech at the Tocqueville Forum, Wake Forest University, April 18, 1988, 8, *Clarence Thomas Sourcebook,* 56.
38. *Dawson v. Delaware,* 112 S. Ct. 1093, 1098, 1101, 1103.
39. The description of the pro–hate-speech position as a "free speech" position is misleading. *See,* Stanley Fish, *There's No Such Thing As Free Speech,* 102, 109, 110 (Fish suggests that the First Amendment has become the "First Refuge of Scoundrels"; that "free speech" fundamentalism rests on "the fiction of a world of weightless verbal exchange"; and that the phrase is merely a strategy to "delegitimize the complaints of victimized groups").
40. *R.A.V. v. City of St. Paul,* 112 S. Ct. 2538, 2551, 2560, 2561 (1992).
41. *Wisconsin v. Mitchell,* 113 S. Ct. 2194 (1993).
42. *U.S. v. Fordice,* 112 S. Ct. 2727, 2733, 2742, 2743, 2744, 2752 (1992).

43. *Graham v. Collins*, 113 S. Ct. 892 (1993).

44. *Graham*, 908. Yet elsewhere in this very opinion, Thomas rails against the "judicial activism" on which the death-penalty abolitionists, he thinks, depended in the sixties and seventies (905). Thomas can himself be read, in *Graham*, as urging states to enact mandatory death statutes. Thomas expressly acknowledged the role that the Supreme Court's "prompting" can have in encouraging potential litigants. He asserts that the Legal Defense Fund did not in the 1960s itself seriously consider a broad offensive against the death penalty "until three Members of this Court, in an opinion dissenting from a denial of certiorari, offered strong foundation for such a strategy" (905 n. 3).

45. *Graham*, 912.

46. *Graham*, 909.

47. *Herrera v. Collins*, 853, 875 n. 1.

48. In *Herrera* O'Connor briefly raised the issue of whether Supreme Court review impinges on the states' "powerful and legitimate interest in punishing the guilty, and the nature of state-federal relations" (16). But each of these questions is clearly within the Supreme Court's competence to decide. Moreover, these state-federal issues are entirely different from the originalist assertions, offered by Thomas and Scalia, about the supposed inherent limits of the Constitution.

49. *Lockhart v. Fretwell*, 113 S. Ct. 838, 842, 846, 853 (1993).

50. *Doggett v. United States*, 2686, 2699, 2700.

51. *Riggins v. Nevada*, 1810, 1812, 1816, 1817.

52. *Hudson v. McMillian*, 995, 1003, 1005, 1005, 1010.

53. *Helling v. McKinney*, 2475.

54. *Lamprecht v. FCC*, 958 F. 2d 382, 383, 393, 398, 413 (D.C. Cir. 1992).

55. *Metro Broadcasting, Inc. v. FCC*, 110 S. Ct. 2997 (1990).

56. *Hazen Paper Co. v. Biggins*, 113 S. Ct. 1701 (1993).

57. *St. Mary's Honor Center v. Hicks*, 113 S. Ct. 2742 (internal brackets and quotation marks omitted).

58. *Associated General Contractors v. City of Jacksonville, Florida*, 113 S. Ct. 2297, 2303 (1993).

59. *Farrar v. Hobby*, 113 S. Ct. 566, 575 (1992).

60. Libertarian political philosopher Robert Nozick, critic of "paternalistic" state redistribution argues, in *The Nature of Rationality* (Princeton: Princeton University Press, 1993), that "symbolic utility" needs to be inserted into social science's models of human behavior.

61. *TXO Production Corp. v. Alliance Resources Corp.*, 113 S. Ct. 2711 (1993).

62. S. Carter, in G. Early, ed., *Lure and Loathing* (New York: Penguin, 1994), 73.

63. Ronald Reagan, July 1984. Reagan, in a widely quoted remark, referred to "San Francisco Democrats . . . so far left they've left America." Michael Dukakis's 1988 campaign, on "competence not ideology," was a direct reaction to this successful Republican tactic.

64. C. Thomas, speech to the Heritage Foundation, June 15, 1987, 10; Speech at Suffolk University, Boston, March 30, 1988, 17, in *Clarence Thomas Sourcebook*, 57.

65. S. Carter, *New Republic*, February 22, 1993.

66. E. Chemerinsky, *The Price of Asking the Wrong Questions,* 62 Tex. L. Rev. 1207, 1231 (1984).
67. G. Spann, *Race against the Court* (New York: New York University Press, 1993), 21. Spann argues that since majoritarian infiltration of the Court is inevitable, minorities ought to abandon the Court for "pure politics." Yet, political and legislative gains ultimately remain hostage to judicial interpretation, a pure politics is unattainable, and valuable arguments can be made that *legitimate* judicial review *must* be countermajoritarian. We ought to press these arguments before abandoning the Court to its habitual, illegitimate, majoritarian ways.

## *Notes to Chapter 9*

1. When Carter objects to "nativism," his focus, ironically, is inward looking. *See,* S. Carter, "Nativism and Its Discontents," *New York Times,* March 8, 1992 (criticizing Patrick Buchanan's campaign).
2. S. Carter, "Going to War over War Powers," *Washington Post,* November 18, 1990; S. Carter, *The Religiously Devout Judge,* 64 Notre Dame L. R. 932, 940 (1989); S. Carter, *Reflections of an Affirmative Action Baby* (New York: HarperCollins, 1991), 144, 146, 253; S. Carter, *The Constitution, the Uniqueness Puzzle, and the Economic Conditions of Democracy,* 56 Geo. Wash. L. Rev. 136 (1987); S. Carter, *Promoting Democracy: A Panel Discussion,* 60 Temple L. Q. 997 (1987).
3. V. S. Naipaul, *An Area of Darkness* (New York: Vintage, 1981), back cover. For a fuller account of Naipaul's status as "expert" rather than mere writer, *see,* R. Nixon, *London Calling: V. S. Naipaul, Postcolonial Mandarin* (Oxford: Oxford University Press, 1992), 4, passim.
4. R. Nixon, *London Calling,* 68, 70, 72; Alfred Kazin, *New York Times Book Review,* May 1, 1977, 21.
5. V. S. Naipaul, quoted by Bharati Mukherjee and Robert Boyers, "A Conversation with V. S. Naipaul," 54 *Salmagundi* 13 (1981); V. S. Naipaul, quoted by Paul Theroux, *Sunrise with Seamonsters* (New York: Penguin, 1986), 93; V. S. Naipaul, quoted by Elizabeth Hardwick, "Meeting V. S. Naipaul," *New York Times Book Review,* May 13, 1979, 36; V. S. Naipaul, *An Area of Darkness,* 227; V. S. Naipaul, *The Middle Passage* (New York: Penguin, 1962, 1982), 74, 247.
6. William Walsh, *V. S. Naipaul* (Edinburgh: Oliver and Boyd, 1973), 15, *passim*; Mel Gussow, "Writer without Roots," *New York Times Magazine,* December 26, 1976, 9; Eugene Goodheart, "V. S. Naipaul's Mandarin Sensibility," 50 *Partisan Review,* 244–56 (1983); Friedrich Nietzsche, *Thus Spoke Zarathustra* (New York: Penguin, 1961), 70.
7. V. S. Naipaul, quoted by Charles Wheeler, " 'It's Every Man for Himself': V. S. Naipaul on India," *Listener,* October 27, 1977, 537, col. 4.
8. R. Nixon, *London Calling,* 55–56; S. Cudjoe, *V. S. Naipaul* (Amherst: University of Massachusetts Press, 1988), 199–200.
9. V. S. Naipaul, quoted by Bernard Levin, "V. S. Naipaul: A Perpetual Voyager," *Listener,* June 23, 1983, 16.
10. V. S. Naipaul, "Jasmine," *Times Literary Supplement,* June 4, 1964, rpt. in Robert

D. Hamner, ed., *Critical Perspectives on V. S. Naipaul* (Washington, D.C.: Three Continents, 1977), 18; V. S. Naipaul, quoted by Ronald Bryden, "The Novelist V. S. Naipaul Talks about His Work to Ronald Bryden," *Listener,* March 22, 1973, 367; V. S. Naipaul, "The Regional Barrier," *Times Literary Supplement,* August 15, 1958, 37–38; V. S. Naipaul, " 'It's Every Man for Himself,' " *Listener,* October 27, 1977, 537; V. S. Naipaul, *An Area of Darkness,* 228; V. S. Naipaul, "The Writer," *New Statesman,* March 18, 1966, 381–82.

11. Peter Nazareth, rpt. in Robert D. Hamner, ed., *Critical Perspectives,* 145.

12. V. S. Naipaul, "A Conversation," 54 *Salmagundi* 20 (Fall 1981); V. S. Naipaul, quoted by Eyre M. Banning, "Naipaul at Wesleyan," 14 *South Carolina Review* 45 (Spring 1982) (emphasis Naipaul's as reported by Banning); V. S. Naipaul, quoted in Bryden interview, *Listener,* 368; V. S. Naipaul, quoted by Adrian Rowe-Evans, "The Writer as Colonial," 40 *Transition* 56–62 (1971); V. S. Naipaul, quoted by Charles Wheeler, " 'It's Every Man for Himself,' " 535; V. S. Naipaul, quoted by Mel Gussow, "Writer without Roots," 8 et seq.; V. S. Naipaul, quoted by Zoe Heller, "Kingdom of Naipaul," *Independent* (London), March 28, 1993, Sunday Review, 2; V. S. Naipaul, "I Cannot Disown Trinidad and It Cannot Disown Me," *Listener,* June 10, 1982, 13–14.

13. T. R. S. Sharma, "Chinua Achebe and V. S. Naipaul: One Version and Two Postures on Postcolonial Societies," in *The Colonial and Neo-Colonial Encounters in Commonwealth Literature,* ed. Anniah Gowda (Mysore: Prasaragana University Press, 1983), 83–93.

14. V. S. Naipaul, "The Regional Barrier," 37–38; V. S. Naipaul, quoted by Charles Michener, "Dark Visions of V. S. Naipaul," *Newsweek,* November 16, 1981, 110; V. S. Naipaul, quoted by Keith Hamish, "The Ridiculous Panic behind Vidia Naipaul," *Trinidad Guardian,* November 29, 1972, 9; V. S. Naipaul, "The Documentary Heresy," *Twentieth Century,* Winter 1964, repr. in R. Hamner, ed., *Critical Perspectives,* 24; V. S. Naipaul, quoted by Raoul Pantin, "Portrait of an Artist: What Makes Naipaul Run," *Caribbean Contact,* May 19, 1973, 15; V. S. Naipaul, quoted by Charles Wheeler, " 'It's Every Man for Himself,' " 537; V. S. Naipaul, "Return to Guiana," *New York Review of Books,* April 11, 1991; V. S. Naipaul, *Finding the Centre* (London: Penguin, 1986). V. S. Naipaul, quoted in "A Conversation," 54 *Salmagundi* 121 (Fall 1981). James Anthony Froude, *The English in the West Indies* (1887), cited as epigraph to Naipaul's *The Middle Passage*; Naipaul, *The Mimic Men* (London: Penguin, 1967, 1969), 32.

15. Edward Said, "Expectations of Inferiority," *New Statesman,* October 16, 1981, 21.

16. Anthony Burgess, "Joseph Kell, V. S. Naipaul and Me," *New York Times Book Review,* April 21, 1991; V. S. Naipaul, "The Regional Barrier," 37–38.

17. V. S. Naipaul, quoted by Charles Wheeler, " 'It's Every Man for Himself,' " 535; V. S. Naipaul, *The Mimic Men* (New York: Penguin Books, 1967, 1969), 146; V. S. Naipaul, *India: A Million Mutinies Now* (New York: Viking, 1990), 9; V. S. Naipaul, *An Area of Darkness,* 48.

18. The blurb is drawn from Lelyveld's review of Naipaul's 1977 *India: A Wounded Civilization,* where Naipaul concludes that the only answer for India is further decay and total collapse and, perhaps, the hope of a phoenixlike rise from the

ashes. And this last hint of affirmation is reduced to mere rhetoric by the tenor of the book as a whole. Naipaul's 1964 book, *India: An Area of Darkness,* more than bleak, evinces an outright disgust with the place.

19. Paul Theroux, "V. S. Naipaul," 93.
20. V. S. Naipaul, *The Mimic Men*; Peter de la Billiere, quoted in *New York Times Magazine,* March 10, 1991, 34.
21. Edward Said, "Expectations of Inferiority," *New Statesman,* October 16, 1981, 22; Earl Lovelace, "Poor Naipaul! He Has Become His Own Biggest Joke," *Trinidad Express,* October 26, 1970, 10.

## Notes to Conclusion

1. Terry Eagleton, *Ideology: An Introduction* (New York: Verso, 1991), 2.
2. Ishmael Reed, *Airing Dirty Laundry* (New York: Addison Wesley, 1993), 32.

# Index

Abortion. *See* Women, right to choose
Achebe, Chinua, 181, 183
Affirmative action, 40; and Stephen Carter, 7; Clarence Thomas's shifts, 6, 122–25, 160–63; distinguished from "preferences," 7; and Randall Kennedy, 54
Africa: and V. S. Naipaul, xii, 177, 191; and Paul Theroux, 191
Ancestor worship, 58–60
Apolitical, myth of, 6, 7, 16, 21, 66, 87, 89, 128, 130, 142, 168
Appiah, Kwame Anthony, 44
Aryan Brotherhood, 147
Atwater, Lee, 120
Authoritarianism versus totalitarianism, 175
Autobiography: and law, 8; of Malcolm X, 8

Backlash: and feminism, 100; and racism, 12
Baker, Houston, 57
Barthes, Roland: and Julien Benda, 19; and Randall Kennedy, 56
Bate, Walter Jackson, 55
Bell, Derrick, 8; and Julien Benda, 23; and Stephen Carter, 45–46, 63, 64, 65, 67; and critical race theory, xii; and Randall Kennedy, 44, 50, 56; and

Thomas Sowell, 46; and Clarence Thomas, 21, 121
Benda, Julien, 10, 19–26; and Stephen Carter, 38–39, 46, 48; conservative ideology, 20–22; and Randall Kennedy, 38–39, 44, 52, 54, 56; and law schools, 73–74, 77, 102; and partisanship, 194; and Clarence Thomas, 127–28; and the U.S. Constitution, 145; and V. S. Naipaul, 181, 184
Black conservatives, lack of constituency, 17–18
Blackmun, Justice Harry: death penalty, 134, 155; habeas corpus relief, 135, 136, 137, 157; and Haitian refugees, 139–40; hate speech, 148; prisoners' rights, 159; standing to challenge minority set-aside program, 164
Black Panther party, 67
Black voice, xi, 44, 52–53, 61
Bloom, Allan, 8; and Randall Kennedy, 51, 55; and Clarence Thomas, 9
Bolick, Clint: and Civil Rights Act, 1991, 12; and Stephen Carter, 12; and Lani Guinier, 12, 169; and judicial impartiality, 169–70; and Randall Kennedy, 12, 13; and Deval Patrick, 12
Brock, David, 13, 125; and Thomas Sowell, 16; and Kathleen Sullivan, 22
Brown, Elaine, 67